PRAISE FOR *FIND A PLACE FOR ME*

"*Find a Place for Me* roughrides grief, anxiety, and an unflagging humor in such a beguilingly fresh approach to love and saying goodbye. This memoir will burrow down deep into your heart, finding its own place of comfort there. I dare you to be able to put it down."

—Noley Reid, author of *Pretend We Are Lovely*

"*Find A Place for Me* is a love story more than anything else, the story of a marriage as one spouse succumbs to a terminal illness. As Fagan watches her husband's daily decline, she "filet[s] herself] one layer at a time," doing everything she can to honor his wishes and savor the moments left, while trying to come to terms with a life after his leaving. She is a reluctant survivor, one with a "mourning season" in the fall, during which she's lost both parents, two brothers, and now her beloved Bob. This memoir is the answer to the title's command, a place where Bob becomes legendary; Fagan pokes "pinholes of light" by telling their story of love and death in painstaking honesty and with surprising humor. She reflects on "liv[ing] death day-to-day" and then "surviv[ing] the end of love," forming a broader commentary on how we judge love, and how death confounds us. *Find A Place For Me* becomes a primer for living life head-on, "instead of putting your shit in your back pocket and pretending it's not there.""

—Katie Kalisz, author of *Quiet Woman*

"*Find a Place for Me* is a luminous and loving portrait of a young family who must quickly pivot to a new normal when dad is diagnosed with ALS. Deirdre Fagan's sweet and straightforward prose is like a conversation with a close friend. It is less than one year that Fagan travels 'the long walk towards Bob's death and our departure from each other.' And in that span of time she conveys not only her own challenges but lets us get close to Bob, whose courage and humor resonates and lingers. This memoir is a journey of a terminal illness where every page is very much about being alive."

—Donna Kaz, author of *UN/MASKED, Memoirs of a Guerrilla Girl On Tour*

"At its heart, *Find a Place for Me* is a love story. Deirdre Fagan chronicles her family's heartbreaking, ten-month journey of caring for her young husband, Bob, as he battles ALS. Juggling her roles as caregiver, wife, lover and mother, Fagan paints a portrait of this intimate time with honesty and heart. In the end, their couplehood exemplified the code by which Bob lived—'with passion, honesty, strength, and an appreciation for each other and life itself.' This is a memoir that will stay with me."

—Susan Pohlman, author of *Halfway to Each Other: How a Year in Italy Brought Our Family Home*

"This book transcends the monolith of terminal illness, chronicling grief through the everyday rituals and meditations of marital intimacy. It's a story of death illumined on all sides by brimming life. Deirdre Fagan has written something profound in its honesty and humanity, celebrating a love that was—is—profound."

—Adam Schuitema, author of *The Things We Do That Make No Sense*

"Lyrical. Raw. Unflinching. Deirdre Fagan pulls no punches in *Find a Place for Me*, her searing memoir of the ten months she and her young family get on with the business of day-to-day living in the shadow of her husband's death sentence after being diagnosed with ALS. Faced with the certain loss of her 'one and only,' the bereft protagonist who has already survived the loss of mother and father and brothers, sends up smoke signals: 'They seek the help of others. They signal life. They signal danger.' Make no mistake, *Find a Place for Me* signals life. How do death and grief morph into a romance that affirms life itself? With honesty, tinged with Irish black humor and a dab of Nietzsche, and the strength of a love that defies human limits, that's how."

—Kathleen J. Waites, author of "Sarah Polley's Documemoir Stories We Tell: The Refracted Subject"

"In *Find a Place for Me*, Deirdre Fagan takes an astonishingly honest look at living with and coming to accept her husband's impending death from ALS. The book is unflinching in its honesty and ranges from the poetic and philosophical to the practical and humorous. The author pulls no punches, whether she is talking about sexual relations between the couple, her personal high points and low points, or the frank discussions she and her husband had about their futures. With honesty, dark humor, and the love of friends and family, the author and her husband 'get busy living' right up until the end and in the process face all the things most of us fear to even consider."

—John Cullen, author of *Town Crazy*

"As much as *Find a Place For Me* is a book about loss and terminal illness, it is also a book about love. Fagan's recounting of discovering her husband's illness, becoming a caretaker, raising children and holding down a job will resonate with anyone who has struggled to keep it all together in the face of such grief. This book brings humor, honesty, vulnerability, and, ultimately, hope in the face of loss."

—Dina Gachman, author of *So Sorry For Your Loss*

FIND A PLACE FOR ME

Deirdre Fagan

Pact Press

Published by Pact Press
An imprint of
Regal House Publishing, LLC
Raleigh, NC 27605
All rights reserved

https://pactpress.com

Printed in the United States of America

ISBN -13 (paperback): 9781646032839
ISBN -13 (epub): 9781646032846
Library of Congress Control Number: 2021949149

Excerpts from MDA's ALS Caregiver's Guide, published in 2013, are used with permission from Muscular Dystrophy Association, Inc.

Cover images © by Suzanne Tucker/Shutterstock
Cover design by C.B. Royal

Regal House Publishing, LLC
https://regalhousepublishing.com

Printed in the United States of America

For Maeve and Liam,
Liam and Maeve

I have told this story from memory while listening to Bob's voice in my mind. Some conversations have been constructed, and some names, locations, identifying characteristics, and details have been omitted or altered to protect the privacy of those depicted.

PROLOGUE

SIX MONTHS INTO THE DIAGNOSIS

"If you think you aren't going to be smoking when I die…"
Bob's words trailed off. I immediately thought, *Smoking as in
being reduced to a pile of ash?* A pile of cremated remains he would
be, and I most certainly would be smoking, both literally and
figuratively, as I burned down. I was already burning down, like
a lit cigarette. When he did die, I knew I would be sending up
smoke signals, hoping someone would see them and somehow
rescue me. I didn't know how I could ever survive this, this
thing that was happening to us, happening to Bob.

Six months into Bob's diagnosis, I broke down and bought a
pack of American Spirit cigarettes. *At least they are not filled with
all those additives,* I convinced myself. *They can't be that bad, right?*
Two weeks into smoking cigarettes only at night after the kids
had gone to bed, one of many crises made me say aloud to myself, "I deserve a fucking cigarette when I want one," and start
smoking in front of the kids. I was still only smoking three to
four a day, but sometime mid-afternoon I'd walk out onto our
Queen Anne porch in the sweltering summer heat, usually with
an iced coffee also in hand, and light one up. The first time my
son, Liam, saw me, he just stared at me. Aged nine, he was more
enthralled than disgusted. I looked at him and said, "What?" He
just stared blankly at me, shrugged his shoulders, and said, "I've
just never seen you smoke a cigarette before."

My daughter, Maeve, aged four, on the other hand, before
long announced, while climbing onto my lap, sweaty from the
Midwestern heat, "When I grow up, I'm going to smoke cigarettes too." I told her I didn't want her to because they are
"icky." After a few more days of watching me with curiosity,
Maeve announced, "I don't like when you go out on the porch

to smoke," which ignited in me the deep guilt I felt for indulging in the practice in the first place. So, the following Thursday I vowed to my daughter and one of my healthiest friends, Kate, that I would quit the habit, only weeks after I'd begun it. But it was now a Tuesday night late in the summer and I was standing, staring at Bob across the living room, in the lift chair that had now become his primary residence, and giving vocal debate to whether I should buy a pack while I was out.

"I really want a cigarette, but I probably shouldn't buy any. I decided I would stop. But I want one. I *really* want one." Bob looked at me as though the answer was obvious, as certain as his diagnosis. Quickly dismissing my concerns about the kids, about my health, he said: "I think when you are going out to buy your husband diapers, you should also be able to buy yourself some fucking cigarettes." I tilted my head to the left and my eyes upward. After some thought, I shrugged my shoulders with a degree of doubt and said, "You have a point." Shortly thereafter I responded: "You are right."

And that was just it about Bob. He always saw things so clearly, so plainly. He called it, whatever *it* was at the moment, like it was. And he was almost always right.

Bob was sitting right next to me when I first began to write this memoir in that recliner lift chair he'd been bound to for months, with the power chair, lent by the Muscular Dystrophy Association, he'd become so dependent upon a few feet from his raised legs. It was August 5, 2012, five days before our eleventh wedding anniversary and just over seven months since he had been diagnosed with amyotrophic lateral sclerosis.

Smoke signals. They signal danger. They request the presence of others. They seek the help of others. They signal life. They signal danger. They signal life. In my life, smoking cigarettes had nearly always signaled danger, or been the result of it.

1

FOREIGN TONGUE

Amyotrophic lateral sclerosis. It's another language, its words so foreign to a layperson, even a layperson with a doctorate in English. I know why they started calling it Lou Gehrig's disease. Not just for all of the reasons they put on the Muscular Dystrophy Association (MDA) website, such as Lou, who also had the disease, was amazing, or because his wife was also amazing, or because Lou made that awesome "Luckiest Man" speech, but because most people just look at you with a blank stare when you say it, like you have just said Suzy sells seashells down by the seashore. It's ironic that amyotrophic lateral sclerosis is a tongue twister, given that before long, the people who get it cannot twist their tongues enough to utter a single syllable, let alone eleven. And it certainly doesn't sound like something you die from. You die from cancer. You die from a car crash. You die when a plane is flown into the Twin Towers. You die in war. You die of a heart attack. You don't die of something called amyotrophic lateral sclerosis. That's something they check you for in gym when you are in fifth grade. That's something that they should just point out, like a curve in your spine, and send you home with or without medication for.

In fact, when the disease was first put on the table, this is exactly how I heard it. I heard them say the words, "Lou Gehrig's disease," or rather, I heard Bob say it. And I saw the words amyotrophic lateral sclerosis (ALS) come up on the computer screen when I typed "twitch in arm" in Google, but none of it registered. From December 11, 2011, when my husband told me he had a twitch in his arm and made a doctor's appointment to have it checked out (and I mocked him for such silliness), until December 29 when he was diagnosed, I uttered the words, but I didn't hear them. I didn't slow down to read what they meant on the screen. I just pushed them and it to the back of my mind as I continued to decorate the house and bake cookies and shop for Christmas for our two children, then three and eight. The furthest thing from my mind was that my husband was dying. Or at least I thought it was.

Looking back now, I realize I was in the deepest denial I've ever experienced in my life, and raw and painful energy was simmering just beneath the surface. If there are parts of our brains responsible for certain things, I locked away the part that could learn anything about this disease, and I went on with the part that thought what we were talking about was something that is really not a fun diagnosis but isn't something that will kill you. I honestly think that I spent those eighteen days in December 2011 thinking ALS was some sort of syndrome that caused inconveniences, occasional pain, and maybe some mild suffering in a person's life, but that is all. Sure, you have it forever, but you barely notice it, and you treat it. It acts up now and then. I actually didn't know anything about any such diseases either, but I had heard people tell me they had various ailments and they went on living, and so in my mind, without acknowledging it by name, ALS became something along the lines of hypothyroidism. I thought that whatever Bob had might make me cook differently, or require him to take some medications or change his lifestyle, but whatever it was would in the end only be occasionally uncomfortable for Bob, but not deadly. And despite my education and being a curious person, that's how I left ALS in my mind and in my conversations with other people from December 11 until December 29. The people we spoke to seemed to also go along with the charade. They didn't inform me about ALS. They probably figured that I, a researcher and Bob's wife, already knew. They assured me that it couldn't be ALS. They played along, as far as I knew. If they were troubled, they were doing a good job of being encouraging and hopeful and sparing me the gory details of this horrid disease.

When I was an undergraduate studying logic, my father used to joke: "Lou Gehrig has Lou Gehrig's disease. Coincidence?

I think not." It always made him chuckle and got a laugh of recognition out of me at the weak thinking implied in such an attempt at reasoning. This joke was pretty much all I knew about Lou Gehrig or the disease at that time.

No matter how much I press my memory, I cannot find any measure of reality about the disease in those few weeks. We talked to everyone about Bob's twitch and said he was seeing doctors and that Lou Gehrig's disease was "on the table," but at no point during that period did I ever stop to do more than say those words. I said them. I ignored them. I researched nothing. I repeated over and over the same lines. I baked cookies and entertained guests and went on.

But some part of me must have been terrified, because I remember spending, for example, all of the two-hour holiday party at my university wandering from table to table greeting people, and when someone asked me what I would be doing over our academic holiday break, I would tell them I wasn't sure because Bob had a twitch in his arm, they didn't know what it was, and there would be tests. I said it over and over in those few hours, clearly carried by some strong current that made me say it and say it, and sort of nod as people said it would be fine, and yet that fear, that deep unknowing, never caused me to seek the words on the screen that would tell me what ALS was or what it would do to decimate my husband and our family. When a colleague stared solemnly at me and assured me she was sure "it would be fine," I agreed, the way I might agree about how the food preparations would go over with guests. I didn't even think about the way she looked at me, until weeks later.

I wrapped presents for both of the kids and Bob. I did everything. I made fancy meals for the holidays with all of the fixings, even though Bob and I were usually the only ones who ate three quarters of it. If I made Thanksgiving dinner, which was almost always just for the four of us, there would be turkey, and stuffing with sausage and sage and water chestnuts and onions and mushrooms, and mashed potatoes, and two kinds of vegetables, usually Brussels sprouts and asparagus or green beans and broccoli, and homemade rolls, and homemade pumpkin pie, made from a real pumpkin with real cream, and homemade gravy and homemade cranberries. When I first tasted homemade cranberry sauce when I was twenty-one and the berries were still partly intact and literally popped in my mouth, I wondered where they had been all my life.

Bob loved food and he especially loved my food, so I would do all of it, even if Liam would eat only the turkey and rolls, and even when Maeve wasn't yet born or later, not eating solid food. I don't remember what we had for Christmas that year. I'm sure I went all out, though, because that's what I did, and it's also what I would have done to pretend everything was fine, just fine. I may even have printed a menu in a fancy font like at a white-tablecloth, five-star restaurant. I did that sometimes.

It wasn't until we canceled our vacation to Florida to go two hours away to St. Louis to see a specialist that something really started to rise in my consciousness. I had nearly lost it with Liam on Christmas morning when he didn't seem as excited as I wanted him to be about getting a miniature Southwest Airlines plane and tickets to Florida for the new year to see his dad's family. We cut the Christmas video recording so I could yell at little Liam about how entitled he and his sister were acting to not be excited about such a thing. Liam was eight at the time and his sister three. Liam was without a mean or selfish bone in his body, but when we both walked down the sixteen steps from the second story on Christmas morning and he saw all of the loot around the tree for the first time, and he turned to me and said, "It's not as much as last year," without any tone at all, matter-of-factly, like his dad, like a mere observation, what I thought he was saying was, "It's not enough. You haven't done enough. You aren't enough."

Looking back now, I realize Liam was simply making a comment. He was always a very observant kid, and I now know he was just making an observation. He didn't have to tell me that's what he was doing—I've never asked him and he likely does not remember—but knowing him, knowing his tone, the expression on his face, and recalling all of that so clearly as we stood on the stairs, I know he meant no judgment or criticism at all. He was just noticing something. And he was right. It wasn't the same as last year. It wasn't the same at all.

But it wasn't until the phone rang on December 28 and the nurse at our local doctor's office, our primary care physician's office, told us an appointment had been scheduled for eight a.m. the next morning in St. Louis, if we could get there in time, that my body began to prepare for the horror some part of me must have been burying in my gut all along. While my mind still hadn't fully kicked in, when Liam came in while we were hurriedly packing for the trip and ticking off all the practical things on the list—diapers and wipes for Maeve, who still wasn't potty trained, sippy cups and snacks for both of the kids, wine for us in the evening, swimsuits for the hotel pool—and asked us to put a bell on the new bicycle Bob's dad had bought him for Christmas (and that we had hidden under a sheet Christmas morning), I blurted out, angrily, viciously, as surprised as he was by what was coming out of my mouth: "Your father might be dying and all you can think about is a bell on your bicycle! LOOK. AT. US!"

Following an awkward silence, during which I felt shame and disbelief about what had come out of my mouth, Bob calmly explained, "Now isn't a good time, buddy. We can do that when we get back, okay? Why don't you help me and Mom get things loaded into the van?"

2

Numb Drive

On the drive to Barnes-Jewish Hospital, I reached over and stroked the back of my husband's neck and his soft, clean-shaven bald head, as I so often did when he was driving, and asked him if he was worried. Bob said, "No, not when we don't know if there is anything to be worried about," and I stared at his profile, amazed.

I believed Bob. I trusted him. I had never trusted anyone the way I trusted Bob. He had never hurt me—well, at least not since the first few months of our relationship when we were both working through our own shit. He had lied about being previously married, out of shame, because he thought, as a divorced man, he had been a failure as a husband. After we worked through that period of trust, things were completely different. Since then I had trusted him with every thought, every feeling I had ever had. There were no secrets in our relationship; there wasn't even anything to be withheld. I had never been more secure than I was when I was with Bob, or more content. If he wasn't worried, then neither was I. I told the kids, exuberantly, turning my head toward the back seats, "If Dad goes to the doctor and everything is okay, we can spend a few days in St. Louis, since we couldn't take the plane to Florida. We can hang out at the hotel and go swimming! It will be a mini-vacation!"

The next morning, everything would change forever, and I wouldn't even begin to realize it until I dropped off my six-foot-five, 240-pound husband at the automatic doors of the looming building. As I watched him from behind, his broad, strong figure walking into that imposing building in his cargos, T-shirt, flannel shirt, and hoodie, I thought, *There is something*

wrong. Your husband wouldn't be here if something weren't wrong. It was
the first time I had let in any fear. Watching Bob walk through
those glass doors, before I pulled away with the kids in the back
seat, was like watching him leave me and enter the gates of a
heaven (or hell) I didn't even believe in. Something in me sank.
Something in me finally knew.

My mind racing and beginning to process the previous few
weeks differently, I drove directly back to the hotel with the two
kids. They entertained themselves with cartoons and playing
inside closets, and our daughter who couldn't read pretending
to read the Bible and the Book of Mormon, while I sat at the
small desk in the room and read and read and read on the laptop about Lou Gehrig's disease, trying desperately to memorize
the three words amyotrophic lateral sclerosis. I couldn't retain
the words. I said them over and over in my head, mispronounc-
ing them. I had been saying Lou Gehrig's disease when people
asked. I hadn't known the actual words because I didn't think
they had been worth remembering. Confession: I didn't want
to know them. I didn't want to think about it. But then, in that
hotel room, on the laptop, reading and rereading, I knew what
the disease meant. I didn't entirely understand what it was, but
I knew what it meant. It meant "two to five years after diagno
sis." Two to five years. My husband was forty-three. Two to five
years. He may be dead by the time he was forty-five. Two to five
years. My son would be no older than thirteen. He'd probably
be ten; my daughter, five. Even my conservative estimate was
wrong.

After almost three hours of reading in that claustrophobic
box of a hotel room, I decided I couldn't take any more slamming of closets or cartoons or laugh tracks on kids' shows. I
needed to escape the room; I needed to get out of the box I felt
trapped inside. We would go wander around the Target that was
partway to the hospital. I had my cell phone. Bob would call me
when he was ready to be picked up. Everything was going to be
okay, I assured myself. It had to be.

We had been inside Target only about ten minutes, my mind
imagining we were going to stay at the hotel a few more days

and go swimming, so I was in the travel-size aisle with a large shopping cart and the two kids in tow, stocking up on supplies, when my phone rang. All the joy had left Bob's voice.

"I'm ready," he said, and I knew. I knew the way I knew Bob. But neither of us was ready for what he sounded like. "Is everything okay? What do they think it is?" "ALS," he said, and this time, I knew what it meant. "No," I said. "No."

My chest seized. I held back the tears that were forming. I stuffed it down. I had stuffed death down before. I told Bob I was on my way. I hung up in shock. I felt more claustrophobic than in the hotel room. I wanted to run. My stomach convulsed and receded. Liam asked what was wrong and I said sternly, "We have to go get Daddy right now, something is very wrong, and we have to go right now." Hearing my distress, the kids were obedient and quiet. I was obedient and quiet. Instead of abandoning my cart, and without the time to put back everything I had mindlessly and optimistically placed in the cart, I became dutiful. I fulfilled the obligation to buy what was in it. I stood on a line. I returned the cart. I carried the bags. Somehow, I managed to get all of us into the minivan and buckle Maeve into her seat.

Those first few moments are partly vivid and partly a blur: My turning to Liam in the back seat and saying, "Daddy is really sick. He's really, really sick. We have to go get him at the hospital," shaking, I'm sure, as I said this. Maeve, there somewhere behind me in her car seat, I have no recollection of—I hadn't addressed her at all, that I can remember. I must have, but I cannot remember. Too young to understand, she must have simply been observing the whole horrific scene. Maybe she was asking, "Mommy, what's wrong?" Or "Mommy, why are you crying?" I can imagine her saying this. I can imagine her curiosity about what she does not know and cannot understand, but for some reason, I cannot recall her.

I was so absorbed in my own shock, so trying to maintain myself in the face of terror, sheer terror at the thought of losing the only person I had ever fully trusted and who had never hurt me, that it was all I could manage to get through the checkout and out of that Target. It was all I could do to compose myself enough to turn the key in the ignition and move from that parking spot. It was all the strength I could muster to acknowledge my children at all, to know that they were there, that they would be a part of this too. Maeve hadn't even been alive to experience the deaths of my father or middle brother, and Liam was too young to recall—he'd been only three when they'd died, the same age Maeve was now.

I know I called my friend Sharon, "Nana" to my kids, whom I had met when I was seventeen. We are bonded by history and time. Her husband had died five months before my mother, when I was twenty-three, and during that time, our families were woven together by crisis, tragedy, and grief. She is a woman who worries. Being well aware of our trip to the doctor, she had been eager to hear the news and had said to call her once I knew anything. Getting the kids into the car robotically, I had picked up the phone and automatically dialed, desperate to reach toward the family I had left, even if we weren't blood relatives. As soon as I began to speak, the horror was released.

"It's Lou Gehrig's disease. It's terminal. Two to five years." I remember the sound of her voice, her horror, and her acknowledgment.

"Oh no, Deirdre. No. It can't be. What did they say? How do they know?" Sharon was a medical transcriptionist. She knew medical terminology. "I don't know. I don't know anything. Bob just called me. I was in the Target. I'm in the van now. I have to go get him." "Where are the kids?" "I've got them. They are here." "Okay. I'm so sorry, Deirdre. Please call me later," Sharon pleaded. I told her I would—I had to pick up Bob—and I hung up.

Before driving out of that lot I remember distinctly Liam, in the back seat to my right, to the right of his sister, rocking back and forth, back and forth, repeating over and over, "I don't want Daddy to die, I don't want Daddy to die, I don't want Daddy to die." The more he rocked and the more he said it, the more my anxiety rose in my body, and the angrier I became, not at him but at the words, at *death* and *dying*.

I whipped my head toward him and shouted, "Stop it! Stop it, okay? You don't know what death is, but I do! You HAVE to stop saying that!" This was one of the most calloused moments of my life.

I was so unsympathetic. I was so horribly consumed by my own devastation in that moment I could hardly be present enough to more than mechanically fulfill the responsibilities before me. I needed to start the car. I needed to put it in gear. I needed to drive. I needed to get Bob. I needed to breathe. I needed to drive. I needed to start the car. I needed to breathe. Everything else needed to be on hold. The world had to stop.

I silenced my son when I should have hugged him. I should have stopped everything and gotten out of the van and gone to his side and hugged him. And where was Maeve? She was there. I don't remember her saying or doing anything. And Maeve always said and did things. She was always the one to demand that her needs be met. Liam was always so independent and so quiet; we often hardly knew he was there. But in that moment, at that time, they behaved the opposite of themselves. Liam was asking for something and Maeve wasn't, and I didn't deliver. I couldn't.

I composed myself and did the only thing I could do. I moved us forward in our minivan, the one that was supposed to hold an intact family—a family with two parents, two kids, and in our case, a dog, a golden retriever named Ivy—and drove back to Barnes-Jewish to get Bob.

The car was quiet. I somehow took a parking ticket from a slot. I somehow parked the van. I somehow walked our two children into the enormous building that I had seen my husband swallowed by earlier that morning.

We walked along a corridor from the parking lot to the main building. The building is constructed like an airport. Walking from the garage to the building, I found myself entering another world, a world of sick people, a new country. A country of people who are ill, who are there only because they are really, really sick or the people they love are really, really sick. It seemed to me everyone was walking around in this haze, in the haze I had entered, looking at one another for a way out of desperation.

The lobby is vast, so vast, the building so grand, that there is an information desk in the center that has a continuous line of people asking where to go. I had never been in a country, on a planet, like this one before. I had been in hospitals, but this was so enormous it was a world unto itself. I was not sure where Bob was supposed to be, but I knew I must find him. Cell phones didn't work in the building—or at least mine didn't—so I couldn't get him on the phone no matter how many times I redialed, which I did, every few seconds. The kids and I walked around the first floor but we didn't see him. We looked in the directory and took the elevator up a few floors to neurology, but we didn't see him. There were acres of offices, doors, and glass windows. We used the bathroom. We went back down to where the information desk was and got off the elevator. The kids were ahead of me, always a few steps ahead of me.

As we came off the elevator, I spotted Bob. I saw him from behind as I had seen him enter the building that morning, but his head was now down, he was looking at his feet rather than forward. He was still broad-shouldered and strong, his feet carrying him as they always did, forward so directly, not duck-splayed like my feet, like the feet of my brothers. He was pulling his shirt down in back, rearranging it with ease. He was wearing brown cargo pants; he had always worn cargo pants or shorts. They had always carried his keys, his asthma medication, his wallet, his change, his tissues, but as we had children, they also carried binkies, bottles, formula, diapers, wipes, Band-Aids…he was as prepared for any given day with kids as he would have been for a day hike on a trail in the wilderness. I carried a purse, but he was always the one with ready supplies.

I told Liam to catch up with his dad, to get his attention, since children can run in a lobby. Though I wanted to run, I felt I should retain my composure, should walk calmly toward the man in front of me whom I loved with all of me and who we now both knew was dying. I should walk calmly to this death even though I wanted to run through glass windows. I should not make a scene.

As though on a movie set, my children—roughly thirty feet ahead of me—threw their arms around their father's legs and waist and shouted, "Daddy!" Bob turned, so easily, so smoothly, as he had been able to do since childhood, in the way so many of us take for granted, as if moving, swiveling in our own bodies is a birthright, and he embraced those kids and looked back at me. As time froze, I walked briskly to him and threw my arms around him, only dimly aware of the nearly fifty people I knew were surrounding us, of their movements, or of their eyes. Standing center stage but oblivious to anyone and any sound around us, in that space we had always been so good at creating when alone, we held each other and collapsed into sobs while the children gripped our legs.

"I love you. I love you so much."

"I love you. I love you. I love you. I love you."

"I love you so much. I'm here."

I gripped his head and his back. I didn't care who was looking.

Walking numbly back to the parking garage, holding hands with Bob, only dimly aware of my own body, we began the long walk toward Bob's death and our departure from each other. I was so incapable of grasping the truth that was breaking through that I could not even manage to work the machine to pay our parking fee without the help of the attendant, and I thought to myself, *This is what she does. She helps people who have just learned that the person they love is dying pay their parking fees. She's used to this. She's so together, whereas I look like I've just been sentenced to a death, which I have, only not my own.* Losing Bob seemed worse than dying.

I have taken three numb drives to death in my life. The first was to my mother's body. The second was to my father's. The third was back from Barnes-Jewish that day, even though Bob was still very much alive and driving.

Sitting in the minivan staring at the many cars on the road with Bob and me, I suddenly became aware of the date:

December 29, my mother's birthday. Her cancer—discovered the month after I had completed undergraduate college—had been the first and last experience I had had with a terminal illness. She had died two months after diagnosis never having known where the cancer originated, since by then it had infiltrated multiple organs around and near the gall bladder.

When we are out on the road passing by houses, we imagine the people who live in them. We wonder what their lives are like, and sometimes whom they love, or how many children they have, or whether they are happy. But when we drive down the road, do we wonder the same thing of the people in the cars beside us? People are driving in all sorts of directions, some of them drifting on their way to work, but others are elated and on their way to lovers or marriages or births, and others are throbbing or numb and on their way to or from hospitals, morgues, funeral homes, cemeteries.

3

ALS?

When Bob and I arrived back at the hotel that afternoon, we were all exhausted. I have no idea what the kids knew exactly, or how their little minds could even begin to process what they had overheard or been told directly. But I remembered some of what I had said to Liam and I also know both Bob and I tended to say what was on our minds, and that while we must have been holding ourselves at least partly together for the kids on that drive home, I've never been very good at hiding what I was feeling or not blurting out what I was thinking.

I have that memory of Liam rocking back and forth in the back seat at Target, saying he didn't want his father to die, and I have the memory of the kids at Bob's legs, squeezing tightly in the Barnes-Jewish lobby, but on that ride back to the hotel my mind was too busy trying to make sense of a suddenly incomprehensible world to be much of a mother to either of them.

Griefs pile up, one upon another. Each new grief is a grief unto its own, but it's also an assembly. The first loss is always the first loss, and those that come later are always in relation to the first and the rest.

Bob's terminal diagnosis wasn't only Bob's. It was ours as a family. Families are like machines that depend upon all of the various parts working in unison to function well. When one part of the family can no longer function, or needs repair or even lubrication, the machine seizes while attention is drawn to the part that needs mending.

In the case of a terminal illness, a machine begins to break down. At first one part may just need more attention, more lubrication, a repair of some kind, but eventually the parts are no longer available, and the machine slows until it no longer runs at all. This was only the beginning, but the machine as a whole momentarily came to a stop that day.

Bob's diagnosis was the harbinger of the end not only of his life, but of every relationship he'd ever had with anyone, including with our children, with me. But it was also, for me, the anticipated loss that made me feel as though all the other deaths I had survived would become unbearable: my eldest brother, Paul, by suicide at twenty-five; my mother, Maureen, from cancer at fifty-one; my father, Frank, from a heart attack at sixty-eight; and my brother Sean from liver failure at forty. I had been eighteen, twenty-three, and thirty-six when these deaths occurred. I had managed to live without them all; I now believed I had survived the final two losses because I had Bob, whom I'd started dating when I was 30 and he 31. I couldn't begin to fathom how I could outlive not only my parents and siblings but also Bob.

In 2006, when Dad and Sean died, people around me began comparing me to Job, to my face. In the Bible, Job loses his entire family as a test of his faith. I had no faith, so it wasn't testing anything but my fortitude. Any faith I had had was gone in my twenties, after I lost my eldest brother and mother. The only faith I had left was dependent on memory and on keeping them alive through the stories I told about them. They existed in nature, the human, and the environment, and this was the only eternity that interested me.

I wanted Nietzsche's eternal recurrence as stated in *The Gay Science* #341. According to Nietzsche, to embrace the eternal recurrence of one's own life—to not only accept but also choose to repeat your same life over and over again—is to fully embrace one's life. I wanted everything that had happened in my life to happen again and for me to choose it. I had experienced pain from what had once brought me joy, but I had also become *me* through those experiences. A repeat of all my life's experiences would cause more pain but would also bring me great joy. Eternal recurrence would also allow me to experience my family members again. As is said, the strength of our love exists in direct proportion to the strength of our grief.

But now the family I had created was going to disassemble too. It was more than I believed I could bear. It was more than anyone should have to, but I knew people had to and did; I knew people had survived worse, but I didn't want to. I wanted to die. I wanted Bob to go on living. I wanted to take his place.

The kids never fell asleep in the middle of the day anymore. At eight, Liam was past daytime naps, and Maeve had never been a good sleeper. When the children's book *Go the Fuck to Sleep* came out the summer of 2011, Bob said he could have written it. Given the word *fuck*, it sounded as though he had, as Bob peppered most sentences with *fuck* on a regular basis.

I always needed more sleep than Bob did. He could rouse himself more easily and more quickly. He was the one who sat up late nights with baby Liam when after a change and nursing, the boy didn't doze back off. They watched the *Late Show* while I returned to REM. Bob was always the one staying up late with the kids, fueled by Mountain Dew. He always said one of the primary ways I needed love was in the form of time to sleep; he knew that about me, and I loved that he did.

After the numb drive from Barnes-Jewish, we found ourselves back in the hotel room near the St. Louis airport, a hotel where we had stayed many times before, as we had regularly had overnight outings in St. Louis to get our city "fix" and to bring the children to various venues: the zoo, the children's museum, etc. When we got back to the hotel this time, Liam and Maeve did something they had never done before and have never done since: they climbed into bed and promptly fell asleep in the middle of the afternoon—and at the same time.

On that afternoon when Bob and I most needed them to, those children climbed into the bed beside ours and dozed right off. It was the greatest gift. Maybe their little bodies were as overcome as ours with the medical news. Maybe, but I couldn't get out of myself to see. All Bob and I knew was that it was a blessing they were asleep.

Bob and I were now alone. We could cry without eyes watching. We could talk openly about what we were feeling. My six-foot five-inch, 240-pound husband, so strong, so muscular, sat curled over with that arm twitching, curled forward, seated at the foot of the queen bed, and in a steady sob began apologizing to me.

"I'm so sorry, Dee. I'm so sorry. I never wanted to do this to you. You, of all people. I never wanted to hurt you. I always just wanted to be there for you, for the kids; now I can't do that. I can't be there for you. I'm so sorry."

"It's not your fault. It's okay. It's not your fault." I stroked his neck, and his back, and his head, sitting beside him.

"You already lost Sean, your dad, everyone. I'm so sorry."

"You are not doing anything to me. This is happening to you. Yes, it's happening to us, but you are not doing anything to me. Look at me." I turned his face toward mine. "It's not your fault. I love you."

Bob was not a disappointment; he was the best thing that had ever happened to me. He was the reason I was still alive. His gorgeous frame sat on the edge of that bed weeping in the position of *The Thinker*, sobbing into his hands while I sat next to him, my own eyes wide open but dry. I wasn't crying. I was soldiering. I was in shock. We then climbed into the bed and held each other as tightly as we could.

Maybe we made love. I'm not sure if we did, but I think we did. I remember Bob on top of me—either because we were making love or because we were embracing—and I remember him looking at me, looking right into me, and I remember gripping his bulging, twitching bicep and feeling his soft, warm, hairy belly against mine while I stroked his prematurely bald head and looked up at him. I remember the sunlight of midday creeping through the windows and the children's restful breaths on the other bed. And I remember very clearly, the most clearly of all, the blue package over Bob's right shoulder on the desk. I had packed snacks for the two-hour trip to St. Louis for the mini-vacation we were now not going to have, and the juice boxes and salty and sweet snacks were all lined up on the desktop.

I was staring at the zipped blue bag of "everything" pretzel crisps across the room and this is what I was thinking as Bob lay there on top of me twitching: *I have three to five years to live* in Morse code from his arm. Well, not exactly Morse code, but just as much as everything bagels and pretzels are not everything, this twitch was Morse code. Until now, he was the only one who had been deciphering the code. *Everything bagels are not everything,* I kept repeating in my head. I don't know why they don't say "all" bagels instead. *All* would at least imply "all" toppings, but everything suggests "everything" topping, which is not correct. And then Bob curled up next to me and fell into a deep sleep. As I lay there, unable to sleep, listening to Bob and the kids breathe peacefully, I stared across the room at the desk with the phone on it, and the row of snacks, and I focused all of my anger on that damn blue bag of pretzel crisps and screamed silently to myself, *Everything chips are not everything! They say they are everything but they aren't!* I wanted to hurt something.

I was angry at the bag for advertising everything because all I could think was that everything, everything in my entire world was in that room, and I was going to lose the center of it: Bob. Since I am a realist, I had decided when we each turned forty that we at least had until we were fifty before one of us would get cancer. Since my mom died of cancer at fifty-one, this seemed plausible. At that time, I was eager to assure myself that we had at least a decade, because having lost the last two members of my immediate family so young, I had calculated that making it to fifty would mean at least fourteen more years without a major catastrophe. But here we were only five years after the last major loss.

When someone you love is dying, "everything" else can go to hell, including that fucking misleading package of pretzel crisps.

Early that morning, I had still been imagining Lou Gehrig's disease as something along the lines of lactose intolerance, but that's not what it is. It's not something you live with—it's something that kills you, incrementally, as your muscles deteriorate and you eventually die, usually of asphyxiation. Bob, who had been born with asthma and been rushed to the hospital regularly as a kid—had had weekly shots, had been burned all over his body at the age of two from accidentally pulling a teapot on top of himself, and still had half a nipple and missing chest hair from the burns—carried in his cargos, along with the baby wipes and binkies, the meds he took daily puffs of, and an inhaler for emergencies, and yet he was going to die because he was not going to be able to breathe. It was the cruelest fucking joke. It was everything. He was my everything.

A means *no.*

Myo means *muscle.*

Trophic means *nourishment.*

No. Muscle. Nourishment.

As I listened to the three most important people in my world breathing in their sleep, I began doing math again. I'm an English teacher. I can't do anything but basic math, unlike Bob who started out as a physics major and could do complicated equations, but I'm damn good at basic math. I handled our bills because, growing up poor, I knew how to handle money and I could do quick math in my head when it came to percentages of sales, mortgages, and the like. I learned math to survive. "At most Maeve will be eight, Liam thirteen. It could be sooner. She could be six—he could be eleven. Some people live longer. They could be wrong. I can't do this."

Calculations. I was doing calculations. I was trying to calculate something that had no calculation, had not been fated, was no punishment for anything, and was no one's fault. It was just what happened. Things happen. Really awful, shitty things happen. I knew this, but I was tired of them happening to me.

"Everything bagels are NOT everything!" I whispered angrily, and then I collapsed into sleep too.

4

THE DIAGNOSIS

Bob had a long sleep. It was probably not more than an hour, but it felt like much longer. Time has a way of changing depending on our emotions. Car wrecks occur in slow motion. A meaningful kiss or good sex that lasts minutes feels like thirty minutes, an hour. We are shocked when we look at the clock and we've been transported there and back and only twenty minutes have passed.

That day seems both long and short in my memory. Waiting in the room while Bob was at the hospital—long, very long. The walk from inside Target to the parking lot—long, very long. Looking for Bob in the hospital—long, very long. None of these took anywhere near the same amount of time. The whole day—short. One day. One day and our lives together had been abbreviated as quickly as placing a period at the end of a sentence. There was an end mark now, and we had a pretty good idea of when it was going to be. When my mother was told she had two more months, I didn't believe it. I thought she would live longer, but the doctors were shockingly accurate. Two months it was. Just two months.

Bob didn't actually get a diagnosis that day. After the nap, he told me that the doctors hadn't issued a diagnosis, and I stared blankly at him, shocked again. My mind began replaying the past few hours of our lives.

"If they didn't diagnose you, then why do you think you have ALS? Why did you tell me you have ALS if you don't know whether you have ALS?"

"They just talked about me as though I wasn't in the room."

"Okay."

"ALS is the only thing on the table; it's obvious that's what I have."

"But how is it obvious? How do you know?"

"It's what I have. They just don't have the guts to tell me. They want to do the tests, but the tests aren't going to show anything. I have ALS, that's what I have."

"I don't understand."

Bob began to explain. When Bob had pressed the doctors for alternative diagnoses, they had none. They just wouldn't commit to ALS that day because there is no affirmative test. It's a process of ruling out other possibilities. Bob couldn't pee on a stick, as I had repeatedly to try to figure out whether I was ovulating so we could get pregnant, or get blood drawn from his arm, as I did to confirm the pregnancy that was such a miracle, or undergo an MRI, as I had just before I was diagnosed with Lyme disease, to know for certain that he had ALS. This seemed absurd to me. Another absurdity.

"They can't know whether you have it? Ever? They just guess?"

"If you want to make a lot of fucking money doing nothing, become a neurologist," Bob sarcastically remarked. "All they do is push and pull at you—shit they did two hundred years ago— then look at what you can already see yourself, and say, 'Yup, your arm is twitching, you are weaker,' and send you home. It's fucking bullshit. They don't know fucking anything about this disease."

But Bob did know something about it. He knew what he had. "I have ALS," he said, and he said it the way he said all things he was certain of, like how far he would go to protect our children or me, or how he would write anyone off if they didn't accept us for who we were, including his own family, or how convincing he was when he told me he loved me.

"But how do you know?"

"I just know."

"How long have you known?"

"Pretty much since the day you looked up the twitch on the computer while I peered over your shoulder in the office."

"When will they know? When will they tell you?" I asked.

"The doctor is supposed to call us later this week, with the results of the tests they did today."

"But you are sure it's ALS?"

"I'm sure. I could tell by the way they didn't look at me. By the way they talked as though I wasn't there. Fucking cowards."

Bob said he knew. And I believed him.

The children were still asleep when the first texts started rolling in:

Did you hear anything?

What do they think it is?

Hey, just checking in. Let us know how it went today.

Some of the texts had come in while we were asleep. I needed to figure out whether to respond, and what I was going to be telling people. I also needed to call Nana Sharon back. It had been quite the phone call I had given her earlier that day in that Target parking lot.

Bob told me I should start telling people he had ALS: "That's what it is. Just tell them that's what it is."

Whom do you call when good news happens? Whom do you call when bad news does? Whom do you call first? Whom we reach toward signals a lot about the relationships we do or don't have in our lives, and these people, or our relationships to them, change. It is in constant flux. We often talk about our lives as having occurred in "chapters." These chapters—which we distinguish in hindsight, of course—are often identifiable by location, proximity to certain other people, or roles that we fulfill at school, at work, or in our home lives.

There was a time in my life when the first person I wanted to tell anything to was my mother. There was a time in my life when the first person I wanted to tell anything to was my father. I can recall distinctly in which directions I reached during every tragedy or crisis in my life and whom I expected to be there and who actually was there. Who we expect to be there for us, and who really is, is often far more different than we can ever imagine. It was time for me to begin reaching, but toward whom?

5

You Will Call

When Bob tells you he has a terminal illness and you can start calling people, you do it. You do it because you believe him and trust him more than anyone you've ever known, not because he's always right, but because he has never once pretended he was when he wasn't. So, you know he's right, and you tell people because you must, because telling gets it out of you, because telling, the adrenaline of launching into 911 mode, the digesting of information for you, comes from saying a thing aloud again and again as a sort of chant, and so you will. You will call. You will tell. You will send your first smoke signals.

Bob knew how much I would need a support system. He knew nearly everything about what I needed before I did. He predicted my needs throughout his illness and he was right; he helped prepare me by being the one to tell me everything first. Soon I would become that for him too. I would be the one who could see from the outside and could predict what he needed next. He told me so and he was right. We propped each other up like this—we always had—and now we were going to do it better than ever before and more consistently and constantly.

Bob told me I should start calling people, but not his family. That could wait until the next day. He would call them himself. He needed some time.

Our hotel room was standard with two beds, a TV, and chair or two, and so the only place I could make phone calls with privacy from the children was in the bathroom. After the kids awoke, ate room service because we couldn't muster the motivation to even leave the room, and got sucked into the television, I walked into the bathroom, shut the door, turned on the fan, sat on the toilet, and watched myself in the mirror as if I were watching someone else's life in a movie. I wasn't in my own body.

Having no family left besides Bob and his family at this point in my life, the only person I had reached toward so far was Nana Sharon. I hadn't felt the urge to call anyone else just yet, though I felt an obligation to respond to the texts and to call our closest friends who were spread out around the country.

One text, from our friend Casey, was received shortly after our return to the hotel. Casey was one of our closest friends at the time, and young, in his late twenties. He was a former student of mine who had become a friend and creative writing peer who stopped by the house several times a week. He knew where we were and why that fateful day. He had, by early afternoon, texted to ask if there was any news. Those texts caused this young man to be one of the first to hear the news and the horror in my voice. I realize now what a burden that must have been for someone so young. But I wasn't thinking. I was reacting and acting. I was going through motions but not able to reflect at all about them. When I told Casey, he immediately offered to watch the kids for us the next night when we got home so that Bob and I could be alone, not on view for the children, able to think and to manage our emotions with privacy, and to begin digesting the devastating news we had received.

I continued to make calls. I don't recall in what order, but I remember who I called—Alyse, a member of our writing circle, who was sure to begin hearing the news and who I wanted to tell first; Steve, Suzanne, and Kate, all of whom had worked with Bob at his previous university. Everyone was sure "the diagnosis must be wrong," that "a second opinion was necessary," that "surely this couldn't be true." I told them Bob said it was so and that I believed Bob. I finally cried, sitting on the toilet, staring at myself in the mirror, uttering the words and maintaining some degree of composure and strength by continuing to remain partly numb through it all. The conversations came with shock, disbelief, encouragement that the diagnosis might be false, or that certainly in Bob's case it would be the longer prognosis, that we could do this, that we were strong.

I finished making the phone calls and left the bathroom and climbed into bed with Bob and became overwhelmingly aware of the twitching in his arm beside me, not only telling me what was, but now becoming an ominous foretelling of what was to come. Exhaustion guided us to sleep and we held each other close, despite the fact that we never used to sleep that way. We were intertwined in every other way, but given Bob's size and mine we could never quite get comfortable in each other's arms in bed. Just as while standing, in order to make our lips meet without craning my neck, I had to stand on a step, in bed my neck always had to be craned to be on his shoulder, and my arms could barely reach over his 40-inch waist when we were spooning, but on this night we held each other all night and slept deeply the way one does after physically laboring all day.

When you have children, especially young children, you are required to keep your own emotions and needs at bay more frequently than not, at least if they are your number-one priority, which mine were. This maintenance of others is exhausting and necessary in order to care for children and accomplish everything that life demands. While we did not hold everything in, as Bob and I believed in at least a degree of controlled honesty, we certainly couldn't curl into the balls we wanted to curl into and just stay in that hotel room alone for an eternity. We needed to check out, drive home, unpack the car, feed the children and ourselves, and generally go on living. I didn't know how I would. Bob desperately wanted to live but I desperately wanted to die.

The next morning it was time to call my dearest colleague and then-chair of my department, Terrence, about spring classes, which would begin in less than two weeks, to let him know that Bob couldn't teach the extra class at my university he'd signed on for as a part-time sabbatical replacement, and that I would want to scale back as much as possible on my responsibilities outside of my teaching in the coming months.

Bob was ready to move forward with the practical matters. He was the one who urged the call about work. I would have been calling Terrence anyway, since he was one of my best friends in Illinois, but that morning I sat in the lobby of the hotel while Bob and the kids loaded the car and got me a coffee, and I cried into the phone to Terrence about the impossibility of it all. I stared at the gaudy carpet that all hotel lobbies seem to have, blinking through my tears, with no regard to passers-by, going over the logistics of scheduling while Terrence, too, expressed his disbelief that this could at all be true. Terrence had known me only a little more than a year when my father and brother died, but he soon became like family to me. He became a combination of father and brother, being more than ten years older than I and sharing many of the same values and appreciation for literature and music that I had shared with my dad and Sean. The phone calls that used to last three hours with my family now lasted three hours with Terrence. We would begin by solving some issue at work, but soon we would be talking about Yeats or the Grateful Dead or our pasts. Just a few years before, Terrence and I had painted my bathroom together while listening to Irish tunes and drinking Guinness.

Terrence was tall, as tall as Bob, even about an inch taller, and when he walked down a hall ahead of me, he looked like my middle brother, Sean, albeit thinner. He even had a bit of that duck gait Sean had had—feet splayed out as he lumbered along. And we had an easy way with each other. We could go to dinner and sit in long silences without the least bit of discomfort. He was family to me—the closest I had to it in the area. I had told him so more than once. Terrence assured me work would be fine and I shouldn't worry about it at all. He would take care of everything; just teach my own classes and he would take care of everything else.

When Bob first received his diagnosis—or should I say, diagnosed himself—in St. Louis, I could not anticipate who would be there for me or for us, but I followed my instincts, my gut, and the unfolding that naturally happens as our molecules bounce from place to place, struggling to survive.

Moments in our lives come to me in flashes—the scene in the Target; in the bathroom of the hotel room; in the hallway when Kate, who hadn't been home the night before, called back and the kids were awake, and I burrowed into a corner near an ugly floral decoration and confessed that Bob was dying, while people rolled suitcases past me toward the elevator. I smelled the wallpaper and stared at the baseboards. Tears ran down my face and started my nose running too. I, a washer of hands dozens of times a day, wiped my nose on my sleeve. I didn't care about anything but that moment, that telling, my Love. I shooed the kids back into the room when they wanted to comfort me, as though they had no idea what was happening.

And then there is the vision of leaving the parking lot that morning. The van was loaded, Bob was driving, and I was sitting in the passenger seat. As Bob took the turn out of the lot—a lot I knew so well from having stayed at this hotel numerous times before—he turned toward me, then back out the window. The kids were surely buckled into their seats, but Bob and I were again immersed in our own world in the front. The early morning sun was shining through the windshield, onto the dash, and into our eyes as he cranked the wheel toward the exit. He glanced at me again, and then, again looking forward, he said, "I want you to love again."

Another blow. Another shock. And dread. And awe. I felt like throwing up.

"What?"

"I want you to love again. I want you to find someone else after I'm gone."

"Seriously? I don't want to talk about this. I'm not ready to talk about this. I don't want to talk about this," I said forcefully, as I gripped the armrest on the door with the sudden urge to exit the moving vehicle.

"I mean it. I want you to go on and love again after me. You deserve love in your life."

"I don't want to talk about this," I said, becoming angry.

"Okay," he said. "But I want you to know that. I just want you to know that."

It hadn't even been twenty-four hours since we had learned he was going to die, and he was already thinking about me and imagining my future. I was still back at Barnes-Jewish hospital, holding him in the lobby, crying in front of strangers, feeling for the third time the aftershocks of sudden loss, even though he was breathing right next to me as we began the drive back to our beautiful home in Illinois.

While the sky was sunny and clear, the roads without snow cover, we drove home in a mental fog. We were exhausted and overwhelmed as we stared ahead at the road knowing what we hadn't known two days before and only beginning to comprehend the truth of it. I'm sure I was interacting with the kids and offering them snacks and generally trying to act as normal as possible, but I don't remember them being there. I hardly remember myself being there.

Bob was barely present in his own body, too, as a ticket sent to us a month later in the mail would attest. He apparently caught the tail end of a yellow light just outside of Hannibal, Missouri, and was issued a ticket for running a red light. Our van was caught on camera and there we were in the image, two shadowy figures in the front seat of a white minivan hurtling toward a future that now had an abrupt stop sign. When the picture and ticket were sent to us, it felt like yet another cruel cosmic joke. It was as though from the heavens, we had been frozen on camera if only to preserve the hell we had suddenly found ourselves in. We now had a concrete image of what it was like to be literally driving toward death—our very own twenty-first-century version of Emily Dickinson's famous carriage ride—and that death journey not only came with a fine to the police department we couldn't afford, and more minutiae to address in the form of various phone calls to the insurance company and a lawyer—it had stolen more of the limited time we now had by transferring it to the ordinariness and meaninglessness of the most mundane aspects of living.

When we arrived back home, we unloaded the vehicle and waited the way one waits for an eagerly awaited phone call for the evening date that would allow us privacy, intimacy, to be alone in the world that existed before children, before the demands that took us from each other daily, before death warrants.

But there is one more thing notable about the afternoon of

our return home that I long to erase, not from my mind, but from that afternoon. While I was busy unloading the vehicle, little Liam threw his arms around my legs and shouted gleefully, "Mom! That was the best vacation we've ever had!" Before I could check myself, and feeling slapped in my face, not by my dear sweet boy, but by life itself, I looked back at him, appalled and dumbfounded, and said, as though I were speaking to an adult, "We just found out your dad is dying, and you think that's the best vacation we've ever had?"

I ache when I recall these words. My poor, sweet boy was trying to make the world whole again, right not only in his world, but in ours, bring joy to us as he always had, and I took a swift sledgehammer to his open-hearted gesture of love. I was so fully aware the world was no longer whole, could never be whole, that I could not be there for him in that moment as I should have been. I was struggling to put on my own oxygen mask. His had to wait.

I'd like to think I said I was sorry after that and held him close. I think I did. I'm almost certain I did. I most often do when I am far from an ideal parent, which I often am, not only when my heart is breaking into parts, but when I'm tired, or stressed, or overwhelmed. I wish I could describe to myself what happened when I held him close and apologized to the top of his dear, sweet head, smelling his young boy smell. I wish I could tell myself for sure I said I'm sorry, but that's not the part I remember.

After the long afternoon of waiting and holding ourselves together, if only moderately, we handed the responsibilities of the kids to Casey around dinnertime, and became for the evening only a couple, a couple before children, Bob and Dee in our own little world, like when we had first met.

6

THE FIRST DATE

I made a reservation with points at the hotel in town where Bob and I often went on dates. I know this sounds really sexy, and it is, but it wasn't ever about sex—well, not entirely, anyway. When you have small kids and no one around to watch them for you, you often starve for alone time as a couple. When we would pay for a sitter and finally have a date, Bob and I sometimes wanted social time with people and would join others for dinner or meet at a bar or go to someone's house, but sometimes we just wanted to return to what we called Bob and Deirdre World—the *we* we were before and the *we* we were when no one else was present. When Bob and I were alone, it was as if the entire world zoomed away and time no longer existed. There was only now, and in that now we were completely absorbed in each other. This is what we wanted on date night.

We brought wine to the hotel as we always had, and I imagine we brought food too. We usually did. Our routine was to check in, order food, pop a bottle of champagne or wine, and have a toast, and then Bob would go to pick up the food while I sipped some more wine and waited. When he returned, we would sit cross-legged on the bed eating and using facecloths taken from the bathroom as cloth napkins, and we would sometimes even watch C-SPAN. We didn't have much opportunity to watch grown-up programming at home with two little ones dominating the set. Then we would turn off the TV, turn on the music, and snuggle and talk. Bob was the music guru. Before I broke the bank getting him an iPod, he stored audio files on his laptop. Since he had an hour-long commute, he would plug in the laptop to the car and seat it like another passenger in the passenger seat. He was always ripping CDs and finding new music for us.

Snuggling and talking would often lead to lovemaking, and then we would be back to snuggling and talking. We had a hotel date at least once every three months for years. We usually had to check out before eleven p.m. to go relieve the babysitter, but even five hours or so of alone time was cherished and worth the points or the dollars. Sometimes, if we could get ourselves up the next morning, we would take the kids back to the hotel for breakfast and the pool just for the novelty of it, and to get a little more use out of the place.

On this occasion, what I remember the most is resting my head on Bob's chest and grieving. I'm sure we made love, I'm sure it was intense, I'm sure it ended in tears. But what I remember most is feeling as though I were somehow responsible for his illness and wishing also that it were me who was sick instead of Bob. This illness wasn't Bob's fault at all; it was mine.

Ever since I had learned that Bob had ALS the day before, I had been worrying that somehow my thoughts a few months before about a man from my past had made it happen—had made Bob have ALS. I lifted my head from Bob's warm, hairy belly on that hotel room bed and told Bob that only a few months before, when our recently widowed friend, Chelona, was telling me about her new relationship, I momentarily wondered what it would be like to feel those new-relationship feelings again. I put myself in her shoes and asked myself, while she chattered giddily away about her new relationship with a man she and her late husband had known together: *If Bob died, who would I harken back to and be interested in?*

There was only one person from my past I could imagine. My relationship with Bob began shortly after the end of a prior relationship with a man I'll call Michael. I knew that Bob and I were so far from those moments that had occurred eleven years before, and yet I also wondered how it must sting for me to say aloud tonight, a day after his diagnosis, "I thought of Michael."

I told Bob that in my mind, as I had balanced the options of first-date excitement with the deep love we had developed,

I had without any doubts chosen him and us over jitters; that when I had had that thought in a booth eating sushi with Che-lona, I was imagining a future at least twenty years ahead of us, not now. I tried to explain why Michael: "See how all the other relationships had had a natural end? See how this one didn't?" I started crying, overcome with shame and guilt and the fear that somehow I had made all of this horror happen—Bob's ALS, a terminal illness, the destruction of what we had built—by having a thought while drinking a martini and eating sushi and listening to the quivers of a widowed woman newly in love.

Bob looked at me with sympathy and stroked my face. "You know how crazy that is, right? To think that you could give me a disease by having a thought? By having a conversation with a friend? You didn't do this to me, Dee. Don't ever think you did anything to make me sick. You didn't do this. Don't do that to yourself. You and I both know that's crazy talk. You can't be the rational, brilliant Dee I met and married and think that you had anything to do with this." I nodded as tears slipped off my chin and onto his belly, but I still felt shame. "And of course you would think of him. That relationship didn't end at the time because you wanted it to—it ended because he ended it. It makes total sense."

Bob knew the disease wasn't his fault, but he felt guilt that he was harming me and the kids by being sick. Searching for an answer as to why he had the disease, I was trying to understand what we could have done differently to keep it from happening. We were holding each other and trying to make sense of what didn't make any sense to us at all. ALS doesn't make sense to most people, especially those without a history of it in their families. No one yet knows what causes ALS, though research-ers are slowly making progress. Ninety to 95 percent of ALS diagnoses are considered "sporadic," meaning not inherited or familial. There is no history of ALS in Bob's family. His case was sporadic. None of it made sense.

We had more people to tell about Bob's illness and more decisions to make, and we were still waiting for the doctors at Barnes-Jewish to call us back with the results of their tests, but for now we were holding each other close and searching—searching our minds for understanding and the internet for anything we could find out about the disease and what the future held for Bob, for us, and for our family. And we would soon begin drinking wine—a lot of wine—and listening to music that allowed more painful releases of emotion. We would soon begin grieving by staying up late, unable to sleep, drinking too much, obsessing about the information and trying to find answers. We were already grieving Bob, as though Bob were already dead. We were grieving together, familiarly.

The next day was New Year's Eve. We were supposed to have taken those little Southwest Airlines planes we gave the kids Christmas morning on their Christmas present flights to Florida, and we were all supposed to be in the sunshine celebrating New Year's Eve with Bob's family for the first time ever. Instead, we were going to be watching the ball drop in Times Square with the sinking feeling that this may be it—the last one. Our journey together was nearly over. Our own ball was about to drop and shatter.

7

THE NEW YEAR

It was now December 31; time to celebrate the new year.

The first New Year's Eve Bob and I spent together in 2000, I was sick, and we were traveling the next day to Dublin for our first-ever big trip together, but we got a bottle of port, which would become our annual tradition. We sipped it while waiting for the ball to drop on the screen of the giant console TV in the studio apartment of Bob's that I had taken over when he moved to Florida for his first teaching position after graduate school. We had already made the decision just days before that I, too, would move to Florida once we got back from Dublin.

While the night went on, we heard neighbors screaming from balconies in the courtyard outside of the apartment, so we would randomly open the door and scream back to no one and everyone, "Woohoo! Happy New Year!"

When the ball dropped in the year 2001, Bob and I joined a balcony party across the courtyard from our apartment. We figured anyone having that much fun would welcome us as long as we brought some port. Bob and I walked over and looked up at the people spilling out of the apartment onto the second-floor balcony. "We brought some port," Bob said and raised his arm with the bottle. "Can we come in?" We spent our first hour of that new year with strangers, raising a glass, hollering, and laughing. I don't remember a single person's name or what any of them looked like, but it was one of many adventures Bob and I would have joining parties.

I wanted to keep our tradition alive, so two days after Bob's diagnosis, we opened a bottle of port and I turned on the TV for us to sullenly watch the ball drop in New York. In all the years we had lived in Illinois, we had always considered it midnight when it was midnight in New York, our state of origin, even though we lived in a different time zone now. Once the ball dropped in Times Square, our phone would ring, and Bob's mom would wish us "Happy New Year!" and remind us that the next day was her dad's, "Pop's," birthday—Pop was the maternal grandfather whose old GM Bob drove when we first met—and then Bob and I would go to bed as though we still lived in New York.

On New Year's Eve 2011, Bob went up to bed around ten-thirty. He didn't want to be there for the ball to drop. The ball had already dropped for him, and while he was doing an incredible job being strong, I guess celebrating the oncoming new year was just more than he could bear. I sat, heartbroken, watching the ball drop by myself for the first time since we had met, feeling forlorn and wishing he were with me. When the ball dropped at eleven p.m. Illinois time, the phone did not ring. I kissed the kids who had passed out downstairs on sofas with me, and then I raced up the stairs and awoke Bob and kissed him. He wasn't going to be allowed to entirely opt out. I was going to make him do this with me.

He lay on his back. I brought my face close to his and cupped my hands on his cheeks. "Happy New Year. I love you so, so much." His eyes slowly opened. "Happy New Year, Dee. I love you too," he said sullenly.

We both looked at each other with pained, furrowed brows and worried expressions, but we also feigned smiles and hugged, and then I left Bob and carried the kids upstairs and tucked them into their shared bed on the floor of our room. I stayed up a little while longer, finishing my glass of port at my computer while crying over one of our songs, "The Best of Times" by Styx.

On 1/1/12, at 2:03 a.m., I wrote Bob an email: *We can do this.* The next day, Bob wrote me back: *With you, I can do anything.*

8

Zero to Ten

"So what do you think it is, Doc? Is it ALS?" Bob asked.

"Well, we don't have the results of everything yet, so we don't know."

"Okay, but given what you do know, what do you think?"

There was a long pause.

"Well, I mean, you are showing the signs of ALS, but it's really hard to say at this point. We have to get all the results in because there's no test to know for sure you have it."

While no one at Barnes-Jewish had diagnosed Bob on December 29, the following week when Bob received a call with some results from the tests, he requested the doctor call him back because he had questions.

The kids were tucked into bed and we were sitting on opposite sides of our huge square kitchen table, with seating for eight, with a phone ready to be on speaker in the center of the table, waiting for the call. When Bob got the doctor on the phone, the doctor reiterated the results of the tests they had already done; I don't even remember what they were—maybe MRIs and blood tests—and then the doctor said they were waiting on some other results from the tests Bob had undergone that day.

"Okay," Bob said dismissively, "but what else could it be?"

"Well, we are in the process of ruling other possibilities, like multiple sclerosis, out, but until I have the results of more tests, it's hard to say."

"Okay, I understand that," Bob said, growing more frustrated. "But given what you know, what are the odds it's ALS? I mean, if you had to say right now what you think it is, what would you say?"

"Well, um, well."

"This is my life, Doc, and I don't want to spend it waiting to find out what the hell I've got. I want to know so I can make decisions and get on with my life. So, I'll ask again: given what you know, what are the odds, say out of one to ten that I have ALS. I'm not going to sue you or hold you to it; believe me, I'd be glad to learn you are wrong"—Bob chuckled—"but I really need to know." Bob paused but there was silence. "This is driving us nuts, the not knowing. You're the doctor, you've seen hundreds of cases, you know what you are seeing. Can you just be straight with me? Between one and ten."

There was another long pause and then reluctantly, the doctor said, "I'd say a nine."

With relief, Bob let out a long breath. "Thanks, Doc. Thanks so much for being straight. That's all I needed to know. Really, thank you. All right then, we will talk to you later. Give us a call when you find anything else out."

We hung up the phone. We had already been hit by a semi-truck days before, so this was not a hit or a blow. This information was met with a sense of relief that we could stop waiting to find out if Bob was right. We now knew, and we needed to start moving on with what it was going to mean.

Actually, we had already been moving on, Bob with so much more clarity than I. Bob, the day after his own self-diagnosis, had already contacted our realtor, Myron, who had sold us our house and told him to keep an eye out for single-level homes. He and his wife had become very good friends of ours since he had sold us our house five years before. We were already thinking we might need to move to a place with greater accessibility since Bob and I were anticipating Bob's use of a wheelchair.

Bob sent an email to Myron on December 30th, the day we got home from the hospital:

> Just wanted to keep you updated on what's going on. It looks like it's a pretty good bet that I have ALS. They're waiting on some blood work, but if anything else comes up, I'm sure everyone involved will be surprised.
>
> Since we're not going to know about the blood work for

about two or three weeks, we were wondering if you could
send us some info on some homes that have only one floor,
and something smaller than what we currently own. If this
thing progresses as we think it will, we just won't be able to
keep this house.

We were thinking quickly and talking a lot. Three days later,
on January 2, we sent another email to Myron:

> We've decided, at least for the moment, to stay put,
> and (if needed) to alter this house for anything that might
> arise. We figured the added disruption to the kids probably
> wouldn't be a good thing. (We know our neighbors, and
> they know us.) Also, we got a great rate on this house, and
> the house is extremely flexible, and can be tweaked here
> and there for stuff.
>
> If the blood work does come back with indirect confir-
> mation of ALS—i.e., if doesn't indicate anything else that
> I might have—then we'll probably head to Rochester, MN,
> to the Mayo Clinic in order to get a second opinion, as well
> as for whatever resources are available.

We were in action, and we were discovering how knowledge-
able many of our friends were—friends we'd met through our
previous lives without each other, and through the life we had
shared, as well as through moves from New York to Florida to
Illinois for work. My father had a friend who knew all sorts of
things about nutrition and would later own a vegan restaurant
in Massachusetts. She wrote me with descriptions of food and
herbs that might help Bob. My brother had a friend in California who was a geneticist; he informed us about the science of
the disease. My father had a friend who had once worked with
doctors in Chicago who might be of help for a second opinion
or more information. People from all different areas of life and
from all over the country offered to help with information,
access to care, and emotional support. Suddenly we realized
how cool it was to have so many great friends with so much
knowledge.

After Casey babysat, Casey and two other friends, Lee and Ping—colleagues from my university—showed up with a bottle of Bogle Phantom, Bob's favorite wine. We raised glasses and made jokes, and while everyone initially seemed uncomfortable when Bob made cracks about ALS, they began to slowly get on board with what was going to be one of our primary ways of coping: humor, Irish humor, dark humor, gallows humor, and joyous laughter as our hearts broke, one jagged shard at a time.

As the first few days of the new year began to pass, Bob started his research, gathering advice pertaining to nutrition and diet. We also decided to seek a second opinion at the University of Chicago, as had been recommended by my father's friend. Bob's dad offered to fly in and watch the kids so we could take two days for the trip.

In Illinois, Bob and I had neighbors on each side with kids—two couples, with five kids on one side and four on the other. They each had taken a turn watching Liam during a crisis—first, when my dad died, then when Sean died. Our kids played together every day. I had to tell them what was going on, and I needed to protect our kids from anything the neighbor kids might say about Bob dying, not because they were bad kids (they weren't) but because they were kids, and kids sometimes said things because they didn't know any better.

I asked my neighbors if I could talk to them without their kids.

"Bob has ALS, or Lou Gehrig's disease," I told them. I could tell by their expressions that they, like me, didn't know much of anything about the disease. "He had this twitch in his arm…"

"We went to see the local doctors, then down to St. Louis…"

"Standard diagnosis is two to five years…"

"We told the kids Daddy is sick."

As I explained what was happening, they looked increasingly concerned. They had been there when I lost my dad and brother five years before and knew I was the last surviving member of my family. They, like so many others, said they couldn't believe this was happening, but especially couldn't believe that it was happening to us.

I asked them to tell their children whatever they felt comfortable telling them, but to know that their kids would likely start hearing things from Liam and Maeve, and to please encourage the kids to be sensitive. I had no idea why I was even saying this, but I was so afraid for my children, so afraid of the cruelty of children. I wanted to protect them, and I knew I couldn't. I didn't want them to lose their dad, as I had fought so hard to find one whom I would never leave and who would never leave me. And now he was leaving, and I was going to end up a single mom after all. I could do so little. I could only attempt to shelter them and hold them close, telling them everything would be okay, even though it wasn't. It was never going to be okay again.

On January 4, I emailed the first set of neighbors, thanking them for their support. I let them know that we would be heading to Chicago the following week for a second opinion. I reiterated:

We want to try to keep things as normal as possible, so please know we still want the kids to come over and play and everything. They are not an inconvenience. If they are, we'll just say they can't come in today, and so on.

In terms of telling them, we trust your judgment. Right now Liam knows Bob is sick and that it's serious, and that it has to do with muscle weakness. Until this thing progresses, we'll just keep it at that.

I wasn't thinking about what Liam had inevitably overheard or what I had said in the Target parking lot about Daddy dying—I was struggling with that reality myself. I emailed a list of items for the grocery store—they had offered to pick up items I had requested: avocado, bell pepper, celery, chard, kale, lemon, spinach, leeks, hummus, almond butter, almond oil, flaxseed, spelt or quinoa rotini, rice or buckwheat soba noodles, a pound each of salmon and trout. I provided a link to a health food list online that we were following. *Thanks again for everything*, I wrote. *We are going to try to get back to functioning today. Liam is off to school until three.*

Reading this now, I am stunned by what I perceive as our

fortitude and resilience, or at least what we were presenting to others as fortitude and resilience. Clearly, we were carrying on with caring for the children and running the errands. I cooked, and we both kept the house clean. Bob did the laundry (I hadn't done any in a few years), and I know we still had a daughter in diapers. But what I most remember of January is overwhelming grief and drinking wine and crying, playing our songs over and over, and talking to friends on the phone. I was filled with adrenaline and exhaustion and pain.

I called Chelona, whose husband had died the summer before, and asked her, "Can you believe this is now happening to me? I can't believe it. What are the odds?"

I called Kate in Florida, blowing my nose repeatedly, and throwing tissues all over the floor of our bedroom:

"I can't believe this is happening. I just took that walk with you at the conference in St. Louis and said that finally, five years after Dad and Sean, we were exercising and eating well and had cut back on our drinking, and now this. I can't believe this. Five years, that seems to be all I ever get before some giant fucking boulder just comes along and says 'Fuck you, sorry, but that's all the good you get to have.' I never thought I'd lose Bob—not in his forties—this is crazy. I thought for sure we would have until at least our fifties. I mean, where the hell did this disease come from? Why Bob? Not that I want it to be anyone's husband, but why mine? I mean, haven't I had enough? I've done my part. Why couldn't it be someone else this time?"

9

OPENING THE DOOR

Bob called his family and told them the news. I don't know exactly how the conversation went, but I do know he told them right away that I would be "calling the shots" on how things went from then on out. Neither of us knew exactly what those shots would be yet, but we knew we had to do it together, and mostly alone, as we had done pretty much everything. Bob's stipulation that I would call the shots meant he would tell me what he wanted—if I didn't know already—and when he was no longer able to speak for himself, he wanted me to be the executor of his choices.

Bob and I were intensely private and mostly quiet people. Those who saw us at a gathering, especially one of the parties we threw at our house, would always describe us as extroverts, and while Bob was far more of an extrovert than I am—he was better able to have brief exchanges with folks at the market, bank, or in various offices at work—neither of us recharged with other people. We always recharged with each other and in quiet. We preferred small intimate gatherings where we could really converse with people and talk openly about the things that mattered to us most: people, ideas, politics, race, gender… all the topics most people consider "impolite" conversation.

These were the sorts of conversations Bob and I engaged in daily and that we wanted to discuss with people when we did get together with them. Neither of us ever had much tolerance for small talk, and the more we grew together throughout our relationship, the less interest we had in spending time in ways we didn't find meaningful. We also found that we gained most of what we needed from each other, and one of the things we loved about getting together with others—especially after we felt like we knew each other completely—was having new things to talk about when we were alone.

Bob and I were also very independent. Part of this was by choice and part by necessity. I had never had much family around, even when I was living with both of my parents or one of them, and the little family I did have was never much of a support system when it came to daily living. By the time I was fifteen, I was almost entirely on my own. My family was small, dispersed, and not the kind that got together to move you, or manicure your lawn, or fix your car. They often weren't there for the big things either. As an adult, my family—which consisted of Sean and Dad by then—would get together to talk. If there was a project to be completed together, it was invariably an intellectual one, like finishing a script or a book together or solving a practical problem. Sean lived on the opposite coast, so the three of us seldom got together. We were usually together, separately. The family I had left—at least when Bob and I first got together—was not a family that lifted things together, unless it was heavy thoughts.

Bob's family might have been the sort to do physical things, but we had never lived near them, nor did Bob wish to. He preferred privacy and, therefore, his family at a distance. Growing up, he told me he felt as if he were on the outside peering in at the others, because he had such different interests. While he was a man of ideas—he studied philosophy—he was also a man well suited to heavy lifting and he had the muscles to do it, having worked out most of his adult life. I came to cherish the peace and quiet of a house of only two adults plus two kids. While we may have lacked help from others, we were also free of obligations. We could rely on each other and do things our way, and that worked well for us.

My father had always been fiercely independent and had forced me to be too. He was always there to hash out ideas and explore possibilities, or to work on research and writing projects. When you grow up in a family that teaches you to do things on your own, or a family you want to distance yourself from, then you do things for yourself.

Bob and I were proud of our independence. When our son, Liam, was born, we were at the hospital for four days and we had only one friend visit us. Later, a couple and their young nieces helped us travel home, brought us Subway sandwiches, and said goodbye. When we had our daughter, one of our neighbors and her small daughter visited the hospital, and we went home on our own. I was at the hospital four days with my son and five with my daughter. There was time to visit but few did, and while sometimes I feel a degree of envy for those that enjoy a visiting throng to welcome new babies, there is a part of me that chafes against it too. I don't like crowds. I never did. I'm a keep-it-intimate kind of gal.

I feel the same way about holidays. If a dinner table includes more than six people, I become overwhelmed. The thought of Thanksgivings where families need multiple turkeys and hams and get out folding tables and dozens of chairs is unnerving to me. The idea of spending a favorite day of the year chatting with Aunt So-and-So from Such-and-Such sounds nightmarish to me. Thanksgiving, for us, typically included me, Dad, Bob, and then Liam, once he came along. When you live your life in small groups, a large group is overwhelming. It feels like the Costco of holidays rather than the intimate booth at the local corner café where I prefer to find myself.

Since Bob and my family had lived this way, it was only natural for us to approach death in a similar way. Dying was not for public display. If I didn't want a roomful of people surrounding me while I was alive, why would I want them surrounding me when I was dead? Bob felt the same way. Intimacy was what we had with each other, and if we were going to stay true to that comfort level, we were going to deal with Bob's death similarly. So, when Bob told his parents and sister about his illness, he also educated them about what he did and did not want.

On January 3, after we received the updates on his blood work from Barnes-Jewish, Bob wrote an email to his parents and sister telling them that while there is no diagnostic tool for ALS, it was pretty much a "lock" that he had it and so he wanted to make some things clear about how things were going to proceed. He told them to visit the ALS Association for more information.

He told them that our "door was always open" if they wanted to visit, but he immediately set boundaries: "Deirdre and I have had many conversations over the years about diseases, treatments, and end-of-life decisions. She is my best friend, and the person who understands best what I want. And what she says, goes." He used the losses of my family members as an example and wrote, "When Frank and Sean died, Deirdre's family [Bob meant the very small handful of distant relatives I had left] pretty much understood that Deirdre was the person in the know and backed-off. I would appreciate the same courtesy with her," he wrote. He still wasn't finished though. This email was all about telling everyone to back off and let us be. He tried to soften the blow by saying that we both loved all of them very much, but then he reiterated, "but the details are ours, and ours alone. We were never the 'traditional types' to begin with, so don't push anything. I can't emphasize this enough," he continued, "If you want to do something to help, we would appreciate it—but if either one of us says 'no,' then drop it, and let it be. Deirdre clearly has other things to worry about, and she obviously doesn't need the extra stress."

Remember that this was five days after Bob realized he was dying. Five days. I'm not sure I could tell my father anything this assertively unless I was pissed off, and Bob wasn't. He was simply able to be of sound enough mind and clear enough head and stout enough heart to tell his parents and his sister what he wanted five days after he had determined he was dying. He was also already worrying about me. This message is about him, but it's also him protecting me and the kids. He ended the letter by writing "At this time (and for the future), supporting Deirdre and the kids would be the best avenue to pursue, and we would appreciate anything you have to offer."

In all the time I knew him, Bob always knew what he wanted.

Bob was a philosopher, and that central fact is a large part of what defined him as a human being. He was an analytic philosopher and that meant one arrives at conclusions through facts and reasoning. I had never met anyone so steadfast. Most of us are at least somewhat buffeted around by our hearts, but Bob was not. I'm not sure he was ever moved by his heart in a direction where his head had not already been turned. This didn't mean he lacked feeling—Bob felt things enormously, and like me, cried, not only during times of trouble, but at the beauty of humanity witnessed through a particular performance or in an artwork, for example. We were both moved by everyday beauty.

When Bob and I visited Paris together for our delayed honeymoon in November 2001, we both sat cross-legged on the floor to stay with the *Mona Lisa* a little longer, just a little bit longer. We watched viewers walk in and snap a picture and walk out, barely studying the image, while we couldn't bring ourselves to leave. When Bob and I visited and then left my father in New York after we had moved to Florida, I would sometimes ask Bob to turn the car around and drive back because I felt a pull in my heart. I would give my father one more kiss, one more hug, and I would often cry as the car began to crest the first hill. I felt this similar feeling trying to leave the *Mona Lisa*. It felt magnetic. I was being pulled, but I was not alone. Bob felt it too.

When Bob was a freshman in college, there was a time when he felt suicidal. He had always loved physics and recalled riding his bike to the town library to check out books on physics when in junior high and high school, so he naturally thought that was what he wanted to study. He headed off to Rochester Technical Institute as an eighteen-year-old and soon found himself miserable, surrounded by people unlike him, drinking a lot of booze, and working out instead of attending class. He even skipped a final once—to go work out (a story he later humorously told many times to his own students as a tale of what *not* to do). Bob was failing school and life had no meaning for him. But then he took a philosophy class and suddenly he discovered there were others like him who worried about the same things and were interested in talking about all of the things he felt were important. He called his father and told him he was going to change his major and get a PhD. He had never known anyone with a PhD, and he really didn't have any idea what it meant, but he had asked his philosophy professor how one makes a living in philosophy, and he was told he should get a PhD; so that was what he did. He made that decision at eighteen, and everything else followed.

In many ways, Bob's decisions about his ALS diagnosis followed the same course. Bob said, "I'm a philosopher; I came to terms with my own death in my twenties," as though that explained everything about the decisions he would make about his illness. And in a way, it did.

Bob knew he was going to die, and since he had come to terms with his own death in his twenties, he was not afraid of death, and he was not going to extend his life and end up like those with late-stage ALS whom he'd seen on YouTube. He was going to play this hand the way he had played all of his hands. The cards were dealt, and it was time to start playing.

My way had always been a bit more meandering, my heart often leading me in directions that my mind knew it shouldn't go, and my educational pursuit consisted of a zigzag of heart, mind, heart, mind. Bob and I, however, were committed to doing this thing—his death—together. I would zigzag more than Bob, and I would be bringing up the rear a bit, but I wasn't going to stop playing. I, too, would play the cards I was dealt, and I had designated Bob the dealer.

After Bob and I had told our inner circle the news, it was time to begin telling everyone else. Some might decide they want to keep something as intimate as a terminal diagnosis a secret, but secrets are rarely good. We tend to keep secret what we want to hide, and if we want to hide something, it tends not to be good, and in my experience the hiding only makes it worse. We keep secrets out of fear—fear of judgment, fear of criticism—but succumbing to such fears rather than facing them also rarely does us any good.

We sometimes keep secrets when we are afraid the telling will somehow jinx us, like when we are pregnant and we aren't sure the baby is going to make it, so we wait until the second trimester to be sure. The thing about this kind of secret, though, is that we often end up bringing more harm to ourselves. By not being open, we offer ourselves no empathy. The thing about shielding ourselves from the pain of sharing that we have had a miscarriage—for example, by not sharing the news of a pregnancy until after we are "sure"—is that, if we do have a miscarriage, no one will have been on the journey of glee and destroyed hopes that we ourselves will have experienced. If a person never knew we were pregnant, how could that same person mourn with us the child we lost? It is only by letting people into our hopes that we can let them into our grief. It is only by letting them into our sorrow that they will feel sorrowful too. I am a very private person, and so was Bob—even more so than I—but I knew that without telling, we would live in total darkness, with few pinholes of light.

As someone who had to work hard to build support groups, I learned that it is only by letting people in that we can gain support. While Bob and I wanted to go it alone, I knew that not everything we would need to do could be done alone, and that the only way anyone would care to help is if they had an idea of how they could help. I also knew that I would need emotional support, someone to talk to, someone to listen to me. Bob knew this before I did.

Bob told me early on, "You will need someone to talk to about me. You won't always be able to talk to me about me."

How did he know this? I didn't. Yet. I wouldn't for a while.

Bob and I told each other everything; the idea that I would be talking to someone else about him—rather than to Bob himself—pained me and made me realize the slow separation we were facing. Our opinion was that once you started talking to someone else about your spouse, rather than to your spouse, you were usually headed for trouble.

10

DECISIONS

After New Year's Eve, Bob returned to the internet to discover what ALS would look like, what it would do to him, and how it would end.

One of the things Bob found was "Often Awesome The Series: An ALS Love Story." The film story began as most stories do, as our story did, with love: "Tim Met Kaylan. They Fell in Love." There are over thirty episodes that follow Tim and Kaylan through Tim's death and past it. The first episode is Tim's diagnosis. By episode thirty-two, which Bob sent in an email to many people, we see Tim in the advanced stages of ALS. This episode is what Bob watched over and over to see what was coming. This is what he showed me so I would know what was coming. This episode is what Bob used to decide how he would approach ALS and his own death.

Each episode begins with Tim's face and his computer-generated voice introducing himself and his ALS. In "Episode 32: A Day in the Life," we see a modest brick Cape Cod home. Inside, Tim is bedridden and being cared for by his nurse, Kim. The video begins at 8:10 a.m. with Kim suctioning Tim's mouth and adjusting Tim's head because he is immobilized. At 8:19 a.m., Tim receives a bowel movement cleanup, wipe-down, and moisturizing. At 8:25 a.m., Tim receives trachea suction. At 8:43 a.m., Tim receives a breathing treatment. At 9:05 a.m., Tim's medications are measured and crushed. Tim needs care twenty-four hours a day. Tim can't move. Tim is in diapers. Tim receives a sponge bath. Tim can't swallow, so his saliva is suctioned. Tim has a tracheotomy so he can breathe. Tim can't speak. Tim takes forty prescriptions a day for depression, anxiety, joint pain, neurological pain, and swelling. He takes his medication and sustenance through a feeding tube directly into his stomach. In order for Kim to brush Tim's teeth, his mouth is held open by a dental device. By early afternoon, the fifteen-minute video is sped up to show the amount and frequency of care in a day in Tim's life.

Tim still has a sense of humor, though. He uses a device to communicate with his eyes, and he jokes, after receiving his medication, that he is on more drugs than a rock star. Viewers watch as Tim receives physical therapy, gets a bath, and so on. Bob and I watched, through sobs for Tim, and sobs for Bob. We couldn't look away. In "Episode 34: The Long Goodbye," Tim makes his last trip to the hospital for an infection that is causing green discharge to pour from his tracheotomy. While at the hospital, Tim decides he wants to die at home. In the final episode, Tim does, surrounded by his loving friends and family. Tim was born October 11, 1979, eleven years after Bob, and he died August 23, 2011, a little more than a year before Bob.

I could not imagine this disease happening to my six-foot-five, 240-pound husband, whom my students in Florida had once likened to a professional wrestler. After Bob had visited my class one day at the University of Miami, one of my students concluded, "Dr. Dre is married to Stone Cold!" Bob, who had been a bouncer in college, was going to be reduced to a shadow of himself in a matter of months or, at the most, a few years. As I watched the story of Tim and Kaylan, I imagined Bob in Tim's condition, unable to talk, trapped in his body, and unable to move. I couldn't imagine not hearing Bob's voice. More than that, I couldn't imagine Bob not having a voice. He specialized in having a voice in all matters. His philosophy dissertation, on mind and language, focused on demonstrative reference. Demonstratives are words that rely on context, and often gesturing, in order to be understood. I always teased him about having written several hundred pages on the word *this*. Bob was also from New York, and he spoke as much with his hands as his mouth. And yet, when he doubled over in laughter, he barely made a sound. His soundless open mouth, his bouncing body, head down, tears running down his cheeks in joy as he was hunched over in infectious laughter, is still one of the things everyone misses about him. Watching this video of Tim, I couldn't imagine Bob in this state—unable to talk to me or the kids—and neither could Bob.

As we watched Tim and Kaylan's story, I thought about Bob, but Bob thought about me.

Bob imagined me suctioning his mouth, feeding him through a tube, cleaning up his bowel movements, and giving him a bath. He watched repeatedly, for several days, and then announced, "That would be no life for you or the kids."

While Tim was still able to communicate, the sheer amount of maintenance to keep him alive took a great toll on those around him. They were willing and able to do it, and they wanted to, and I wanted to, for Bob, but Bob could not imagine that life for me, for us.

Because of these videos, Bob was able not only to imagine his own death, but to almost watch it happen, and he did, numerous times. He used it to tell other people not to give him false hopes about his diagnosis or about this disease; he forwarded the link to many people. He used it to face the reality of his own diagnosis and to make his choices early rather than late. He used it to accept reality. We both used it to grieve. Every time we watched Tim and those around him, we not only felt for them, but imagined ourselves, and we mourned it all. We faced the reality of ALS over and over and over by clicking the mouse on the desktop.

In early January, Bob began deciding what choices he would make for himself about his own care, and he placed the kids and me at the forefront of those choices. He was dying, and there was no denying it, and everything we had learned about ALS had taught us there was nothing he, we, or anyone, could do about that. But certain things were still in Bob's control. He could still make some decisions about his life, and he could make some choices that would help those of us who were not terminally ill to live when he was gone.

It wasn't long before Bob decided he didn't want to be what he called "a watermelon on the counter" watching his life go by.

"Dee, I'd be trapped in my body. I'd have all these thoughts and I wouldn't be able to express them. I wouldn't be able to help you with the kids like I've always done. I wouldn't be able to hug you or kiss you. I wouldn't be able to make love to you. You know how I would miss that," he teased.

"I know, but you'd still be here. You could see us. You could see the kids grow."

"But I'd be a watermelon on the counter. I'd be watching, but I couldn't do anything. I couldn't even give advice. Forget the physical stuff. I wouldn't be able to share any of the thoughts I was having or help anyone in any way."

I listened, trying to imagine this new life he was describing.

"And what kind of a life would that be for you? You'd have to be home all the time. You and the kids couldn't go anywhere. All the things we have loved to do—taking the kids on trips, introducing them to new foods and places, going to see theater and music, getting them out of this white town—you couldn't do any of that."

"But we'd have you. I mean, it would be okay. We could do it."

"The kids would have this dad in the other room, but I wouldn't really be adding anything meaningful to their lives. I would just be something to take care of."

He paused and searched my eyes. "I don't want to live like that. That's not living. My whole life is about making meaning. This is the shit I teach about. I've thought about this for a long time—what makes a good life. Living isn't just about being alive, it's about what you can contribute to those around you. It's about making the world better while you are here. We've made a good life. I love this life and you and the kids, I fucking love you like crazy, and I sure as hell wouldn't be giving it up if I had a fucking choice, if it weren't for this fucking disease, but I don't want to extend this shit. If this is how it's going to go, I'm getting out as soon as I can, and that means saying no to anything that's going to extend this shit once life isn't life anymore." I nodded. "Watching the kids grow but not being able to do a damn thing to help them or you. That would be worse," he said. He didn't want our lives to become about suctioning his mouth, draining his catheter, feeding him through a tube, staying home every day of our lives, unable to even go to a store or a restaurant. Our lives would become nothing but maintenance of his limited life, and he didn't want that for us. He wanted us to go on living. He wanted us to thrive.

I didn't know what I wanted. Well, I did, but I couldn't have what I wanted. I wanted Bob back. I wanted our lives back. I wanted this outrageously cruel fucking disease to go away. But most of all, I wanted whatever Bob wanted.

"I will do whatever you want me to do when you want me to do it. I am here, and I want to do what you want to do. You say I'm calling the shots, but you are calling the shots. You just tell me what you need and I will do it. I will be who you need me to be as long as you need me to be it. We can do this thing, whatever it is, the way we've done everything else: together. I love you."

"I love you too."

I held his hands in mine. We leaned forehead to forehead.

11

HOLDING HANDS

When we lose someone from a terminal illness, we lose them one bit at a time—first emotionally, then physically, or a combination of both. Whatever the combination or order, it's excruciating. When someone's skin is your own skin, losing them a bit at a time is like fileting yourself one layer at a time. There were times during Bob's illness when I likened losing him to tearing off a painful bandage one millimeter at a time. But I could no longer deny that we were of two bodies, one ailing and one growing stronger in order to carry the other. I was also already becoming his voice, long before he began losing it, as I began carrying the news to others and becoming the communicator of all things to all people, including the children. Words were leaking out of the house—they had to if one of us was going to survive.

When life brings us joys, we want to share them, and when life brings us sorrow, we tend to fold in on ourselves, lie in bed, and generally try to shut out the world. Bob and I did this. We did this in the beginning. I told those I had to tell, and then I hid. We hid. From early January until school started again and life had to go on, we hid. But we didn't hide as much as we wanted to because we had to stand up for the kids. We had to face what was leaking out the sliding door and into the driveway and would soon become visible to all.

When we received the horrid news of Bob's ALS and eventual demise, he died. He didn't literally die, but a part of him, of us, died in that moment.

When you are diagnosed with a disease that not only is terminal but has no treatment at all, there is no hope. With some diseases, like cancer, there is treatment. The treatment may not work. The likelihood of recovery may be slim. But there is hope. When my mother was diagnosed with cancer and given two months to live, I thought she might have three, maybe four months, so I delayed my entrance into graduate school until the spring term, which would begin in January. She died at the end of August, as the doctors had predicted she would, but for a little while, at least, I was able to hold out hope.

When you are diagnosed with ALS, you are told you are going to die, soon. There is no question whether you will die from ALS; there is only a when. Two to five years from diagnosis is accurate most of the time, and when Bob pressed the doctors on what that actually meant for him, it was a much shorter time. The doctor said two to three years, and when Bob asked how many of those would be good years, the doctor said maybe one. Having lost my mother, I knew the time assigned was likely to be accurate. Everything we read said it was so. There was no treatment. There was no hope.

When we were told Bob was dying, it was as if we were told he had died, but that we were given a furlough to grieve together before he had to go. Bob and I had grieved before, and if it hadn't been for our small son, Liam, and then an unanticipated miracle pregnancy with our second child, Maeve, we probably would have struggled even more to come out of our grief. When my father and brother died two weeks apart—five years before Bob's diagnosis—we found ourselves putting all of our energy into just getting through the day, the way one manages to wade through the most humid of days—clammy, disoriented, and numb. We managed to go through the motions of life, day to day, and then we fell victim to our own pain at night.

My father had died unexpectedly of a heart attack on September 22. My brother had died unexpectedly of liver failure on October 6. October 6 was the first day I had returned to work since my father died. After Sean, I didn't return to work until January. I just couldn't.

I also couldn't shop at the same grocery store. My father and I had shopped there on the last day he was alive. Dad had made some jokes in the produce aisle that no one got. It was the fall of contaminated spinach, so he hollered across the aisle to me, "Don't forget the spinach!" He made the same joke at the register: "Did you remember the spinach?" The cashier got the joke. For the first time in the few months he'd been living in the Midwest, he felt like someone "got" him.

A week after my father died, I tried to return to the grocery store, but upon entering the produce aisle, I began to have a panic attack. There was a seizing in my chest and in my stomach and my mind kept shouting, *Get out! Get out! As fast as you can! Run!* I speed-walked my way back to the minivan, barely present in my body, and when I got back in and closed the door, I collapsed into sobs over the steering wheel, much as I had done in the parking lot of Target. It was all too familiar.

I didn't shop at that grocery store until the following summer—at least nine months later. I couldn't shop at all for several months; instead, we ordered takeout almost every night. Bob and I gained a lot of weight eating nachos and chicken fingers and french fries from the restaurant that was closest to our house and drinking too much, drinking way too much, after Liam went to bed at night.

For months after my father died, the grocery store became a disturbing place where somewhere among the avocados and lettuces, my grief was waiting to be consumed, and I wasn't ready. I couldn't stomach it.

From the day of Bob's diagnosis onward, I baked, I cooked, I fed him all the foods he loved: my homemade spaghetti sauce and meatballs, grilled steaks, soups and chili, pie and cookies. But I began losing my appetite along with him as his symptoms progressed.

Initially, we were trying to plump Bob up so that when he began losing weight, he'd have some extra to lose, but I began starving myself, just as I had when my mother died. By the time Bob died, I had lost thirty pounds from the stress and from being unable to eat. Bob didn't drink while I was pregnant, and I didn't eat when he couldn't. The less he could eat, the less I could eat. There would eventually be no joy in food. There

would be only limited pleasure in life and guilt at savoring anything other than Bob.

Bob and I drank and cried together the rest of that January
holiday break, knowing life would soon have to go on, and we
would have to march with it, but for now, we were consumed
with thoughts of his dying and how we were ever going to manage our way through the pain. The one thing we knew was that
whatever we were about to go through, we were going to do it
the way we had done everything: together and holding hands.

12

GETTING BUSY

When we drove to Chicago for the second opinion, it felt like a date because we were never alone unless we had paid someone to watch the kids. Bob and I hadn't been away for two whole days without the kids since my brother Sean had died and we had to fly to Florida to drop Liam off with Bob's family, then fly to San Francisco to identify my brother's body, pack up his apartment, make arrangements for his cremation and the ashes to be shipped to our local funeral home in Illinois—the same one that had just taken my father's body two weeks before—and then fly back to Florida, get Liam, and fly back to Illinois.

We took the long ride up to Chicago in our Toyota Camry. On the ride up, I stroked Bob's head as he drove. We talked, but there was no discussion of what to expect this time. We didn't even talk about ALS. I don't know what we talked about—what we wanted to do after the doctor's appointment? Jokes about how his dad would handle the kids without us? Neither of us was expecting any different news, but we did think we should at least follow through on the advice of others and get that second opinion, though the University of Chicago won out over the Mayo Clinic, since it was closer.

While we were at the U of C Medical Center, I watched as the doctor did all the usual tests that Bob had described to me as archaic after his local neurology appointment and then at Barnes-Jewish. Push here. Pull there. Get up and walk one foot in front of the other, and so on. As I watched Bob, I could see that his feet weren't lifting the same. I noticed that he didn't appear as strong. I was aware and surprised, looking at him in this context, that his body had changed, which seemed so strange given that it had only been a few weeks since he'd first identified the twitch. Since he had been working out regularly before the diagnosis, his biceps were still as big and his chest as muscular as when we met, but his gait wasn't right.

When you have children, you often don't realize how they've changed or grown until you see a photograph. We are so used to being around them every day that small changes are difficult to notice. The same was true for me that day. Place Bob in a sterile medical office and watch him walk, and suddenly I saw that his symptoms were more than the twitch in his arm.

"So, what do you think, Doc?" Bob asked.

"I think you probably have ALS."

Bob laughed. "Thanks for saying it."

Thankfully: a straight shooter.

"We thought so," I said. "Well, actually Bob thought so. He diagnosed himself before anyone else would commit. Thanks for saying what you think instead of trying to protect us from the truth. We can take it. That's why we are here, because we want to know. We don't want to pretend. We want to get on with what we can get on with."

The doctor nodded, then leaned forward and addressed Bob, looking him squarely in the eyes.

"So, this is what I think you should do. Some people will leave here after I tell them this, and they'll go home and shut the doors and turn out the lights and wait to die." There was an emphatic pause. "Don't do that. That's not what you should do. You need to take this news, know it's there, and then put it away and go on with your life. You clearly both love each other very much. Enjoy the time you have together and enjoy your life as much as you can. If there is something you've always wanted to do, do it. Don't wait. This isn't a disease where you can wait. If you want to do something, go do it. Do it now. Live your life."

"Get busy living instead of getting busy dying?" Bob asked.

"Yes. Now, I'm not going to take up any more of your time. Go on, get out of here; enjoy your life."

He shook Bob's hand and then rose to leave. "We do have someone from the MDA who would like to share some information with you before you go, though."

13

REALLY GETTING BUSY

The MDA—the umbrella organization for ALS— representative provided us with a packet to take home, complete with a handbook and a video. The video taught me about a website that I could use to request assistance as time went on, but also provided a way to communicate with folks via one bulk email or a blog post. Communication, while at first cathartic and emotionally helpful in terms of repetition and release, can become exhausting as people ask how the person is and you find yourself having to repeat over and over the same information.

We spent that night after the doctor's appointment at a hotel just outside of Chicago and made our drive home the following day. The hotel gave us a huge suite, and it felt like one of those hotel date nights where we would have checked in and had our own little party. While our spirits weren't up for it, we went to an Italian restaurant around the corner and enjoyed a nice meal and wine. For now, we were still able to savor the food as we always had, before Bob would inevitably have difficulty chewing and swallowing as all of his voluntary muscles deteriorated.

We tried to have a good time. We were morose, but we picked up another bottle of wine and sat in the hotel room drinking out of plastic cups. We weren't much in the mood, so we didn't make love even though we had a huge room to ourselves. (By morning we would decide we needed to seize the opportunity.)

Bob's arm was still twitching like crazy when we went to bed that night; it wouldn't stop for the rest of his life. Those twitches were his body's way of signaling something was wrong—like a fire alarm—and are often one of the first symptoms of ALS. They indicate that the signal from the nerves to the muscles is becoming increasingly disrupted. I snuggled up to him, wanting to feel the twitch, wanting to somehow be in this with him, or to even transfer the illness to myself. I still very much wanted to be the one to die, and told him so, regularly. I would rest my head on his hairy chest and say, "Why can't it be me? I want it to be me. I can't do this." I couldn't imagine how I could ever go on without Bob by my side. He was the love of my life and my reward for all of my other disappointments and losses. Why couldn't he be the one to stick around and go on? I was too tired already.

Even though we usually weren't snugglers at bedtime, I put my head on his arm that night and felt the twitch and tried to communicate through those rhythms. *I love you. Please let me die instead. I am here. I am here. I am here. I love you,* I thought, to the rhythm of the twitches.

We went home, Bob's dad left, and I decided I had better start reading the materials the MDA had given us. I got up one morning and sat in my Valentine's Day hearts-covered pajama bottoms and poured coffee into my sock monkey mug. That mug brought whimsy when I needed it most. I was dressing for happiness even though I was anything but.

I sat down at the oak kitchen table—with all of the scratches and dings of our writing circle, friends, family, and the kids—and started to turn the pages of the MDA handbook. The spiral-bound book was titled the *MDA ALS Caregiver's Guide* and it was created by the ALS Division of the MDA. It had chapters on everything that it pained me to know, but everything I needed to learn if I was going to be all of the things I had promised Bob I would be as we went through this together. It had sections titled The ALS Caregiver, Daily Care, Respiratory Issues, Communication Issues, Nutrition Issues, Emotions, Financial, Legal, and Medical Issues, Finding Caregiving Help, and End-of-Life Issues, in that order. I was now an ALS Caregiver, and I needed to learn all that I could. I sat at the table alone, reading. It was all so difficult to comprehend and imagine. Bob was still walking around and speaking clearly. Other than the twitching, nothing much else had really happened yet. I noticed he was a little weaker, a little less stable on his feet, but life was pretty much as it had always been. It was hard to imagine him ever becoming so dependent on me. He had always been the "heavy lifter" in the relationship; I did the fine tuning, but he lifted heavy things. When we were first dating in Albany, New York, he sent me an adorable email where he wrote, *Cave Bob love Cave Dee wants to have Cave Kids with Cave Dee, Grunt.* When people called, I was referred to as "The Brains of the Operation" and he called himself the one who lifted heavy things. *Grunt.* According to this guide, I was soon going to have to be the brains and the brawn.

I read about drooling and choking and lifts and pressure sores and anger and depression and voice banking…it went on and on, for over two hundred pages. I sat sipping my coffee and flipping through the brightly colored pages, my heart sinking with each turn of the page. This was what I was doing first thing in the morning. This was what we read now. This was what life was.

Then I found the section titled, "Marriage." Under this heading there were two sub-topics: "Changing Roles" and "Intimacy and Sex." Clearly the MDA wasn't encouraging patients to have sex and intimacy outside of marriage, since sex was a subheading of marriage. This struck me as odd. An actual section titled, "Marriage." Strange. In any case, I began reading.

Bob and I had always been intensely attracted to each other and rather proud that we had defied the rule of "no sex on a first date" if a relationship is going to last. We not only had sex on our first date, but we had it multiple times. Our sex life had always been a point of pride for both of us because we could be screwing the hell out of each other one minute and talking philosophy and poetry the next. Many of our early emails to each other were filled with flirtatious comments on each other's bodies and how eager we were to be intimate again. The one weekend Bob stayed in Florida instead of coming to Albany—while we had a semester-long distance love affair— we had phone sex.

The section on intimacy begins innocently enough, describing how sexuality will inevitably change as the disease progresses:

"Caregiving can provide for a special kind of intimacy. Intimacy isn't only sex—although ALS doesn't end sexuality. Times of closeness and romance can come during special meals, dates or anniversary celebrations, or simply from talking, touching, laughing, hugging or sleeping together. A couple can enjoy the moonlight, favorite music or affectionate kissing. One woman found that feeding her husband was a comforting and cozy time for her. Reading to him, while holding hands, also became intimate and precious."

It was sad to imagine us limited to only touching, but it was also encouraging that we might find other ways to be intimate. I kept reading with a combination of curiosity and appreciation that the guide was addressing such issues. It was refreshing that the MDA was informing readers, because for many in American society, sex talk is so taboo. No one, for example, ever talks about elderly sex. Sure, there are Viagra commercials and subtle references to feminine dryness, but until we age ourselves, we are kept in the dark. No one really informs us what sex as an older person is going to be like, or if we are even going to have it. We don't talk about sex with disabilities either.

The last page of this section begins, "Some spouses find it difficult to maintain a sexual relationship because they see the partner in a clinical way or are too exhausted," but within a few paragraphs the mood changes entirely. It's a short section—only three pages altogether. For a book with so much detail, readers are given little, but what they are given is very important. The section continues:

"A person with ALS needs to give his or her spouse affection and time to be intimate. If a caregiver provides chores all day, and then is expected to 'perform' sexually, it becomes another task, not lovemaking. Both partners can make romantic gestures through words or planning a time for intimacy. Catheters, vents, and immobility make it necessary to adjust sexual positions and actions, but offer a great opportunity for imagination."

This made a lot of sense to me, but the word *imagination* struck me as odd and leading. I thought, *Way to go, MDA! Nice job encouraging sex and intimacy!* but none of the language or tone before that word *imagination* prepared me for what came next:

"One couple took advantage of the times the partner with ALS fell on the floor and was uninjured, and another man says, 'Thank God for sturdy ceiling lifts.'"

I doubled over with laughter, imagining a contraption dangling from the ceiling like a swing in a sex club. Bob came in from the living room to see what was going on—nobody had laughed like that in the house since the 29th of December. There had been no room for laughter. ALS was not a laughing affair; or was it? "What's going on?" he asked.

I pointed at the page, trying to catch my breath. "Look," I gasped. "Read this." And I kept laughing, awaiting his response.

Bob read the section aloud and then smiled, raised his eyebrows, and began swinging his hips and arms in a suggestive fashion, making porn music sounds: "Hey, Dee, buck a bow bow, buck a bow bow." He chuckled. Then he winked at me and nodded his head up and down as if to say, *Yeah, baby.*

"Honey," I declared, "I can't wait until you fall on the floor!"

The caregiving guide had just poked a giant hole in the tension that had been building in our house since we'd received the news. All the gnashing of teeth and clenching of our fists and maudlin crying to love songs—it wasn't going to end, but we felt a great release when we were able to stand back and see the absurdity of the entire situation through the guide writer's choice to include these memorable quotes. We were facing a miserable fucking situation, but dammit, we had a choice about how we were going to handle it, and since when had Bob and I ever gone home, turned out the lights, and shut ourselves in a room as a way to deal with reality? Sure, we'd done plenty of metaphorical yelling and pounding of our fists as we faced obstacles—like Bob's vasectomy reversals, not being able to conceive children initially, or the money struggles that inspired moves, or the losses of my dad and brother—but we'd always kept fighting the fight and laughing. We'd always kept laughing. Now was no time to stop.

Bob and I never did buy a sturdy ceiling lift or do it on the floor (after he had ALS, anyway), but it turned out it wasn't the specific advice we needed from the MDA, so much as the spirit of the intimacy section. We needed to be reminded that we could and should laugh, and we needed to know that lovemaking was going to be possible. We needed hope and relief.

Later when we thought back to this time, we recalled another time when the pressure had built, and we'd lost our humor for a short time but were able to reclaim it.

When my father moved to Illinois and felt like a fish out of water, it was with good reason. The Midwest is different from New York. In New York, people are direct and private, and while they will always help a person in need, they like their fences. When we lived in Illinois, there were no fences, and people rarely said to one's face what they were thinking—or that was our assessment anyway. We were direct people. Even too direct for some people.

When we first moved my dad in, we had to take our van to the auto shop for an oil change and general check-up. We had a local place and we'd gotten to know Jim, the local guy who owned it. My dad sat in the passenger seat with me in the back, as we both waited for Bob, who had driven the second vehicle, to drop off the keys. Jim was passing by our van when he suddenly yanked the passenger side door open, reached his hand toward my father, and said, "Pleased to meet ya! Welcome to Illinois!" as he firmly and vigorously shook my father's hand up and down. My father was totally jarred. Dad had practically been assaulted, by New York standards, where fences were fences and doors were doors. He responded in kind, the mechanic shut the door, and then my dad said, once he was out of earshot, "What the hell was that?" It was classic small Midwestern town stuff, as far as we were all concerned. We had a good laugh.

About a week after my father died, Bob was pumping gas on the same edge of town as the auto mechanic while I waited in the car. When Bob got back in the car, he turned to me before turning the key in the ignition and said, very seriously, "I just figured it out."

"What?" I asked.

"Jim killed your dad," he said, deadpan.

We didn't start the car for about five minutes. I couldn't stop laughing, and I imagined my father in the car laughing with us. "Delayed heart attack," I added. "It only took a week!" My body shook up and down.

My father would have loved it, loved us, in that moment, carrying on the family tradition of humorous responses to tragedy.

14

JUICING

Time crept forward as we absorbed the devastating news, and before we knew it, it was mid-January and school was back in session for me, Bob, and Liam, who was in third grade. We decided to keep Maeve home because Bob wanted to soak up as much time with her as possible. We had to go forward. We needed to get busy living. Bob and I had classes to teach and kids to raise, and we needed to get Bob's health on track with good food because his body was attacking itself. ALS attacks motor neurons in the brain and spinal cord, eventually impacting all voluntary muscle movement. Voluntary muscles are ones we control, muscles we use to do things like lifting our arms or legs, speaking, or breathing. Muscles we can't control are ones like our hearts. We can't hold our heartbeats the way we can hold our breath.

We had a membership to a big-box bulk-food place; Bob's folks had given it to us when Liam was born so we could get cheaper formula and diapers. When I got home from work one day that month, there were huge quantities of vegetables all over our kitchen table. Bob was juicing. His dad had gifted us a Breville juicer because our friends had told us juicing was the quickest way to get good nutrients into Bob's body. The juicer was whirring like crazy, and Bob was standing there in a pair of cargos, a tank top, and a flannel shirt—his usual attire.

"Hey, what's going on?" I asked.

"I'm juicing!" he said ecstatically

"I can see that," I said, surveying the mess in the kitchen. Giant bag of sweet potatoes. Carrots. Celery. Kale. Spinach. Peppers. There were so many ingredients and peelings and bags everywhere.

"There's a video I want you to watch. I left it on the computer in the office," Bob said, shouting over the juicer without skipping a beat.

"Okay."

"Go watch it."

"Okay." I laughed because he looked a bit nuts as he kept feeding the machine its vegetables. "I'll be right back."

"Great!" He was so enthusiastic that he was almost maniacal.

I watched the video and it explained what he was doing. Bob had found a woman on YouTube who said she had reversed her multiple sclerosis with her diet. He was going to try to reverse this son-of-a-bitch disease with food. I walked back into the kitchen, where Bob had a giant pitcher full of juice. It was at least a gallon's worth. The kitchen reeked.

"Did you juice the onions?"

"Yup!"

"Seriously? You juiced the onions?"

"Hell, yeah!"

"Oh no, Bob. That's gross. You *eat* onions. You eat them raw; you can cook them. You don't JUICE onions. That's going to be disgusting. It's going to take over everything else."

"Oh shit, it is?" he said, dumbfounded. Bob could boil pasta and heat stuff. He made mean scrambled eggs because he had the patience to cook them on low, but Bob was no cook. I once had him mash the potatoes, and those fresh, delicious babies were mashed so well that by the time I realized how long he'd been mashing, they had turned into those boxed, made-from-potato-flakes mashed potatoes dished out in school cafeterias.

"You've got to be kidding me. Let me smell it." The container was a Hulk green, and the smell of onions was overpowering. "Yuck! I can't believe you are going to drink that!"

Bob smelled it. "Oh shit." These spaced-out moments were the Bob moments that were unforgettable and delightful. "Did you watch the video?" he asked.

"Yes, I get it. It's pretty amazing. It's worth trying. Let's do this thing."

"Well, I'm not going to waste it. I guess I've got to drink it.

Here goes." Bob plugged his nose, and began downing the entire jug, taking breaks to shake his head and wince. He managed
to drink that entire fucking onion thing. He was going to slow
this "ALS fucker"—as he often referred to it—down, dammit.
We were going to fight this damned disease.

15

Laughter Medicine

January was the month of several doctor's visits: one in Chicago and another in St. Louis. In St. Louis we met with a physical therapist and the MDA representative who talks to ALS patients about various forms of support, including support groups. Our town, we learned, had one, with three members, all much older than ourselves, given that the average age at the onset of the disease is fifty-five. We decided a support group wasn't really for us—both of us regularly repeated the Groucho Marx line that we didn't want to be associated with any group that would have us as a member. No one in that support group would be able to relate to a woman who had a three- and eight-year-old at home. What I really needed was someone who understood what it was like to lose their entire birth family, and then learn their husband was dying too. In America, finding someone like that in their early forties—I was only forty-two—would be difficult, especially in our little predominately white town of 40,000, where the majority of family reunions held in local parks had upwards of 100 attendees, and the local paper regularly showcased five generations as someone reached a milestone birthday or had a wedding anniversary open house.

While meeting with the MDA representative in St. Louis, we were asked whether we had received the MDA materials—the ALS guidebooks and the video.

"Yes, we have," I said emphatically. "Have you *read* the section on intimacy?" I began laughing, and Bob did too.

"Um, no," the representative said, curious. "Was it useful?"

"Oh, it's useful all right." I raised my eyebrows and smirked.

Bob leapt in with his porn music: "Buck a bow bow. Buck a bow bow." He didn't do the hip thing, because we were sitting, but the representative recognized the music. Somehow Bob's porn theme invariably seemed recognizable as a porn theme.

The representative's ears perked up as she looked at us quizzically.

"Um, yeah, you may want to read it," I said. "It's got some, uh, really interesting quotes from various couples."

"Yeah, interesting," Bob said. "I think what Deirdre means is, it's sort of the porn section."

The MDA representative began laughing, awkwardly, and somewhat aghast, hand covering her mouth. "Oh, uh, sorry...I guess I better read it," she said.

"Don't be sorry! It's awesome that the MDA even wants to talk about this stuff. I was just surprised when I learned that when the person with ALS falls on the floor, I should see it as an opportunity, to, you know, *get it on*," I said.

"Oh no, I had no idea!" she said, laughing.

Bob winked his *yeah, baby* wink.

"I was reading it over coffee one morning, feeling super depressed, as you might imagine, and then I was laughing so hard tears were running down my face. It's great, don't change it!"

Soon we were all laughing.

We had made the woman's day. She told us so. Her job was dealing with people who had just learned someone was dying, so she certainly didn't spend much time laughing, but as Bob and I switched back and forth, filling in the gaps in the story about what we had read in the book, we had her cracking up, in shock and in stitches both.

"And hey, Dee," Bob said with a wink. "I'm eager to need the lift! Buck a bow bow. Buck a bow bow."

"Uh, yeah, there is a mention about how much a couple appreciated the *sturdy* ceiling lift."

Later, the representative wrote emails to Bob, telling him she'd told her colleagues all about us—and that they all knew us as "the porn couple."

The humor that we brought to our visit with the MDA we also brought to the visit with our primary care physician. She had been our family doctor since we'd first moved to Illinois.

The kids never had a pediatrician—we all went to her. We loved that she could treat the entire family because, as an author I'd once read pointed out, a family is like a mobile, and when one piece is off balance or removed altogether, it causes the entire family to become off balance. I had always thought of families in general, and ours specifically, in this way, even before we knew we would lose Bob. I figured if we all had the same doctor, then not only could we be treated individually, but she would be aware of issues that affected us all. When we took the kids to the doctor, we all went. When Bob or I went, we went together. We communicated about everything, which meant being there to be each other's voice when one forgot something, or each other's memory when we needed to recall what the doctor had said, or to just hold each other's hand through the painful parts, like gynecological exams and spinal taps.

Bob and I had always been fierce in our dealings with doctors; Bob had taught me that. He insisted on doctors who answered questions instead of those who insisted on talking to us as if we were idiots. He insisted on being present as much as possible for anything that happened to me, and I did the same for him. We agreed that a good bedside manner was incredibly important in a doctor, and if one treated us as if we were unable to understand them, then we didn't want to see them again.

When I had an MRI while being tested and treated for Lyme disease, the reps took images of my brain, and Bob, forever fascinated by science and the human body, asked for a CD that he could take home. After watching both my C-sections, Bob used to joke that he had seen all of me and loved me anyway, adding, "No, really, I've seen *all* of you. I've seen your liver. I love you inside and out!"

Bob was never one to shy away from looking at anything directly, or addressing anyone directly. It was one of the things I most admired about him. He was unlike most people, who tend to avoid what makes them uncomfortable, especially regarding any form of conflict, and who will sometimes keep the peace at the expense of creating greater problems. I know people who think if they ignore something it will go away, and I've known people who tried to keep so many people with disparate needs happy that they ended up making no one happy. Bob and I used to like to say, "Instead of putting your shit in your back pocket and pretending it's not there, get it out, put it in front of you, and address it so you can move on." We all have a bunch of baggage; pretending we have none just makes us look foolish as we drag it around tripping on it as it batters our heels.

At our visit with our primary doctor—a doctor we'd selected because of her knowledge and bedside manner both, one who was about our age and had children about our children's ages— we told her how amazing she was and how grateful we were that she got us to Barnes as quickly as she had. It was still early in Bob's illness, and Bob said he wouldn't be going to doctors for long. There wasn't anything they could do except check his breathing and monitor his muscular weakness, both of which a patient knows well enough himself. Also, Bob's increasing lack of mobility was soon going to make it harder for him to go anywhere. As ALS develops, you need much stuff ordered— like bed rails and walkers and commodes and wheelchairs and special utensils for eating, feeding tubes, tracheotomy tubes, catheters, and so on, and you need in-home care or hospice. We weren't going to be visiting our doctor's office much.

This was one of the last times—if not the last time—I remember being in one of our doctor's patient rooms together.

"You rock! And I was your first Lyme patient!" I said proudly, expressing our gratitude for the quick ALS diagnosis, even though she didn't really diagnose him. As a family care physician, she wasn't in a position to diagnose ALS, but she did send Bob immediately to a local neurologist.

The more Bob and I read online about ALS, the more we learned that ALS is often misdiagnosed. Many people spend the first year or more just trying to find out what is going on with their bodies, which is a big waste of time when a person is looking at a two-to-five-year remaining lifespan.

Bob—upping the ante on my comment about being her first Lyme diagnosis—said, "Yeah, but I'm her first ALS patient and mine's terminal, so I win!" Bob winked at me and raised his one eyebrow at the doctor (a talent only Maeve has inherited). Bob and I glanced at each other flirtatiously as we continued to playfully banter back and forth.

"Oh, sure, just because I had Lyme, and I didn't die from it, you had to go and get ALS. You always have to win!"

The doctor, surprised and pleased, said with a laugh, "It's so great that you two have such a sense of humor about this."

We eventually learned that the "twitches" were medically termed *fasciculations*, which were the spontaneous firing of a motor unit, a group of nerve and muscle cells that work together to contract a muscle. Later that year, when we needed our doctor's notes to apply for disability, I read through all the medical details. When Bob had seen our family doctor for the first time in December, she had identified fasciculations in his tongue, which means he had bulbar onset, as opposed to limb onset. The corticobulbar area controls muscles of the face, head, and neck. Bulbar onset also progresses the fastest of all ALS cases.

16

Bob's Muscle Team

We were grateful to welcome our first visitor, Natasa—a friend we'd met in Florida who now lived in the Midwest—in late January. When she heard the news, her instinct was to come as soon as possible, and we welcomed her visit greedily. She took care of us by making sweet and savory crepes, giving Maeve piggyback rides, and generally entertaining the kids. She was also an empathetic and thoughtful listener. There was both celebratory and melancholy wine pouring.

Anticipating many more out-of-state visitors, by February 6, 2012, Bob decided we should begin setting the tone for how he wanted others to interact with us. Dark humor, Irish humor, gallows humor was where it was at, but we also wanted a degree of normalcy.

After a month of conversations about medical updates, I sent out my first posting through the website—a mechanism that would help prevent expending all of our energy on constant and repeated in-person or phone updates. This practice also helped us avoid having to deal with platitudes or advice from well-meaning colleagues. A woman at the university once told me, "Someday you will be able to look back and know that it was all for the better." I blinked at her, twice, and said, "Uh, yeah, I don't think so." *How could there ever be a day when I would think losing my husband was a good thing?* I wondered. *How does one even delude themselves into this way of thinking?*

We decided that Liam and I should begin having a weekly chat routine to get him to open up about his feelings. So Liam and I would go upstairs to the master bedroom to talk. He was beginning to notice platitudes too. His teacher, he explained, often said, "Life is good," and another proclaimed, "Life is easy."

"But life isn't always good or easy," he remarked thoughtfully. At eight, Liam already understood that glossing over reality wasn't good for anyone and could easily be perceived as ignorant or insensitive. He reminded me of Bob, who'd always hated the name of the store "Life is Good" for precisely that reason. "Yeah, life isn't good for everyone," he used to say.

The first email I sent out, Bob and I composed together. Subsequently, we would either compose the messages together or I would compose them and have Bob proofread and edit them, adding and removing information. For the most part, Bob would sign off on what I wrote because we were like-minded in most things. The people on this list grew over the months Bob was ill as I ran into new people who wanted updates. "I have an email update list," I told them. "Would you like to be added to it? It's called 'Bob's Muscle Team' and it's on a website where we can post updates, send bulk emails, and later, when we need some help, have a calendar where we can ask for things like, 'Could someone pick up the kids from daycare/aftercare today?' or 'Could someone come hang out with Bob because I'm at work?' or 'Can anyone deliver groceries?'" The email list began to include people who weren't among our closest friends, but those whose knowledge of what was going on would benefit us, or because their understanding would be necessary for us to continue to support Bob through the process, such as a superior at work or an acquaintance eager to help.

In the first email we sent out, we didn't offer much in the way of reservations. Here is a truncated version of what I wrote:

February 6, 2012

Part of why we started this page is to keep everyone apprised of Bob's health and our general well-being so that when we have an opportunity to see you or talk to you, we can spend our time talking about more interesting things, like the weather, or what you had for breakfast, or better yet, music or Nietzsche. Time is valuable and we would like to spend it enjoying life with each of you and laughing rather than recounting the latest developments in our business of loss and grieving.

Around the house, Bob's able to do most of the things he always did, but he gets tired more easily and some things take more time than they used to. There are also some things he can no longer do, such as lifting heavy things, like the kids. He has lost some of his fine motor skills. He has difficulty opening water bottles or pinching open clothespins, for example. He also takes the stairs more slowly. His speech is mostly unaffected, although when he is tired, it can become a bit more nasal or his words less clearly enunciated.

Bob and I have our good days and our bad. We are trying to embrace every day and appreciate it. Some days this goes well. Other days it is harder. In addition to talking and crying, we spend a lot of time listening to music, making off-color jokes, and laughing. Our shared humor makes everything more possible.

We went to the doctor in St. Louis last Thursday, so here's the latest in terms of the prognosis:

Bob's breathing is the same as a month ago—which is great!

Bob's likely to lose the use of his arms first, since that's where the weakness began.

Bob is likely going to have one to one and a half years of quality time.

Now that you know all of this, please feel free to call Bob and talk about yourselves. I will occasionally need to talk, and I will find you (I know who you are!).

Reading this now, what I notice most is our honesty, our directness, and the playful attitude we brought to the entire enterprise. There was also an effort, however—at least on my part—to act as though what was happening inside our home was the same experience everyone was having outside of it.

I look at this now and think it was my way of being gracious, but also of rallying support. It was partly selfless and partly selfish, partly politeness and partly a survival mechanism. This is the most dishonest aspect of this entire piece: my humility.

As the months went on, I was always reminding everyone that we were all in this together, as if we were all experiencing the loss equally, but really, we weren't. While everyone who loved Bob was going to lose him, to some this was going to matter more than to others, and for some it would be a loss felt every day, whereas for some others it would be a jolt, a general sympathy, or a reflection upon their own mortality, and then Bob and I would recede from their minds almost completely. I don't blame people for this; I understand it. I have been on that end of this sort of thing too. I am reminded of the line of the grieving mother in Robert Frost's "Home Burial" where she laments and resists how quickly people seem to return to their own lives shortly after a death.

I imagined Bob climbing into the grave without me every day, and every day I found myself climbing in with him. Since we had met, we had been—as Nana Sharon often said—two halves of the same body; if he was the right hand, I was the left, and vice versa. I could not imagine it ever being otherwise.

Bob's parents were going to lose their child whom they had known thirty-one years before I ever entered the picture. They had memories of his infancy and childhood, his first marriage, and the transformation of Bob into the man, earringed and tattooed, whom I met in 2000. They had created him, nourished him, and watched him grow. They had a relationship at once closer and more distant than the one Bob and I shared. They held the reserved space all parents hold regardless of distance or time, whereas I had had only twelve years with Bob. But I had also become his best friend, his confidante, and his lover, and he had told me he had been his more authentic self with me than with anyone else.

Bob had a gruff exterior, one he had cultivated through not only his choices in attire and accoutrement, but also his way of walking. He didn't hold his shoulders back—they rolled forward—and he tended to walk looking at his feet more than looking straight ahead. He presented himself as someone "not to fuck with," as he would say. With his six-foot-five stature and his piercing green eyes, he came across as intense and a bit scary. He didn't always smile at strangers initially, not until prompted to do so by a friendly gesture. He wanted to be "left alone," as he put it.

Bob's family moved from Long Island to Buffalo, New York, when he was in high school, where he was taunted for his New York accent. When he grew to his mature size, he wanted two things: 1) to avoid being bullied by keeping people a little intimidated and at a distance; and 2) to defend those who were bullied by stepping up for the underdog. Once, when a strange dog wandered into our backyard, frightening the kids who were playing there, Bob raced out of the house, his hands high in the air, making himself appear at least seven feet tall, and ran at the dog, growling and chasing it into the street. When it came to defending who and what he loved, Bob had no reservations about his appearance or the judgments of others. He looked like a wild man running like an animal that day, growling and grunting, and he didn't care at all.

Bob's parents were losing their baby and would forever have an ache they could not soothe, but I imagined they had grown somewhat accustomed to only talking to him monthly or seeing him once or twice a year, with the combination of familiarity and distance that loving someone for a long time but not being a part of their daily life creates. His absence would be felt every day, because while he was alive, they knew he was "out there" and he was "okay"; he was, after all, their baby, their son, but they had had time to get used to not having his daily presence.

This loss, the one parents experience, is one I have not experienced and therefore can hardly comprehend; I can only recall my own parents' separate reactions to the loss of my eldest brother to suicide, and, terrified, imagine it myself. And when I do, I am utterly broken. Losing a child has been one of my greatest fears since I became a parent. Even uttering the words is terrifying.

Bob's only sibling, a sister, was losing her brother. Having lost two, I could identify somewhat, even though it is not only the relation of someone to us but the relationship we have to them that we grieve, and this is something so individual it is like snowflakes. Some we knew were going to lose a friend or a colleague; this I have done, and so I can not only imagine it, but summon the memories in my nerves of what it felt like and how I grieved. I lost my parents as an adult—albeit a young one when my mother died—so I can't even begin to know what it must be like for my children to have lost their father at such young ages.

What I did know indelibly was that I was losing my husband and I would have to go on and raise children alone, and this I knew no one else was experiencing. No one was just going to move in and be the mother and the widow for me. Also, no one else was in our house. No one else would continue to live the loss every day in their home with their children that I would have to endure. No one else would be grieving in the same way I would, except Bob, who was already grieving with me, but would then have relief. Bob and I both believed that when a person dies, that's it. It's the end of suffering. It is not suffering itself. And there is no hereafter. This is it. This is the life we have, and we have to make the most of it. As Vladimir Nabokov pointed out at the start of his memoir, *Speak, Memory*, most do not worry themselves over the time before their own births, doubled over in angst over what they did not experience, nor should they imagine such a time after their own deaths and be troubled. As Epicurus made clear, death is not experience, it is the absence of experience. Soon Bob would have peace from this suffering. I would have to endure.

I sometimes resented that there would be an end to Bob's grief, and I told him so. I even joked when our youngest, Maeve, was being difficult—she was a challenging young one—"I know why you got ALS. You don't want to be here when Maeve is a teenager. Thanks a lot." Bob truly got the joke.

But Bob also would never learn who Maeve would become, who she would be, how she would change and grow. We always thought her strong, independent spirit would better serve her as a woman than as a toddler, but Bob would never have the chance to know, and he thought a great deal about what he would miss out on with both of the kids. He wanted me to remind them later that "it goes both ways"—he would be missing out on them just as they would be missing out on him. I was not yet focused on what Bob would miss out on, however. I was focused on what he would not have to experience.

There would be no end to our children's grief or mine. I was trying to be gracious and humble about the loss to the outside in my update letters, but on the inside I, too, was beating my fists like a toddler. I wanted someone to be the mother, not to the kids, but to me, and somehow make everything better.

17

You Know Me

During the fall I was turning forty, the mourning period of my immediate family took on an even greater magnitude than it had the previous fall seasons. My mourning season began with my mother's death on August 30, my father's on September 22, and Sean's on October 6, and it went through to Paul's death on October 31. In 2009, though, three years after Sean and Dad died, I barreled toward my fortieth birthday, feeling the full weight of my family on my shoulders. Soon I would live longer than both of my siblings. There was something so wrong about this, and it overwhelmed me.

I had once had two older brothers, and now it was just me. I picked up smoking again. I had a bit of a midlife crisis. I didn't buy a fancy car, and I didn't dye my hair as I had done after my divorces. I did, however, indulge in wine and cigarettes, and I went out dancing at a college bar without Bob. I wanted to be young again, dancing with Sean in bars, existing only for a moment in the pre-time of loss. There was, too, a young man who appeared to have a crush on me, often being the one to invite me to meet him and a group of friends at the bar. And so I went, and developed a bit of a crush in return. I was running out of my house and toward something—youth, or maybe just somewhere I could ignore the pain of imminent loss. I wasn't really running from anything in the house. I certainly wasn't running from Bob. I was running from time. I was running from aging.

Bob and I seldom went out. We had two kids, one of them under two. I'd had two kids from C-sections and my jeans were getting tight, and this young person seemed to think I was fascinating.

So, I would be in my sweatpants, hanging out with Bob after the kids went to bed, and a text would come in from Billy inviting me along to the college bar a few blocks away.

"Billy says everyone is going to the bar," I'd tell Bob.

"Do you want to go?" he asked.

"Yeah, if it's okay."

"Go."

"Are you sure?"

"Yeah. If you want to go, go."

"I feel bad."

"Don't. Someone has to stay here, and I don't mind. You need this. Go. Have fun."

"Thank you. I love you."

I would give Bob a kiss and then bound up the stairs in excitement, as if I were in college again, throw on some jeans, throw on some makeup and do my hair, come down, ask Bob again if he was sure, and be out the door in ten.

I would stop for cigarettes if I didn't have any. Billy smoked too. It was all very exciting and spontaneous, and there wasn't much room in my life for spontaneity anymore.

It was never just Billy and me at the bar. Everyone was always there—a large group of at least five or six people I knew—but he was the conduit getting me there. He was the one inviting me. And Bob knew I was going through something—cigarettes were always an indication I was going through something. And Bob felt the impact of Sean's demise just as much as I did, and he knew that autumn, my "season of mourning," always killed me. And Bob always wanted me to have whatever it was I needed.

One night, Billy and I stood outside the college bar, smoking a cigarette under an eave during a rainstorm. We had just heard "our" song on the jukebox—he'd selected the song and introduced me to it, and somehow without saying, it had become ours, if only in my own middle-aged mind. It was Kings of Leon's "Use Somebody," a popular song at the time and regularly on the radio. The lyrics were easily conveyed from an early-twenty-something mouth to a near-forty-year-old English

professor's ear. Lady Gaga's "Bad Romance" was also a hit regularly played on the radio, and over and over in my mind, and
another we'd danced to at the bar.

The night was a stage set for romance. A downpour. Temporary shelter. The light from a few streetlights silhouetting our
faces as we dragged on our cigarettes, quite alone. For a few
moments our gaze held just long enough for me to decide. The
desire was there—I was feeling lust for someone other than my
husband for the first time in more than a decade, but reason
prevailed. *This is infatuation,* I told myself, *not love. I love Bob and I
would do nothing to hurt him.*

I wanted to kiss him, though, and that was enough.

The next night, I talked to Bob about it all.

"So. I've been going out a lot. And thanks for letting me do
that. It's felt good."

"Good. I'm glad," Bob said.

"And I've felt young again, like I'm in college again, not
about to turn forty. And it's not that I don't like my life but
because I just miss all the excitement of being young. The new-
ness, the intensity. The way the whole world dissolves when you
are a little intoxicated and on the dance floor and the way I feel
when I know I look sexy."

"Yeah. I get that. I'm glad you are having fun. You deserve it.
I know this is a shit time of year for you, and I know this year
is especially hard. That's why I am glad you've been getting out.
You need it."

"Yeah, but there's something else I need to talk to you about."

"Yeah?" he said, raising that eyebrow of his.

"I've, uh, developed some feelings."

"Okay." Bob waited.

"I'm not proud of them, and I know they are temporary,
and empty, but I'm having them, and I need to talk to you about
them, even though this isn't going to feel good. I know if I
don't talk to you about them, they are just going to get bigger,
and I know it's bullshit and I want to diffuse it. I know it's
imagined, not reality, and I don't even want it to be reality, but
the more it's a secret, the more it grows."

Bob looked at me with curiosity. "Okay, hit me with it. Who is it? Billy?"

"Yeah."

"I figured."

"You did?"

"Yeah. It's kind of obvious." We both laughed, awkwardly.

I felt the emotions for Billy already beginning to deflate. Bob got it. He knew. He already seemed to understand.

"I haven't done anything. I'm not going to do anything, but it makes me feel good to have someone else desire me and want me. At least I think he does. It seems like he does. And when he texts and invites me out, it's nice. It's nice to be with all the young people. I don't know what I'm going through exactly, but I know I don't want to lose you, or mess up anything, or really do anything with him at all, but I feel lust. I do. I will admit that. And I feel like shit about it. I feel like shit about having any feelings at all."

"Look, Dee," Bob assured me, "it's natural. You've got a hot young guy paying attention to you. That's awesome. I'd be bull-shitting you if I didn't admit it *does* make me a little jealous, but I totally trust you. I know you'd never do anything to jeopardize us. I know you, and I love you."

"I love you too, and I'll stop going out if you want me to. I will. I'll just not go anymore."

"That's not going to matter. Whether you go or not isn't the issue. You have to work through this stuff. I trust you. Go out. Have fun. Flirt if you want. That's all fine. Just keep talking to me about it." I nodded. "And don't do anything," he said and laughed. And then I laughed. A burst bubble.

"I feel better already. I knew if I just outed these feelings I would feel better about the whole thing and see it more for what it is. It's just a crush. I know that intellectually, but emo-tionally, it's just, it's just fun. And I like the feeling…I love you."

"I love you too."

We sat there a minute in the space that was just us again. Bob and Dee World.

Then Bob added: "Just don't fuck him."

"Yeah, Bob. Duh. I won't. Ha!"

Bob winked at me. I walked over to where he was sitting and bent down to him. We kissed deeply. I climbed on his lap and we hugged. He was my favorite place in the entire world.

And then I kept going out. And nothing happened. And life went on. And my birthday came. And Billy came to the party I threw at my house for myself and brought me "Cupcake" wine, which was relatively novel at the time. I kept the bottle around for a long while, a souvenir from one of the best birthday parties I had ever had and as a reminder of the fun of that late-night flirtation. And more cigarettes were smoked that night, and more dancing ensued, and another friend even gave me a cigarette extender, which really made me laugh at myself as I imagined myself as Mrs. Robinson in the movie *The Graduate*. By the end of the night, that extender was gone, and by the Day of the Dead, my mourning season had once again passed, and by the holidays, the entire episode of my craziness that fall had eased up. By January it was nearly past, and by spring the cigarettes were gone, and I saw a boy standing before me who seemed so young, so very, very young and cute, but not sexy anymore, just a boy, and the character he had become in my imagination the previous fall had completely dissipated. Bob and I were as solid as ever, and some of that early relationship giddiness for each other had perhaps even been revived.

One day the following summer, I mentioned how nice it had been to just feel young and sexy for a while before my fortieth birthday.

"Y'know, I'm still a bit jealous," Bob responded.

"You are? Of Billy?" I was surprised.

"No, silly, of the fact that you had some young hottie hot for you; I wish some hot young chick wanted my ass."

"Yeah, I guess it was nice. But just remember who has all the chili peppers on Rate My Professor. It's not me. They do all want you. You just don't hang out with them because we live here an hour away, so they don't invite you out. And besides, while it was nice for a while, I don't think I want that ever again. I'm done. I'm good."

"Well, that's a relief," he said, smiling. We both totally got it.
"I love you."
"I love you too."

I had been sitting with Bob's diagnosis for over a month, and
we had both accepted it was inevitable, and now I was trying
to imagine how I would live when Bob was gone. How would I
go on without him? I couldn't imagine that, but I could imagine
Michael being there because, well, he was familiar, and he'd
always been around there, somewhere, in the past, both family
and friend and former sexual interest, and if I could imagine
being with him, then I could imagine living. I was harkening
back in my mind to the conversation with my newly widowed
friend over the martinis the previous fall. Just as a dance floor
and a crush helped me outlive my mourning season the fall of
my fortieth birthday, a crush might just help me outlive Bob.
Of course, Bob was aware of how much time I was spending
on Facebook Messenger, but I was going to have to tell him
how I was feeling about Michael soon because that's who we
were, that's how we rolled.

Not everyone rolls this way. In my experience talking about
such things with others, it seems most people don't. I subscribe
to the idea that truth and knowing are always better than igno-
rance. Bob and I both did. It's part of why we both gravitated
toward philosophy. Bob and I agreed we couldn't deal with or
grow from what we didn't know. Relationships of all kinds are
built on trust. I firmly believe that it is by *not* outing such information, even in relationships we are committed to maintaining,
that we grow more and more distant from our partners. Not
telling Bob would have made—in the case of my fortieth-year
crush—a mountain out of a molehill. Keeping that crush to
myself would have helped those feelings to snowball, instead
of Bob and me melting them together. Hiding and not telling
never seems to do much good in any situation.

Honesty and trust were at the center of our relationship. We
knew each other completely and were wholly ourselves with
each other, nothing held back or hidden. While Bob was sick,
I remember thrashing about one night, crying. He assured me

that I would go on and that he wanted me to find someone else to love. I told him I didn't want to, and then said, exasperated and desperate, "No one will ever know me the way you know me! I don't want to do all that work again anyway, telling someone *everything.*"

"You have to not see it as work. It can be fun. You can teach someone about you. You will get to tell your stories again."

"I don't want to. It sounds exhausting. And besides, you know me."

Bob looked at me, with those piercing green eyes. "I don't know you," he said, deadpan.

I was momentarily stunned, and then I was rolling around on the bed laughing. That was the most hilarious thing I had ever heard.

Bob was dying and we were both learning how to live with it. In the next few weeks, we would be jarred more and more into reality, and we would work more and more to express to each other how we would each play our hand.

18

CHECK IT AT THE DOOR

By the beginning of March, we were almost to the middle of our respective semesters; both of us had managed to continue to teach. Our new normal was our new normal. Dostoevsky was right: human beings really can get used to anything.

Bob's department ordered a machine to help him project his voice, and Bob's pacing lectures became standing ones. He didn't tell his students much about his illness. The show just went on.

I found that it took all my willpower to go to work and teach poetry, but I had committed to checking my life at the door. None of my students knew my husband had been diagnosed with a terminal illness, and so for the time I was at school, I was able to pretend it wasn't true. How else could I have read aloud lines from poems like Whitman's from *Leaves of Grass*: "to die is different than any one supposed and luckier."

In October of 2006, after Sean died, I had to participate in the student senior seminar topic that year of "The Elegy," selected by my colleagues shortly after my brother's and father's deaths. One colleague later stated that the topic was chosen because they all thought it would be good for me. Later I heard students recount how painful it was for them to know what I had been through, which they knew because I had taken leave and because it was such a small town. I decided the only way to teach well while Bob was dying was for my students not to know Bob was dying. If they knew, they would surely seize up. Lips would tighten. Words would not be uttered. They would be afraid of speaking out of turn or of triggering my emotions, especially when discussing poems with death as a subject.

I vowed to myself to check my emotions at the door, and that I did. In hindsight, I realized it also helped me. I split myself into two halves. I needed to protect my students, I told myself, but I now know I was also protecting myself; if I didn't have a place to forget ALS, I would not have a way to face ALS.

During the few campus hours, I was Dr. Fagan, I was not a woman whose husband was dying. I was not a woman whose children were losing their father. Well, at least not until I ran into a colleague who asked about Bob's health, and I quickly added them to the bulk email list so I wouldn't have to talk to them. If I could avoid colleagues, then I could avoid the pain, if only for a few hours. I was most grateful for the colleagues who didn't offer pained looks or empty-headed clichés about God's will.

We made it to March, which brought Liam's ninth birthday and our friend Kate—the one who had helped create the Gay-Straight Student Alliance with Bob at his former institution; the one who had babysat Liam as we packed to move to Illinois; the one at whose house we spent our last night in Florida before the moving truck arrived—came to celebrate with us. She was one of my closest friends, the one I had confided in from the hotel in St. Louis when we first learned of Bob's illness. She was the one I talked to in January while throwing snotty tissues all over the floor of the second-floor bedroom.

A video of Liam's birthday shows Kate, Bob, and me laughing amidst the free chatter of the neighborhood children. Bob's parents had gotten us a video camera when Liam was an infant. We weren't very good at getting it out during typical days, but we were good at getting it out on Christmas, birthdays, and other special occasions. People told me to begin videotaping everything when Bob was first diagnosed. I would want the videos later, they told me. They were right, but I didn't listen. It felt too awkward to put my ailing husband on view like that.

I had splurged on an iPad at Christmas, days before Bob was diagnosed, and then almost returned it because I felt guilty about the expense. The iPad, however, friends told me, was a handy device for taking along to doctor's appointments, useful for notetaking, keeping in touch with folks via Messenger, and snapping quick shots of the kids and the occasional video of Bob when he didn't know I was doing it. They were right.

Everyone needs to get in the habit of taking notes at doctor's appointments, and it is better to start young than wait until you are diagnosed with a disease. So much terminology and details will be thrown at you in medical jargon, and unless you, too, are a medical doctor, you won't be able to retain most of it. Every other word will be in Latin or medical language, and you will not likely be fluent in that language. I had to memorize amyotrophic lateral sclerosis. I had to memorize plasmapheresis, which Bob gave a grueling shot. I had to learn words and procedures I had never heard of before, all under the pressure of a life depending on it.

So, I kept the iPad, and I took notes, if only to reiterate to others what we had been told by the doctors. I was unable to videotape Bob regularly throughout his illness, however. We wanted to be in the moment and experience it, rather than behind the camera recording it. Today, however, I wish we had more video where Bob is in front of the camera rather than behind it. Bob videotaped and I took still photos. This is what we had always done as parents; after all, the focus had been on the kids.

Bob and I had never much worried about getting us in pictures; we figured we didn't change all that much. We mostly worried about getting the kids in pictures. I now realize that was a mistake. What will your children most want when they grow up? Endless pictures of themselves, or some more pictures of their parents? They are most likely to lose their parents before they would like to, even should they live to an old age. Children are more likely to outlive us than we are them, although it doesn't always happen that way. Nature sometimes reverses itself.

I have so few pictures of my own family members, since they largely lived in a pre-cell phone era, without the selfie and pic-taking mania of present day. Now billions of photos are uploaded to Facebook every day. While I doubt we need quite the deluge of pictures that are going to be left behind when we die, I would have liked to have a few more of Bob.

Two of my favorite grainy videos I took with the iPad are 1) of Bob doing the dishes; and 2) of Maeve sitting on his lap watching TV and eating popcorn. I don't know why the quality of the videos isn't very good. It might be because it's an old iPad. It might be because I didn't know what I was doing. Either way, I love that both of these videos are of everyday actions, and in neither one did Bob know I was taping, at least at first, and when he did realize it, he just kept on doing what he was doing. They are both short. In the first one, Bob's just been diagnosed and so he can still stand and do the dishes, and I love that he's standing.

It wasn't long before holding the sponge tightly enough to clean dishes was a thing of the past for Bob. By Liam's birthday, it was already past. But in this first iPad video, Bob is doing the dishes, his back to me, in his baggy cargo pants, his "no-butt" and his long, tall back facing me. I am making jokes about his lack of an ass. Bob always made jokes about not having an ass.

Because Bob did dishes after dinner nearly every night of our marriage—if you cook, I wash—and because we are joking with each other the way we always did, I love this video. In the other video, the one with Maeve on his lap, she's so tiny, the big plastic Walmart popcorn bowl is so big, and Bob is so happy just to have her sitting there, even though his fingers are curled and he can't lift her anymore, or especially because of these things. He had held and carried those kids through their infancy. Ask anyone who knew us then and what they first recount is how they remember Bob always carrying one of the kids. Not being able to lift those kids anymore, or do any of the lifting as he once had as my Cave Man Bob, was one of the ways the disease robbed Bob of his identity, robbed Bob of a quality that made him not want to live as a "watermelon on the counter," as he still frequently put it.

19

THE ENDLESS PARTY

March to April were always busy months for us because we had Liam's birthday, then St. Patrick's Day, then Maeve's birthday, and Easter thrown in there somewhere too. In early March, Bob decided that having Maeve home with him when I was at school was becoming too much for him, so we transitioned her back to daycare—a difficult decision for Bob. Despite how exhausting it was going to be without Bob's help, I was focused on keeping our lives moving forward as they always had, so we were preparing for our St. Patrick's Day party, the largest party we threw annually, which we had thrown every year since 2002. We were also preparing for another round of visitors, this time the five members of Bob's sister's family: his sister, her husband, and their three kids.

From the end of January until September, Bob and I had well over a dozen sets of visitors. I write *sets* because sometimes it was one person and sometimes it was five. Some flew, some drove, some stayed a night, and some stayed a week. They came, and I cleaned sheets and towels, cooked, baked, and made our house the best Bed and Breakfast I could, frequently with bottled water and folded towels and maybe even a chocolate waiting on the pillow for their arrival. I was outdoing myself. I wanted everything to be perfect. I wanted everything to be normal, better than normal.

My goal was for Bob's illness to be one endless party, until he decided he'd had enough. We didn't want his light going out without some last hurrahs, and we didn't want melodrama or mourning to be the center of what was happening. "Check it at the door," Bob had said, and "Get on board with our dark humor."

The entertaining was taking its toll on me, though. I am an introvert by nature, so there were times I just had to check out. I needed quiet, more quiet than I was getting most of the time, so sometimes I would just disappear upstairs for a short time. This became more and more necessary as time went on. A short car ride, a short walk, an hour or two hiding in our room was sufficient recovery time for me to get back into the game, most of the time. These were my moments of solace. I was smiling and doing my best to hide the stress, but it was there, and it reared its head when I least expected it. The week of Bob's spring break, I was still teaching three days a week, and we not only had Bob's sister's family's visit, but we had Bob's lumbar puncture, and an open-door St. Patrick's Day party that brought around forty visitors. It was definitely one of those weeks when I reached a boiling point.

When Bob and I decided we wanted to have children, we also made decisions about how to raise them. We were not religious, and so we didn't plan to celebrate the usual religious holidays in the usual religious way. In the beginning, we weren't even sure we would celebrate the holidays we ourselves had grown up with: Christmas, Easter, and so on. We had a lot of talks about lying to children about Santa Claus, the Easter Bunny, and the Tooth Fairy. We didn't believe in lying generally, and we really didn't believe in lying to children. If we were supposed to be the people they trusted more than anyone else, why would we want to jeopardize that truth by intentionally giving them false information? Bob said, "How could they trust us to know other stuff about the world and be honest with them about the other stuff if they couldn't trust us with some basics?" And how could we not only lie to them about these things, but lie to them repeatedly about these things, year after year, day after day? We would let the kids discover what they thought about things, and we would be there to answer their questions or teach them to research and read and explore as they grew.

Bob and I decided that since we weren't going to buy into the usual stuff, we ought to have some celebrations that were a part of our own family identity, and so we happened upon St.

Patrick's Day as one of them. I had fond memories of wearing matching "Kiss Me I'm Irish" shirts with my mother and going to parades and eating corned beef and cabbage in bars while listening to live or recorded bagpipes. My mother loved bagpiping, parades—pretty much everything about St. Patrick's Day. Our annual fest would be a tribute to my mother, who had been far more gregarious than I and had always managed to feed people even when she was broke. She always stretched food well and people were always welcome at our home and table no matter how broke we were. Mom even made slow-cooker dishes of food to bring to the local pub on holidays. She took great joy in feeding people, and she was a marvelous cook.

Bob and I determined that on St. Patrick's Day, we were going to make corned beef and cabbage, wear green, and feed people. This would be our thing, and it would be the one time every year Bob and I would open the doors to friends and acquaintances alike and throw a huge party, despite our introverted natures.

The first St. Paddy's party took place in our one-bedroom apartment in 2002. We had a glass coffee table as our only place to eat, and about ten people came. They sat on the futon couch, in the one beat-up recliner we had, on the floor, and in a rolling office chair pulled over from our computer, and we ate and imbibed. Two years later, we had a 1,300-square-foot, three-bedroom apartment and a new dining room table, and more than twice as many people came. In the years since, the party has been mostly annual. I skipped the first year we lived in new towns, the year I was recovering from pneumonia, and the first year after Bob died. Other than that, the show has gone on.

The year Bob was sick, his sister and family decided to come for the party. They had always known about the party and wanted to make those memories with us. Falling on March 17, we had had parties in Illinois when it was still snowing and parties when it was sunny, but the last party Bob was going to have was the year spring decided to come early. The daffodils bloomed along the driveway, and the magnolia in the backyard was filled with delicate pink-petalled flowers. While visiting that week, Bob's brother-in-law generously did for us what Bob and I would have typically done ourselves—he mulched the entire backyard where Bob and I had erected a wooden playset for the kids two years before. That week, he and the nephews also erected the basketball hoop Liam had received for his birthday two weeks before. I cooked daily and baked pies and took care of Bob while Bob's sister and his niece helped to entertain the kids.

Sometimes our weakest moments are just our weakest moments. Sometimes we have nothing left to give anyone else, and we want to scream at everyone, "Can't you see what's happening here? Can't you feel the pain that is oozing from every pore of my body? Don't you know what it's like to lose the love of your life and the father of your children? No, not just a husband. Not just any husband. Not an ordinary husband. Certainly not that awful husband who beats you or the one who makes love to you as if you aren't there. Not even the one who is nice and kind and maybe even wonderful, but doesn't get you. I mean the one who *is* you. The one who *is* you! I'm dying over here!"

This is what I wanted to scream that week, but it's not what I actually screamed. I screamed other things instead. Teenage behavior that might have once been barely noticeable suddenly incensed me. I say incensed because, just as I don't always see when I've reached my limit with my own children's behavior and suddenly blurt out something unexpected, I didn't see I had reached my limit with the world. It had not yet been three months since Bob's diagnosis and I'd done my best to hold my head up and keep my foot on the pedal of life, but it was taking a toll I hadn't been entirely willing to accept. Maybe it's because Bob's sister's family *is* family that I let the dam go, but for whatever reason I did, and it wasn't good. It's not how I wanted it to be.

Bob's nephews were eighteen and twenty at the time, and Bob felt that they had not really wanted to come visit. He'd encouraged his sister to let them stay home, but she had insisted they accompany her. In any case, the family arrived, and the boys did what I supposed many boys that age did—they hung out on their computers, watched television, and did runs for junk food, despite the fact that I was baking pies. They didn't like pie. They weren't sure they wanted to eat most of what I cooked, and they looked at the array of dishes with suspicion. They wanted McDonald's and Hot Pockets. They were fish out of water in someone else's house for a week, a house that they had never been to before, with an uncle they saw once a year at most, who was, this time, dying, and a couple of young cousins who were underfoot, and me, the aunt who was beginning to reach her limit.

Our house had three bedrooms and a sunroom. Since our kids were sleeping on the floor of our room on a futon, I was able to give Bob's sister and brother-in-law Liam's room, and our niece Maeve's room, which left the sunroom for the nephews. It had no vents and no blinds or curtains, and it had floor-to-cciling windows on three of the four walls. We provided them with a fan and a way to prop the door open and suggested they keep the fan pulling the heat out of the sunroom during the day and blowing the air conditioning in at night. It was unusually warm.

Bob had a lumbar puncture scheduled that week to try to see if his spinal fluid would tell us anything new. His lumbar puncture was like getting sap from a tree. Following the puncture, he was supposed to remain lying down for the rest of the day, eating salty foods and drinking caffeine to stave off headaches, though he would still manage to develop one and need to call the neurologist for pain medication. The day I took him for this procedure and hauled him home was also the start of March Madness, and when we returned, the boys were watching a game in the living room. Bob and I didn't watch sports, but Bob yielded to the speakers blasting basketball as he lay on the futon couch in the living room all afternoon, recovering from the puncture. Both of us were trying to be good hosts.

As the days wore on, my impatience with the boys began to dwindle. For some reason they became the target for my exasperation with all I was doing to try to keep house and Bob and the kids while having visitors. I wanted them to eat the pie and the homemade food I was cooking, help out Bob, and in general make life easier, but I also wanted them to notice us, and value what we were doing by taking on visitors and a party in the middle of a life that was caving through the floor. This was an awful lot to expect from young people—way too much, really. How could they have any idea about any of it?

When I came back from a shopping trip for the party and found our eldest nephew on his computer at the kitchen table, everyone else gone but Bob and the house freezing, I was perplexed. I checked the thermostat; it was about five degrees lower than where we usually kept it. When I asked Bob's nephew why it was so cold, he told me he had turned down the air.

"Why?"

"Because our room was hot."

"Yeah, so, you blow the hot air out of that room with the fan I gave you. You can't just lower the air. It's just going to go out of the room. The room is all glass with no insulation and it's on the second floor. The thermostat is on the first floor. It's still going to be hot in there."

"Well, it was hot," he said, appearing somewhat defensive and maybe a little annoyed.

I went from zero to sixty in about two seconds. I didn't even realize how fast it was happening. "Don't touch the thermostat," I said calmly but firmly, in a tone I had never used with him or anyone in Bob's family before. Inside I was steaming, the anger bubbling up. He gathered up his computer and went to the front porch, which was where he and his brother would retreat for the rest of the trip when they wanted to make themselves scarce.

I walked out on the porch in the sweltering heat and found him sitting with his laptop on his lap. I looked Bob's eldest nephew in the eye. "Look, if you don't want to be here, there are several hotels I can recommend, but if you are going to stay here, then you need to follow the rules." I was shaking as I said it. I will confront someone when pushed, but I really don't like confrontation. It's hard for me, as it is for most people. He looked shocked, stared at me with a sort of blank look, and said, "Okay." We were both frozen, but likely in different ways and for different reasons.

I went back into the house and told Bob what had happened, and then I told him I had to leave. Adrenaline was still running through me. "Okay," he said. "Do what you've got to do."

I paced, trying to figure out where I could go. I ended up texting Casey, who lived in an apartment around the corner and a few blocks down.

Are you home? Can I come over? He replied, *Sure.*

I grabbed a bottle of wine and my purse. I kissed Bob good-bye. "I don't know when I'll be back," I said.

"Take your time," he said. Bob always knew when I needed some space.

I went to Casey's and we drank the bottle of wine and talked. At first I ranted, and then our conversation wandered to books and other things we had in common while we sat on his couch. When we ran out of wine, we opened a couple of beers. Time passed, I calmed down, but dammit, I wasn't going to go home and make everybody dinner. They could just fend for themselves.

At some point, Bob called.

"Hey."

"Hey."

"So, uh, we're going to order some subs from Subway. Do you want anything?"

"No, thanks. Is everyone back?"

"Yeah."

"Okay. I don't want to come back yet."

"Okay."

"Are they wondering where I am?"

"I think so but no one is saying anything."

"So, I'll just come back in a little bit."

"No worries. I just wanted to see if you wanted anything. I'll be up when you get here."

"I just didn't want to make anyone dinner. I'm still pissed off."

"Enjoy yourself."

"Thanks. I love you."

"I love you too."

In hindsight, it would have been better if I hadn't taken on so much. No one told me I had to cook for everyone and bake pies, and I could have been clear about our needs and booted everyone out of the living room while Bob was recovering from the lumbar puncture instead of steaming on the inside and expecting everyone who had just parachuted into our lives to know what I wanted, and what Bob needed. But I was trying to be the best hostess. I wanted everything to be perfect for Bob. I wanted everything to be as it used to be. If I hadn't put so much on myself, I wouldn't have felt so put upon when people didn't just love everything I was doing for them, for us.

The boys, after all, were losing their uncle and had been thrown into a situation in which nobody is comfortable. Many people fled from us, just as many had done when my mother was dying, including me. I had to run from my mother periodically in order to take my own breaths. It was excruciating watching her dying. She lived in a small town, I knew no one, and there was nothing to do, so I smoked, I slept, and I ate barely enough. And then when I could no longer breathe the air of the trailer without feeling that my lungs would collapse, I fled to the house of a cowboy several hours away and killed time there. One time, my mother called me to ask me when I was coming home. That tug of war is inevitable when we live death day to day. No one parachuting in could know what Bob and I needed, and we were running as fast as we could to keep up—both of us emotionally, and me physically, too—and not even always knowing what we ourselves needed. How could I ever expect any of us to get any of it right? There was no "right."

It's my own theory that the people closest to you are the very people who can't be there for you when you need them, and it's for that very reason they are closest to you. They are grieving the loss themselves and can't see past their own loss to yours, just as you can't see past yours to theirs. The people who tend to step up and help the most are the ones just close enough and just far away enough to be able to handle facing the realities of it all with you. During all the times of loss in my life, the people who showed up were hardly ever the ones I expected; they were nearly always a surprise.

St. Patrick's Day finally came, Bob's nephews kept to themselves; his niece and sister helped with preparations by peeling the vegetables, helping with the kids, and decorating; his brother-in-law put the final touches on the outside landscaping; and I cooked the twenty pounds of corned beef and the cabbage, turnips, onions, parsnips, carrots, and potatoes I always cooked. Family then mingled festively with friends. The voices of partygoers filled the house and spilled onto our deck. People were on the porch, on the back deck, in the kitchen and living room, and even on chairs in the driveway. It was March 17, but the weather felt like late April. It was one of the largest St. Paddy's Day parties we had ever thrown, and it happened to fall on the most gorgeous of days we could have imagined.

During the party, someone walked through the screen door going outside. A few hours later, someone walked through the screen door coming inside. We decided it wasn't a party until someone had walked through the screen door. I took a piece of electrical tape and wrote: NO PIXILATED ENTRY on it in permanent marker and placed it at eye level on bent screen that we had managed to shove and push back into place. When I was young, my mother had always referred to her own intoxication as her being a "little pixilated." I found the word fascinating. Now when I say it, people think I'm talking about pixels. Pixilated in the 70s meant "crazy or confused."

I have a friend, Kristin, who has had multiple sclerosis for more than two decades. She used to like to get "pixilated" at our house, because she could feel safe and spend the night. Since the alcohol affects her more with her MS, it was always good for her to have a few drinks with someone strong like Bob around, and with friends she trusted. One night, she got up from the kitchen table to use the restroom when she had a fall. She caught herself with her hands and was just fine, if a little embarrassed. Bob leapt into action, helped her right herself, and said, "Kris, it's not a party until someone falls down!"

After reading the ALS guidebook, however, we realized we had so much more to learn about falling down, the opportunities it afforded, and its pitfalls.

I sent out my next update letter shortly after the St. Patrick's Day festivities. Bob had always joked about how ironic it was that St. Patrick's had become the holiday our family was known for since we weren't religious. He'd say, "St. Patrick drove the snakes out of Ireland. You know who the snakes were, right? The heathens! So, yeah, he killed the nonbelievers, and so...we drink!" he'd say sarcastically, and then he'd raise his glass and say, "Slainte!" the Gaelic toast for good health he had picked up from my brother Sean.

20

COPING

Bob had continued to issue warnings to people about our sense of humor. If it weren't for our humor, we didn't know how we could get through any of this. We were constantly making wisecracks to each other. The levity was all.

When our friends Nader and Brian arrived, Brian, who was also Irish, immediately got on board. Nader, being Palestinian, told me in confidence that he was really struggling with our jokes. He knew intellectually that it was healthy, and he didn't want us to stop, but in his culture no one would ever have said such things, he explained. Indeed, for most people, death was no laughing matter.

Nader and I had known each other since college, and we made sure to have some quiet time to catch up, just the two of us.

"How are you *really*?" he asked.

"I feel like I'm dying. You know how hard it was for me to find Bob. And you knew Sean and my dad and how hard it was for me to lose them."

"I know."

"And I just can't believe this is happening."

"Deirdre, I'm so sorry. I don't know how you are doing any of this. I don't think I could."

"Bob says I've done it before and I can do it again, but it's so fucking hard."

"I can't imagine."

"Do you remember Michael? The friend of my brother's I went out with just before meeting Bob?"

"Yeah."

"Well, we've been talking a lot. He's been helping me."

"Oh?"

"Yeah. It's weird, but he just gets it. I mean, I guess I have always felt close to him, he's sort of like a brother and not at the same time because we were involved, but he's like family, sort of."

"That's nice. I know he must make you feel connected to Sean."

"Yeah, it's that, but it's also…I'm having feelings for him again."

"Oh?"

"His mom is dying, and I've been talking him through it, and he's been talking me through Bob…and I guess it has me wondering…maybe…just maybe after I lose Bob we could…I don't know."

"Wow. How are you feeling about that?"

"I don't know. I feel bad having feelings like that or thinking like that, but it's so nice knowing he's there, and we have that history, and maybe he's changed…maybe he's more capable of a relationship now."

"Maybe…have you told Bob?"

"He knows. I mean, I haven't said everything, but he knows we are talking all the time and it doesn't bother him. He knows we are friends."

"Yeah."

"But I feel guilty. I hate that I am thinking this way, but it's hard not to. I'm losing Bob and I guess it's just nice to think maybe there is someone out there."

"Listen, if this is what you need right now, then just do what you need to do. You are going through hell. This is awful. Anything that can help you, you should do. It doesn't mean anything is going to happen later. I mean, he may not even be that guy. But if he's helping you, I'm glad. I wish there were more we could do. I wish there was something to do."

"Well, Michael is coming here in a few months with Sean's other two friends. I guess we'll see how it goes."

"Really? That's going to be a bit strange, no?"

"It will be okay, I think. It will be good. I mean, Bob and I both love all of them. They helped so much when Sean died. We want to see them. We'll see about Michael."

I was certain Michael had gotten one thing very wrong, though. Back in January we were chatting one night, and I was so distraught, nose running, chest heaving, as I cried quietly over my laptop at the kitchen table while Bob was in the other room, and Michael typed, *This is the worst part*, and I had gotten so angry.

How can you say that? How can you say this is the worst part? Bob is dying. The worst part is going to be when he dies, I typed angrily.

I thought Michael was so wrong.

Kate, too, had been understanding, but she wasn't convinced Michael would suddenly step up and be who I thought I wanted him to be, later, when Bob was gone. "It's okay," she told me. "Don't feel guilty about it. It is what it is. You are doing so much. If it helps, let it help. If he's helping, good."

21

ALS Awareness Month

From April to May, Bob continued commuting an hour and teaching using a voice projector. We tried plasmapheresis on his non-teaching days, a process that was thought to help with an immune disorder, one that either coincided with or preceded his ALS. Plasmapheresis is a process by which approximately 3,600 ml of blood is removed from the body, spun through a machine to remove the plasma (which holds potentially harmful antibodies), and funneled back into the body with a plasma solution and an anticoagulant. While plasmapheresis would do nothing to halt Bob's ALS, one doctor had wondered if the rapidity of Bob's progression was due to an immune disorder. Maybe if the immune disorder were treated, the progression of ALS might slow down.

The first time Bob went for plasmapheresis, we spent several frustrating hours at the hospital trying to get his veins to cooperate and then had to reschedule to have a dialysis catheter placed in his neck by a radiologist. After the appointment to insert the catheter (which could stay in for up to two weeks), the plasmapheresis treatments began. Bob had three treatments and each one took four to six hours. The idea was that if Bob felt better and his symptoms were diminished at all, then we would schedule more treatments and maybe even continue to do plasmapheresis on a regular basis, just as one does kidney dialysis. Where the catheter was inserted in his neck, there was a green label that read *Do Not Inject*. As usual, we found humor in this and made the remark that with St. Paddy's having recently passed, this warning served to keep future partygoers from injecting Jameson whiskey directly into Bob's veins.

On Bob's non-teaching days he planned and created videos

while I was at work: one for each of the kids and one for me. I told him I would not watch them until he was gone.

We moved through Liam's birthday in March, St. Pat's, then Maeve's birthday on Easter Sunday in early April, and then the speed to the end of the term began. For Maeve's birthday she received a doctor's kit because she had been playing doctor a lot since Bob's illness. My stepmother and her husband, Phil, visited shortly after Maeve's birthday and Maeve treated them, and Bob and me, to shots while we sat on the front porch drinking wine. Maeve also recommended we all get up and walk around a bit to get some exercise. Maeve wanted to fix her daddy most of all. Her kit made her feel empowered. Bob would later write a poem about Maeve using her kit to try to make him feel better, and all the heart wrenching emotions those moments evoked.

In April, Liam asked Bob to visit his school for "Special Person's Day," but Liam was worried about Bob's ability to climb all the stairs in the building. When we registered Liam for kindergarten, I noticed—as we lugged Maeve's stroller up and down stairs multiple times in order to check in with the school nurse, visit his teacher, and see his classroom—that there were accessibility symbols on the bathrooms on the second floor but no elevator in the building. When I pointed this contradiction out to the school nurse, she shrugged her shoulders. Students who became disabled had to transfer schools, she explained, and parents who did, or already were, had to meet their children and their children's teachers in the cafeteria, coming in from the loading dock out back. We were incredibly proud of Liam when, after realizing the hardship his third-floor classroom posed to Bob, he contacted the principal and recommended the school raise money to install an elevator through collecting Box Tops and other fundraising activities. While nothing came of the suggestion, we were very proud of Liam, as was Liam of his dad when he managed to make the climb and be his special person for the day.

I now recall the rapidity of those holidays, the continual stream of visitors, and the end-of-term rush, and I am exhausted. During the end of the semester, every term like clockwork, the dust and laundry pile up, the errands are placed on hold, and the takeout increases. The workload is so heavy with preparing examinations and final papers and then reading and grading those examinations and final papers that it is all we professors can do to keep from drowning in the sea of work. Every year Bob and I would try to find ways to make it easier, and every year it would remain just as difficult, and we would be surprised once again by how exhausted we were—and this was when we were all well and young.

To imagine that we were facing this onslaught while struggling with ALS is even more unthinkable. The fact that Bob was still commuting an hour and teaching in April and early May, even when he needed nine-year-old Liam's help loading the car with his materials, is astonishing. Liam and Maeve had both been learning to pitch in those past few months. Even they realized it was going to take all of us now. Liam and Maeve began unloading groceries, Liam brought in garbage pails, and we all started helping Dad with whatever he needed. Bob had started to need additional assistance. While he was using a voice projector already, he was starting to lose the use of his left side. And yet, he went on. Both arms were increasingly hanging limp. He had lost dexterity in both hands and his fingers were starting to curl, but he said his left side was weaker than his right. With what strength remained, right-handed Bob relied more and more on his right side. Bob taught. We both taught. Somehow, the wheels kept turning. These holidays came and went. The class days passed. The visitors came. One, a former student of Bob's and a good friend, Liz, embracing our dark humor, even ordered a white "Happy Plasma!" cake decorated with blood-red icing while we were at a plasmapheresis appointment. Liz also cooked for us and helped me to plant pots for the deck as I always had in spring, by Bob's request. He wanted to be surrounded by living things, he said.

The momentum of visitors and work carried us through, somehow, until May.

As I was trying to control what was within my power to control, Bob had been taking control of his illness. He made decisions about what he did and didn't want. When he decided he needed a voice projector, he requested one. When he decided he needed to park closer to conserve his energy, he requested an accessible parking tag that allowed him to do just that. When he decided the focus on nutrition wasn't helping, he gave up juicing and just ate as much as he could while he still had a fair ability to chew and swallow. Bob was calling the shots. He was still able to, but soon I would have to begin calling the shots for him.

May is ALS Awareness Month. I withheld the information about Bob from my students until the last day of school, and then I told my upper-level students. I wanted them to know because some of them would be having classes with me again in the fall, and I had no idea what summer would bring for me and Bob and the kids, and I wanted the students to be aware of the possibilities before us. I taught at a small school and was considered a senior professor, having earned tenure, so students majoring in English took many courses with me. Some of them had also taken a class with Bob when he was a philosophy sabbatical replacement.

My students stared at me, dumbfounded, when I told them the news. They had had no idea that anything unusual had been happening in my life. I had succeeded. If there was something I could be proud of in relation to my teaching that spring semester, it's that. I wasn't able to protect my own kids from Bob's illness, but I had protected my surrogate kids.

It was ALS Awareness Month in 2012 that we became more aware of what ALS was going to mean for us as a family. We had finished our classes, and now we could focus all of our attention on what had been happening to Bob, to us, to our family since Bob first noticed the twitch in his arm in December. The speed with which the disease was advancing was giving us whiplash, but I had scarcely had time to slow down myself and pay attention.

Unfortunately, this sudden respite from work also meant more frustration came bubbling to the surface, as it had during St. Paddy's week. Some local friends decided to participate in an

ALS Walk in honor of Bob and had asked his permission when planning to do so. Bob thought it was nice and so did I, but as the fundraising began and the plans were posted regularly on Facebook, I began to grow resentful about the entire event, and felt guilt because of my anger. While my update letters made it sound as though we had all sorts of help, none of it was consistent. We had lots of visitors from the end of January on, but they had nearly all been from out of town. Sure, they helped, but mostly we wanted to visit, not ask them to do things. There were a few people in the town where we lived who dropped by with a meal or ran an errand, but most of our guests came for a few days from many states away. The group who had decided to fundraise and walk to raise money for research into the disease lived in our town.

I felt horrible that I was angry about this kind gesture, because who was I to dictate how they expressed their grief or their love for Bob? But I desperately needed help. While the letters and our daily lives were efforts at staying upbeat and positive—and as Bob and I liked to say, "Continuing to raise a glass of champagne despite the sinking of our very own *Titanic*"—what I really hear in my group mailings is cries for help cloaked in my prideful attempts to do it all myself. I was detailing what was going on, but I was also indirectly, very indirectly, saying: *Help us*. I was never very good at asking for help and I certainly had not yet learned.

The date for the walk grew nearer, and with each post and plea for fundraising, I turned to Bob.

"But don't they realize we are going to need an elevator installed on our deck? Don't they know how much all of this is costing?"

"They may not know. They aren't thinking about that."

"Okay, but don't they know we have just been charging expenses as they come up, things you never know you need until you need it, like a riser for the toilet seat, or a better pillow to sit on, or shoes with Velcro because you can't tie your laces, or special foods, or takeout because I'm too tired to cook, or clothes that you can put on because you can't lift a shirt over your head, or a bed rail to help you pull yourself up in bed?"

"No, they probably don't know. Maybe you should tell them?"

Of course, no one really knew these things, and even when I was saying so in my update, I wasn't directly asking for help. In an effort to stay positive, I wasn't really telling most people what was happening. I wasn't really asking for help.

"Don't they know I need help cleaning and doing laundry and running the kids places, and that we'd love to have more people watch the kids so we can have some precious time alone? Don't they know that we just want company, someone to drop over and hang out with us? Hardly anyone comes over. Why would someone drive four hours round-trip to go walk and raise money for something that's never going to help us directly, instead of coming over and spending the eight hours here?"

"Because it's easier," said Bob. "Here they would have to look at me and confront their own feelings about it and it's just harder. It's easier to go do that than to come here."

"I know you are probably right, but it hurts me, and then I feel guilty for being hurt, and I don't know what to do about it. But right now we are facing a lot of expenses and what we really need is real daily help. A walk is great to do in your memory, but you are right fucking here."

"So tell them."

"Tell them? I don't think I can. They'll be hurt. They are trying to do something nice. It's just not what we need. It's nice, but it's not what we need. We need real, actual things, right now."

"You need to tell them," he insisted.

Following Bob's prompting, I contacted one of the people planning to do the Walk and tried to explain as best and as carefully as I could what I was feeling with the most sensitivity I could. This person spread the word and reported that the response wasn't great. I guess at least one person did not realize we needed money, partly because we were planning a family vacation. I was exasperated: "When your husband is dying, you spend money you don't have. You charge the fucking vacation because it's the last fucking vacation you are ever going to have. It's not that we have the money, it's that we are spending it anyway to try to make some lasting memories. This is our last fucking vacation."

As professors, I think people always thought we made more money than we did. Our profession comes with prestige, but it often doesn't come with pay equivalent to that prestige. To further this perception, we lived in a large house because the cost of living was so low in our small Illinois town. We took a 30 percent pay cut when we moved from Florida to Illinois, partly because Bob stopped teaching more than half a dozen extra classes per year. In Florida, where the cost of living was so high, our salary was barely sufficient to afford a small apartment. In Illinois, we could afford a house with a three-car garage. We had nice things, like books, paintings, and antique furniture inherited from my father's family. Also, because I like nice things myself, I saved in order to buy them and in the long run saved money, because I tend to buy them only once. I grew up poor, which made me appreciate and desire nice things, but it also made me very frugal about how I spent money. I do not want dozens of pairs of the cheap shoes I had had to wear as a kid; I want a few really good pairs.

In the end, the walk happened, and life went on.

How could our friends know what I wanted when I hadn't told them? I had never been good at asking for help. We were all doing the best that we could, and I was sending out updates that sounded as though things were going swimmingly, even when they weren't.

I felt very alone, despite the kind gestures coming from so many directions. The fact was, on a daily basis we *were* mostly alone, especially once summer came.

In May, while the kids were still in school, we squared away all practical things like life insurance, social security, benefits from Bob's university, and so on. I had always paid the bills and managed our financial affairs, so we went back over all of our accounts and made sure I had all the information necessary to contact various entities when he died. I knew I was going to be in no condition to handle much.

We planned to go to the Social Security office together, and I made a list of every document I would need to bring with me, as well as a timeline of what could be required later. One of the bizarre things about death is the expediency with which you are expected to handle all the affairs when you are quite literally out of your mind with grief. It almost seems as though some companies hope you will fail just so they won't have to pay out. Social Security is one of those places with a tight deadline. If you don't go during that window, you are shit out of luck.

Knowing this from experience, we got everything in order that we could think of, made lists, and put them in our fire safe. We also contacted our lawyer and updated our wills, the wills we had created after my dad and brother died. We made sure that all things were in both of our names. We made sure Bob's life insurance that we had also purchased when I was pregnant with Liam was current. We did all these things because we had been left to pick up the pieces of my dad's and brother's affairs; while my father's estate had been left in order, except for an unsold house and a few loose ends, my brother's affairs proved more complicated. I didn't know the passwords to his email, or to his accounts or phone, so I had trouble even figuring out how to notify people that he had died. I had his postal mail forwarded to me so I could try to figure out the paper trail. It was a mess. Bob wanted to spare me that confusion at least.

I tend to avoid giving advice about childrearing to other parents. I think every kid is different and every situation is different, and if someone wants to know what I think, they'll ask. But the one piece of advice I give to new parents is: get life insurance. While Bob was dying, we didn't have to worry about whether I would be able to keep the house or our car or be able to stay afloat financially. I'd had the fear of death put in me at thirty-six and had lived in poverty for part of my childhood and had experienced the effects of that. We were living paycheck to paycheck, because of student loans, low salaries, and the inevitable costs of raising two kids. It was going to be all I could do to get out of bed in the morning; I didn't need to be worrying about where our meals were coming from or whether I needed to move and sell the house. Also, the kids needed some degree of stability after their father had been ripped from their arms. This financial security we had taken care of through life insurance; there were at least a few things within our control.

We also talked about who would get the kids, again. Our friends Glenn and Trish and their family were visiting, and they were the folks we had designated as Liam's guardians years before Maeve was born; of course, the will applies to any future children as well, but we were updating it anyway.

We were all sitting in the living room one evening, Glenn, Trish, Bob, and I.

"So, uh…now that the odds have increased, and there are two, you still want the kids?" Bob smirked.

"Of course!" Glenn and Trish said in unison.

Glenn and Trish had been together since undergraduate years, and Glenn had gone to grad school with Bob. I knew about Glenn and Trish the way I knew about Bob. They would raise those kids in a way that would have made us proud and the kids happy—and who could beat a philosopher and a pediatrician as the pair to inherit your kids? Bob, though, was very focused on me and my needs to ensure as best he could that would never happen, but he was right. The odds had increased.

Sometime in May, after classes had ended, Dave, a professor in computer science and a friend from work, began to pop in. He happened to be riding his bike by one evening when Liam was playing on the front lawn with the neighbor kids. "Are your parents home?" he'd asked, and then he just rode up the driveway on his bike. He wasn't one of our closest friends, but we had been colleagues for six years and he had always been invited to our St. Patrick's Day parties. We'd met through a mutual colleague who had since left to take another job, but with whom he had played racquetball, and it was Dave who delivered our Ping-Pong table when that colleague had moved and given hers to us. After all, Dave was one of the few people anyone at work knew who owned a pickup truck.

Bob and I didn't know much about Dave. We'd never known whether he had a partner, but he never showed up with anyone. We didn't know whether he was gay or straight. Our conversations had been limited to small talk and school. Dave didn't reveal a whole lot about his personal life when we were at gatherings, but he always contributed homemade bread when he came to St. Patrick's Day and he was always very good with the kids.

One of the first times we met him at a mutual friend's house, he'd taken Liam outside for a game of catch, and there were pictures of him teaching Maeve how to make noise by blowing into a beer bottle at a St. Patrick's Day party when she was a toddler.

It turned out that Dave's Tuesday night bike ride took him right down our street every week. He would break off from his bike group and head home right down our block, so he started stopping by for an hour or two around the same time each week. He came sweaty and in his bike clothes, carrying his water bottle and a Subway sandwich. I'd offer him a drink, but he'd already have his water bottle. I'd offer him leftovers, but he'd already had dinner or was going to eat when he got home. I'd offer him homemade pie, and he'd never say no.

Once school was out, I thought I'd have time for more frequent updates, but once Bob stopped teaching, ALS decided to remind us just how fucking fast it was intending go and, indeed, had been progressing all along when we were trying not to notice.

We were finally home together all the time and could focus on each other, but the stress was becoming more and more intense. Bob decided it was time for me to contact my old therapist, the one in New York, the one I had met with when I left my first husband, the one I had gone to see just before marrying my second, the one I had returned to when leaving my second, and then the one I had paid out of pocket to have long-distance phone therapy with after my dad and brother Sean died. She'd been with me through it all, the two marriages that had each ended in under a year, and the deaths, and she wouldn't need a lot of backstory to become just the person I needed to talk to about Bob. Michael's visit was coming up soon, and Bob was walking with a cane. It was time to call her.

22

THE LAST VACATION

My update letters were growing infrequent. Bob needed more care. I needed more care. School was out for summer, and if it had been a typical summer, we would have had more time for such things as reading books and letter writing and our own writing projects. But this was a most unusual summer and what quickly became clear was that Bob had made it to the end of that semester out of sheer determination. He had commuted for over an hour to stand in front of his class, teach his students, and bring home a paycheck and health insurance and a retirement package for his family. He had made it. We had made it. We could now be together all the time, or at least a lot more of the time.

Bob started complimenting me on the most mundane things: "Way to pick up that quarter with your thumb and forefinger, babe!" "Great walking!" "Awesome sneeze!" The more Bob lost his own abilities, the more he noticed mine, and the more he kidded me about them.

When I first contacted my therapist in New York, she couldn't believe what was happening. Having been the first person I had ever really talked to about my childhood, and the person who held my hand as I worked through those early losses of marriage and death, she couldn't believe I was losing my husband, that loss was happening for me again, and so soon. Of course, it was primarily happening to Bob, but as I had said to Bob, "But you don't have to be here to go on." Fucked-up thinking to some, but it made a kind of sense to both of us.

It seemed selfish, but I couldn't help it. I resented that my family members had left me holding the bag, so to speak. Death is an absence of feeling; suffering does come to an end, whereas I had to go on suffering and was convinced, this time, that I would die of grief, like the *Deirdre* of Irish lore. I certainly wanted to. Every time I expressed this to Bob, he assured me, "You can do this. You've done it before and you will do it again. I believe in you. It's not going to be easy, but you can do it. Don't doubt yourself."

Bob had given me so much confidence in the time we had been together, with two failed marriages behind me. Naturally enough, I had suffered from low self-esteem and a lack of confidence when Bob and I first met.

It was difficult, at times, not to wallow in self-pity. Sometimes the way people respond to my history, while intending to demonstrate sympathy, shocks my system and reminds me how alone I feel in my difference. "You've lost *all* of your family members? Oh my god. I'm so sorry." Or, the best one: "You are like Job!" Or as Bob once said of the way people looked at him after he became ill, staring back at them was like looking "into the eyes of a chicken."

Intellectually, it's never very difficult to find stories of similar and even far greater loss—horrors unfortunately abound—but emotionally, it is sometimes easy to become solipsistic and entirely self-absorbed in one's own traumas. Healing requires us to be self-absorbed for a short time, but eventually we have to look around, and when we do, we notice that we aren't as alone as we feel. Others are with us, and they help us get up and get moving again. Otherwise, we are no good for anyone, especially ourselves. It's like forgiveness. People always seem to focus on forgiveness as something that is done for other people—as though they need our forgiveness and, therefore, we should withhold it if they have done us wrong—but forgiveness most benefits the person doing the forgiving, because they are better able to focus on the present. Forgiveness, to me, isn't even about expressing anything to the person who caused the harm. It is about knowing what was and finding a place for it so we can focus on the now instead of the memory. It is about not giving energy to past hurts and anger. It is about taking care of ourselves. As Bob and I had often said, "Get that shit out of your back pocket and look at it." Forgiving gets that shit out of us, so we can look at it and learn from it, instead of ignoring or hiding from it, and then we put it somewhere else, in order to no longer harbor the grudges and feelings that cause ourselves harm.

My therapist and I decided I would call every two weeks at first, and, as things worsened, we could increase our conversations to weekly or twice weekly.

Between May 3 and June 8, Bob and I managed to finish classes, hold finals, submit grades, and have more visitors. Our first visitor was our dear friend Lynn, whom Bob had also taught with in Florida, who visited during finals week and commencement—always Mother's Day at my university—and Bob's mom and uncle, who came to visit shortly thereafter. Lynn made and froze stew, bought adorable Mother's Day gifts for me from the kids, and spent time playing with the kids. Bob's mom and her brother found various ways to make life easier for us, including Grandma giving Maeve the final push with her potty training and the two of them spending an afternoon fixing our "pixilated" screen door. Soon we would journey to our week-long vacation at the indoor water park and then home again to more visitors.

That summer, knowing that I was probably planning our last vacation, I began my usual searches for hotels along a beach, any beach, anywhere that might take my accumulated credit card hotel credits. After searching for beach hotels for a few weeks, I had reason to pause. As Bob's ALS progressed, I began to think more carefully about it. He had trouble walking on flat land. He could never walk on sand. What had I been thinking? I had been experiencing denial again, or at least a separation from reality.

"I've been looking at beach hotels," I told him.

"Yeah? Did you find anything good?"

"There are some that look nice."

"Great. Where?"

"Different places."

"And?"

"Well, I was thinking. I mean, you are walking with a cane. And it's been so fast. I mean, we don't know how you'll be by the end of the month."

"True."

"And so, does that make sense? I mean, if we had a wheelchair, how could I push it? Also, can we drive that far away? And flying, how could we afford it? And that would be hard too."

"Yeah."

"And unloading a van every night at a hotel if we drove and reloading it again every morning. I don't know if I could do all that unloading and loading myself."

"True."

I looked at Bob. What we both realized in that moment was that Bob would never see an ocean again. He had insisted over the past months that I was going to sometimes be ahead of him. I would see things he couldn't see, just as he would see things I couldn't. We were going to have to do the hard work of pointing difficult things out to each other, and I just had. I felt sick to my stomach.

When Bob was first diagnosed, I had grilled him about where he might want to travel. Did he want to take a trip? Did he have places on his bucket list he wanted to go? Things he wanted to accomplish? We had made a bucket list when we were first together and skydiving had been on it for me, but not for Bob, who had jumped from a plane five times before we met. We had planned to jump together, but given our fertility issues and ages when we met, we had been in a rush to have children, and once Liam was born, I was no longer willing to take the risk. My luck, I figured, would make me one of the few to die the first time jumping tandem. Bob said he had no destination on his bucket list more important than being home with me and the kids.

I put my mind to solving our vacation problem. How could we go somewhere close, have water, and also make all this easier? A friend suggested an indoor water park, so I started searching the web for water parks within driving distance.

I found one just outside of Chicago, a five-hour drive away. We had always taken our vacations in early June, before peak season, after we'd had some time to recover from the semester, but that was too far away. Every week counted right now.

Liam, too, was much more aware of his father's illness and counting every moment. He told me that he wished there were a fairy who could take away his dad's ALS. I had shared in an update that we all felt the same way. "So, if you come across any fairies now that many flowers are in bloom, please whisper in their ears for us."

I planned the trip to begin Memorial Day weekend. We needed to get on the road as soon as possible, and also in between visitors who had already planned trips.

The minivan loaded, we set out on the road. Bob had always driven and I had always been the navigator—he had no sense of direction. It was a running joke.

Bob said he could still drive, and he wanted to, at least while we were in the country with few cars on the road. He said he would let me take over when we reached Chicago. I have video footage of that trip. I knew that just getting Bob on video behind the wheel was special. He's just driving along, but he'd always been behind the wheel. It was an angle of him I knew well, the one I looked at as I stroked his head and neck on so many drives, and I wanted to preserve it. The kids were super excited. I asked them where we were going on the video, and Liam shouted in his little boy voice, "To. The. Water park!"

What I hadn't anticipated was the sheer size of an indoor water park, or that the hallways would be as long and gaudy as those in *The Shining*. I even snapped a picture of an empty one and posted it online with the comment "Redrum." Our room looked like Florida, complete with pineapple lamps, and it was a good size, but I hadn't thought to request an accessible room, and I hadn't realized that even the accessible parking would be many corridors away from our room. The idea that Bob was disabled, despite a hangtag that said so, was still distant. I made about five trips to unload all our belongings, especially since in order to save money, I had packed our own wine and

snacks and juice boxes and cereals and all other things the kids
wanted: toys, books, dolls. Given Bob's stature, 2XL shirts and
40X34 pants, his clothes alone took up space. Bob sat on the
bed, apologizing for not being able to help. "Don't be crazy. It's
fine," I said, as I made half a dozen breathless trips to the van.
I felt strong and capable and proud that I could take care of my
family this way.

I had been working out regularly when Bob was diagnosed;
it was part of our "getting back to health and leaving depression behind" process after I got pregnant with Maeve and
stopped drinking—which wasn't difficult. With each baby, my
body knew I was pregnant before I did and I just lost interest
in alcohol. But after we had Maeve and I recovered from my
second C-section, I started working out again. At first I didn't
even tell Bob. I exercised on my days working from home—his
days at work—for about six weeks before 'fessing up. I was
worried I would stop, and I didn't want to out myself if I did.
Bob had always been a consistent exerciser. He prided himself
on being able not only to emotionally care for me and the kids,
but to physically protect us too. He wanted to use that big body
for good.

By the time Bob was diagnosed, I had been exercising three
days a week for about a year. Our home gym boasted an elliptical, free weights, and resistance bands, and Bob helped me pick
out a punching bag, which came in especially handy when Bob
was sick. I would go downstairs to the basement to exercise,
and I would picture the word *ALS* or *Death* on that bag, and
then I would beat the shit out of it. All of this to say I had
started to become the lifter of heavy things. I was now the one
who was going to have to "kick ass," as Bob would say.

I took some short videos and photos on the iPad at the water
park. I got some of the kids playing while we sat poolside sipping some slushy alcoholic drinks. I got some of them making
stuffed animals at one of the shops inside.

I also took one of Bob navigating the hallway of the water
park arcade. In this video, it is clear how little balance Bob had.
I can't imagine the determination this vacation required of him.

He had to manage some gentle inclines indoors, and some that were slick, like those poolside. He had Velcro sandals with fair traction, but he walked with a hitch. He looked as if he could tip over with just a push of a few fingers. While there, I started to bubble up with anger again when I watched him try to navigate the crowd. I raced ahead to protect him, like a watchdog. I wanted to raise my hands above my head as he had done that day he'd run the stray dog off of our property. I wanted to growl at the people around him who were so oblivious to his lumbering self, so awkwardly trying to navigate around unsupervised toddlers and oblivious adults. I wanted to bulldoze a path clear through them all.

As my update at the time reads, we ate good food, we had some good laughs, we watched as the kids went it alone. I joined them a few times, after they begged me to, while Bob went it alone. We got very little sleep because the kids wouldn't go to bed at night, especially Maeve, who would wake up at an ungodly hour and ask to head immediately to the water-park slides first thing. We did all of this, in this sterile environment, as best we could, laughing when we could, and faking it through the rest.

And then we had an unforeseen incident. Bob used the bathroom, which meant sitting, and then used the towel bar to help him rise to his feet. Bob had been sitting on a toilet to pee since early in our relationship when I pointed out that "just because men *can* stand to pee doesn't mean they *should*." I further explained, "There are lots of things we can do that we don't do. Just because we can do something doesn't mean we have to. Standing is gross. You can hear it in the other room and it splatters all over the place. Yuck." Bob's life was about reasoning. He listened, assessed, and agreed. That was that. No more standing. And guess what? We didn't have pee all over our floor, and the toilet seat was never left up. And by the way, since three out of four times someone is using the toilet it requires sitting, the seat should just be put down. It's courtesy. Enough said.

So, Bob leaned on the towel bar, and yes, down went the

towel bar, down went Bob. I could lift some heavy things, but nothing quite so heavy as Bob, from a sitting position, on a floor, in a hotel, right in front of a toilet. Try as I might, I couldn't get him up. It was humiliating for him. The kids went in and sat on the floor to chat with him. He managed to shimmy on his underwear with my help, which were luckily boxer briefs, but he was going to have to spend the night, and perhaps the rest of his life, there, until we could find someone to get him up. It was horrible for Bob, the original lifter of heavy things.

I called the front desk. "My husband has ALS, Lou Gehrig's disease, which means he has lost control of some of his muscles, and he has fallen on the floor in the bathroom, and I can't get him up. He also took down the towel bar. I'm so sorry. Is there any way you could send a few people here to help me?" They were very kind. They said someone would be over shortly. I was expecting two, maybe three people to knock at the door. Instead, I opened the door to the Incredible Hulk. You think I'm kidding, but I'm not. He had to duck to get in. He was two Bobs, not high, but across, and definitely had inches in height on him too. He came in, introduced himself, stood behind Bob, and picked him up like a rag doll. He picked up Bob more easily than I could pick up Maeve. He just picked him up. Just like that. Done. "Need anything else? Have a good night."

We had as great a time as could be had by a man on his last vacation and a woman on her last vacation with him. I don't think the kids had any idea this was the case. Bob and I were exhausted. So were the kids. They wanted to go home. They wanted to see our dog Ivy. We checked out early. There was only so much fluorescent lighting and chlorine air freshener and pineapple lamps we could take. I was the one to drive us home in the minivan, glad we'd taken the vacation, but also glad to be going home.

23

SOMEBODY I USED TO KNOW

And we kept going.

I came back and readied the house for another round of guests while my colleague Terrence began painting the porch, hoping it would be dry enough for us to entertain on when the three California boys arrived. Kind, dutiful, hilarious Terrence poured his love for us into the paint he was carefully applying to the porch in the heat of summer, just as he had when he helped me paint the downstairs bathroom on St. Patrick's Day the year I was recovering from pneumonia and didn't throw a party.

That summer of 2012 was the summer Gotye's "Somebody That I Used to Know" hit the charts and was played repeatedly on all of the pop stations. The music video also went viral and Maeve was absolutely in love with it. She would play it over and over again on my iPad. The somebody that I used to know, Michael, soon arrived with Dave and Steve from California. Steve bestowed party gifts: fantastic coffee, divine chocolate, Cuban cigars—all the ingredients for the party we were determined to have while the "California posse" was visiting. Steve pulled me aside. "You know, if you ever need anything, we've got your back." These three men, for me, were extensions of my brother. They had all met Sean almost two decades before. Steve had been the one who found Sean's body when he died, Dave had been the one to call me, and Michael and I had had our well-known, short-lived, incredibly intense love affair. All three were brothers to Bob, and brothers to me, for all they had done, and yet Michael and I also shared a separate bond that was bound up in memories of a before time.

The visit was emotionally intense. It was all things beautiful and ugly. We had our belated "Lobster fest," a smaller, delicious affair of decadence where we cracked Bob's lobster and fed him until he was stuffed on the combination of lobster and the American and Chinese dishes Lee, Ping, and I made. We drank. We got hold of some local weed and learned that now that alcohol was starting to affect Bob as it had affected our friend Kristin—a few sips were like drinking three glasses—weed was the better choice. Bob learned that a small drag on a joint could relax him the way a drink used to, but not further interfere with his abilities. He had an easier time still managing to get around on weed, and yet it allowed him to be a part of the party. From then on, I would keep a little in the house, though it didn't take much and it had never been our drug of choice. It made Bob feel a little more normal.

My emotions were so close to the surface the entire three days, as were Bob's, because we all knew this was it. This was the last time we would ever all be together like this. And Bob loved them all, loved them all for who they had been to Sean, for how they had been there for both of us when Sean died, and for saying they would be there for me and the kids when he was gone. Bob was so broken that he was going to leave me untended, as my own family had done.

And there was Michael. I felt close to him. I observed him. I wondered about the "after time" and what it would bring. I wanted to imagine there was a way we could somehow come full circle and be a couple again because he was familiar, safe. Maybe he could be that person. I didn't know whether he could or whether he wanted to, but he was so wrapped up in my family history, having known my father and even visited him in upstate New York on his own once, having been so close to Sean, having known Bob and embraced Bob for what he had given me that he wasn't capable of (or interested in) giving me. It all seemed like it could, maybe, just maybe, work.

There were many times during the short visit when my emotions were so raw, I needed to step away from everyone. I felt as though the love and the sorrow were so large inside me, I would burst open or break into flames. I would go to my room to breathe. One time, I stepped outside and paced. The energy inside me was huge, but it was uncomfortable energy. Distraught energy. I started walking and managed to walk six blocks. When I came back, I learned that everyone had been wondering where I had been. I didn't have the words to express what I was feeling; I was just so overcome.

That weekend, I bought a pack of cigarettes and I smoked, and it was as if I were twenty-five again. It was like when I used to party with the California boys when I visited Sean in San Francisco. It was as if for one weekend we were all young again, Bob wasn't sick, illness and death and age were far in the future, and we were going to party like it was 2000.

24

MOVING FURNITURE

Bob had had trouble with the stairs before the California boys came, and I knew it was just about time to move him to the first floor. No doubt the three guys arriving would have been happy to help relocate Bob, but I decided against making their visit any kind of work. I wanted their visit to be one giant party of joy. The morning they left to return to Chicago and catch their flight home, Bob and I were filled with such sadness. There were many hugs given and pictures taken. When Steve, Dave, and Michael pulled out of the drive that morning, Bob and I hugged and cried in the kitchen. It was the beginning of a looming end for us. One of the last hurrahs. And we knew Bob would never see them again. The rest of the day was sullen as we sat on our porch, listless, no longer relishing the joy but harboring the sorrow.

The next morning, I started heaving furniture. I dragged the dining room table with seating for six to the enormous living room. I dragged the sideboard. I moved the couches and chairs in the living room to make room. I dragged our futon couch, which had been moved to the living room so Bob could nap instead of taking the stairs, to the dining room and laid it out flat, and dragged another futon mattress down sixteen steps and threw it on top of the other futon mattress from the sunroom to raise its height.

When Bob got up that morning, several hours later, the china cabinet had also been moved. I had texted Casey, and after he and I had tried to lift the glass cabinet top ourselves, I enlisted a neighbor's help too, and the three of us got it done. The dining room was almost a bedroom. I just needed to get a dresser and end table to the first floor. With the drawers emptied, I could do the end table myself, but Casey helped me move the dresser before he took off. This wouldn't be the first time I was moving furniture to create a space to accommodate Bob's changing abilities and our ability to stay close and keep the kids close. By this time we had had various configurations in the living room for Bob to be able to sit and nap comfortably. The night after the California boys left, Bob slept downstairs, and I with him, in our new makeshift bedroom. The kids slept in the living room, since they didn't want to be far from us. Now all I needed to do was raise the chandelier so Bob wouldn't hit his head, and add a bed rail so he'd have some help lifting himself up. I was grateful that our town was only ten minutes long from one end to the other, beginning with the Mississippi River and the Missouri border and ending with cornfields. The hospital was three minutes away and so was the medical supply store. We had good credit because we had paid off most of our student debt by teaching extra courses, but we were racking up the bills. There was no time to go through insurance. There was no time.

While I had become very good at getting things as quickly as I noticed Bob would need them, I had still not become very good at recognizing my own needs or when we needed help. I was, however, slowly learning how to ask for it. I was now talking to my therapist every week on the phone, and she was teaching me how to ask for help and urging me to do so. Therapy was another expense without insurance, but it was one we were willing to pay since I was the cog in this machine that could keep the machine running. Bob knew it, and he was going to be greasing that machine as much as he could to keep it going through talk and suggestions since he could no longer do the physical work of our team. I was still processing the reality of Bob's demise and doing so through the lens of my previous losses, as well as trying to imagine a future, while continuing to chat with Michael through instant messaging, and talk to others about him. Michael didn't know I had come to think of our past as a possible future, but nearly everyone else did.

During my visits with numerous friends, I would somehow wander into the territory of Michael, and before I knew it, I would explain all about our breakup from years before and how he was helping guide me through some difficult days with sound advice. I would recount the past and share some anecdotes from the present, and then shrug my shoulders: "So we'll see." When one of our former female students was visiting, I reiterated the tale to her one night over wine on the deck, while Bob rested inside. She looked at me in disbelief, not about the way I was thinking about and talking about Michael, but at my ability to do so. She had fallen in love for the first time with the man she would eventually marry, and she couldn't imagine surviving the end of love.

She remarked on how she didn't know how I'd done it—rebounded from earlier love affairs enough to find Bob and be happy—let alone how I could imagine doing it again. "I don't think I could do it," she said. I assured her she could, because what's the choice? We aren't always given a choice. Sometimes I had a choice, but this time I did not, at least not one I considered an option with two kids depending on me. If we hadn't had them, I would have been ready to die, but we did, and even when I wasn't sure whether they needed me, Bob reminded me they did.

Our friend Gio had been after me for several months to begin a fundraiser. We were going to need financial help, she said, and people would be willing to help. She said she would set up the entire thing and all I needed to do was say yes. She said it was okay to ask for help. People wanted to help, she said, they just didn't know how. The best week to launch a fundraiser, she told me, would be Bob's birthday week because people would want to do something to make Bob's birthday better.

I had tried to do it all myself and had reconciled myself to paying for what we needed on credit. I didn't know how long Bob was going to live, but I knew we had life insurance and somehow, some way, I would one day pay for all of these things. We could do this alone, too, as we had done all the other things.

But then I realized I couldn't. I was getting tired. We were struggling to meet payments. We needed help. My father had been weird about money; when we were adults he had made my brother and me pay back every cent he'd lent us, by handing us the returned checks he'd written when we were young and needed money—so accepting money wasn't something I was accustomed to. But we needed help. Bob needed to be able to leave the house if it was on fire, and I thought about that, a lot. Not a likely event, but a person needs to be able to leave a building. I finally told Gio yes after about a month of her prodding.

The deck lift and a lift chair were going to be funded by the fundraiser, and it would be all set up to launch at the start of the week of Bob's forty-fourth birthday. I was reluctant, but Gio assured me it was a birthday gift for Bob; I could get on board with that.

25

Hidden Inside

Father's Day, June 17, had come and gone, and now Bob's birthday was less than a week away. For Father's Day, the kids and I gave Bob the best card and a thermal cup (with the necessary straw) that read: "World's Greatest Dad." Bob could no longer sip from a cup. It took both hands to hold one, and his lips could no longer move well enough to sip. Straws were necessary. I took a video of Bob opening the card, which he loved because of its layers of meaning. It's a *Star Wars* card with a recording. On the front it reads: *In a galaxy far, far away, two droids are discussing their most dangerous and difficult mission ever.* And when the first flap opens, *raising kids,* and when the second flap opens, C-3PO says: *How did we get into this mess? We seem to be made to suffer…it's our lot in life.* Was this card about raising kids or about ALS? We loved that it was about both.

Truth is, I wanted to choose death. I really did. While the update letters make it sound as if we were surrounded by love, which clearly we were in so many ways, so much of that love was far, far away. There were many people who did not inhabit our daily lives. We lived in a quiet house with each other and two kids in an isolated town in the Midwest and had our small but intimate writing circle that blew in every few weeks. In between, it was just us. No grandparents for the kids on my side at all and the two on Bob's many states away. No siblings on my side at all, and the one Bob had and her family, many states away. No cousins that were part of our lives. No aunts and uncles on my side that were part of our lives. No relatives at all, actually, except for Bob's immediate family and his one uncle—his mother's brother. Bob, too, had some distant relatives, but I had only met some of them a few times, and others, never. It was summer, we were home all the time, it had gotten too humid and hot to be outside, and the days were becoming long and lonely between visitors.

Much of our shared family had been chosen, and they were a gift, but chosen families have their limitations. When it comes down to it, no job is going to give you time off, no paperwork is going to outline what policy applies to your most valued friend-ships, no anything is going to tell you your chosen family is family in the traditional sense when there aren't blood relatives. And most of our chosen family had their own blood relatives even if I didn't, so they may not need or want me in that same way when the need arose for them. I was on my own entirely, except for the kids, who were going to be (and already were, except for some armchair advice, as Bob would call it) entirely dependent on me.

People had their own lives to live, their own hardships, their own blood families to worry about, and without a relative of Bob's living in the same town, or many of our oldest friends, I would have to go it mostly alone, and I didn't want to. I wanted to dig myself a hole and climb in it, but Bob said I couldn't. He said I could do this. And my therapist said I could do this. And Michael said I could do this. Everyone said I could do it but me. Inside there was a small girl with bunched fists still screaming, "Maybe I can, But I DON'T WANT TO!"

Every time I would iterate that I could *not* do this, my ther-apist would tell me about "a small box hidden inside" of me. "In it," she said, "is the strength you need to do this. When the time comes, that box will open, and you will be able to, but you don't need it yet. Right now, Bob is downstairs, alive, waiting for you. Don't spend your time thinking about when he dies. He's going to die, but he's not dead yet. He's very much alive. Go be with him." And she was right. While I was gnashing my teeth upstairs on the phone to her, he was downstairs waiting for me. And so I went to be with Bob, except when I couldn't bear it anymore, and then I would slip away to get a coffee, or groceries, or just drive around in the car and flick cigarette ashes out the window for half an hour now that I was smoking again. It was only one or two cigarettes a day, unlike the pack a day I was smoking when my mother was dying, but I was still smoking. I would run away, just as I had when my mother was dying, only for much shorter periods.

A short ride in the car mid-afternoon with some music blaring on the stereo, and I was twenty-something again, alone, facing the world without a mother, or driving cross-country alone as I did at twenty-three, and then trying to figure out how to survive the looming world where I would be without a husband. When I got on the elliptical in the morning, I blasted "I Will Survive" first, and tried to believe I would and could. At night, when all was quiet, I sat on the deck and had a glass of wine and a cigarette. It was Deirdre Time, and the wine served as a little sleep aid so I could rest well and begin again. Everyone believed in me the way they had when my mother died, but I wanted to be weak and cared for, and Bob so wished he could give me that care the way he once had, or at least I believed he had. "You've always given me credit," he said, "but you did it all yourself. I was just there, cheering you on." Bob did his best to keep helping me every day. He gave me armchair advice, and he told me not to focus on what our friends and family couldn't do, but on what they had done and were continuing to do. Dave, for example.

Our friend Dave raised the chandelier above Bob's new bed when he dropped by one night on his bike ride. He had noticed that the front door needed slamming to shut, and he fixed that too. When he dropped by weekly from then on, he often homed in on something to fix or something to do. He was a "doer" like Bob's mom, someone who wanted to leave the house a little better than he had entered it. He let Maeve draw smiley faces on his kneecaps. He played with Liam. Mostly, he kept showing up.

When someone is housebound or ill or grieving, regularity helps enormously. After Sean and Dad died, my stepmother, Terry, began calling me every day around dinnertime. Sometimes the conversation was brief and sometimes it wasn't. Sometimes we rehashed the past and sometimes we stayed in the present. I didn't realize for months that she was doing it every day. I was in too much of a fog to notice. After a while I realized it was every day, or nearly. After about six months, I somehow "graduated" and she didn't do it anymore. It was as if her job was done. Somehow, though, she had known that was the sort of help I needed, and she could provide it for a time, even from a distance.

As Dave was leaving one night when we were all on the porch, Maeve—proud of being fully potty trained—shouted to Dave, "Goodbye, Dave! I love you! Next time you can poop on my potty!" Dave cupped his ear, trying to hear what she had said. Bob and I laughed and laughed. I couldn't wait to show Dave Maeve's "princess potty" the next time he came round, with the magic twinkling sound when it pretend-flushed.

When Bob was first diagnosed, he said, "I just want Maeve out of diapers by the time I die." One of his goals had now been met.

26

Just Here for the Cake

Bob's birthday was on a Friday in 2012 and so the fundraiser was launched on Monday of his birthday week. Gio set the fundraising goal at $10,000. I shared the Bob's Muscle Team email list with Gio, and she sent out the link and a plea, encouraging everyone to share the link widely. Every message, every donation—some from people we had never met—moved us to tears, laughter, or both every day of that week. Many people also sent donations separately to our house in a card or with a note. The outpouring was so unexpected and so entirely unbelievable. By Bob's birthday, the fundraising goal had been met: $10,000 in five days. We were speechless.

Giovanna upped the goal to twenty thousand.

Bob had requested a quiet and simple forty-fourth birthday, with just the kids and me. A friend offered to take the kids for an overnight the day after his birthday. Twenty-four hours alone = Bliss. Bob had wanted a quiet evening with sushi on his actual birthday, but I didn't always do what Bob wanted.

On the evening of Bob's birthday, I placed the order for sushi and chilled a bottle of Moet & Chandon. The timing of eating the sushi had to be precise. I returned home, and I set Liam to taping on the iPad my popping the champagne bottle and giving Bob a kiss, and then we all sat down for the quiet, lovely dinner for four he had requested.

The writing circle crowd was set to assemble on the front lawn with plastic champagne glasses, more bubbles, balloons, and other birthday paraphernalia thirty minutes after our scheduled dinner. Then all ten or so would arrive en masse on our back deck and yell: "Surprise!"

Bob was very surprised and squinting as one by one they

began climbing the deck stairs and coming through the sliding glass door carrying their glasses, and he laughed hysterically at the birthday bag that read: *Your Fucking Birthday Gift*. The balloon attached to the bag was black and had a picture of the Grim Reaper holding a cupcake with a lit candle who appeared to be about to blow it out: *Relax...I'm just here for the cake*, the balloon read.

We could always count on our writing circle friends to "get" our humor and run with it; after all, it was one of them, Rebecca, who was gleeful about Bob's fall at the water park and what it could signal as an opportunity for "buck a bow bow." We spent as much time in that circle laughing, dancing, and imbibing as we did critiquing writing. A sense of humor was one of the primary gifts we each brought to the table. The actual gifts they brought to the table the night of Bob's birthday included a fake weed necklace that Bob wore all night, a potato gun and the potato to go with it, and a back scratcher. When Bob saw the potato, he gestured toward a friend and made a kinky crack, "Hey, Jeff, you and me later?" When Bob first removed the weed necklace from the bag, he said to the crowd, "Well, I'll see y'all later," to much laughter.

After the writing circle friends arrived, Bob thought that was the surprise, but then colleagues started arriving from his university, an hour away, and mine nearby, and other friends also started filing in. A few of his colleagues had come to our St. Paddy's party, but otherwise, we'd never had his work friends visit. It was just too far a drive. We usually saw them once a year at his department chair's house for a holiday or end-of-the-school-year party. Bob just kept looking at me and shaking his head and grinning, and then looking at each visitor who appeared in the doorway with surprise as the evidence mounted that I had planned this party. He quickly forgave me for not following his wishes.

Bob was seated at our large kitchen table throughout the entire party, or at least for the first part of it. People kept filing in, and despite the ample room of our 3200-square-foot house, we all stayed in the kitchen. People leaned on the counters and took turns sitting in the seven remaining chairs while Bob held court from the eighth. Bob still seemed like his normal self, except for a little more gray in his hair, his increasingly nasally voice, declining muscle mass, and curled fingers.

When he needed to use the bathroom, Bob rose slowly, grasping the table and back of his chair for balance. Then he proceeded to make his way around the table, using the table as a toddler does to steady himself. The room, which had been so loud with so many conversations a moment before, fell silent as all eyes landed on him. People had clearly been unaware of how much Bob's disease had progressed as he sat greeting friends and making jokes. His struggle to walk reminded them of the reality of ALS and they were speechless.

He picked each foot up slowly and the top of his foot dragged along the floor before righting itself. Dropped foot, it's called. He had to move his knee higher to get his feet to work at all. "Move along, nothing to see here," Bob joked, gesturing with his curled hand. I ached for him in the continued silence and tried to help by inserting humor: "Just keep talking, everyone, it's fine. Bob's just going to the bathroom. Well, not yet, but once he gets there." There was uncomfortable laughter but it died down quickly.

That week leading up to Bob's birthday was the week when reality settled in and would never leave again. Bob now slept in the dining room. He could no longer climb stairs, and that life up there, where the only shower was, was over forever.

There were three bedrooms upstairs with no one sleeping in them, but we were grateful. We had not had to move house. We were still in our home. We had a large enough home to accommodate my father and all his belongings when he moved in, and we had a home accommodating enough to create a bedroom on the first floor for Bob. Our home truly had become "The Homestead." But as I lay there next to Bob in the makeshift bed with an open futon couch base and an extra futon thrown on top to raise the bed high enough for Bob, I grieved.

I had had to make this ad hoc bedroom so he wouldn't have to climb the stairs, but in my expediency I had not yet had a chance to slow down and think about what we had just lost. I'm sure Bob had spent the day thinking about it. The more immobile he became, the more time he had to think. Meanwhile, I had become the "doer," who could let truth break in only when I stopped moving and stood still, if only for a moment. Thinking too long would render me paralyzed. Must. Keep. Moving.

Our homestead needed a few additions, however, as Bob's ALS progressed. We needed a lift chair because it had already become difficult for Bob to get himself out of a chair. He would need one to lift him to a standing position. Our future would also include a wheelchair, and we had a house with front and back steps too high for a ramp. We needed a deck lift and a lift chair, and soon. And our debts were racking up. Insurance doesn't cover accessible vans or elevators, even when it covers a wheelchair, which makes no sense. Gio had taken the lead, and all of our other friends and family, and their friends and family, came to the rescue. While the momentum of donations had slowed after Bob's birthday, the donations were still coming in regularly.

The day after Bob's birthday, our kids were whisked away by our writing circle friend Alyse for twenty-four-hours—a birthday gift to Bob—and Bob and I opened a bottle of Opus One we had purchased several years before for a special occasion. We had hoped to make it to our wedding anniversary on August 10, but we now knew there was no time like the present for anything.

Bob couldn't drink very much wine anymore, so I drank most of it. We poured it into our fancy decanter, savored its deliciousness, and recalled the lovely evening we spent in Albany just before he moved to Florida, the final celebration of our summer of falling in love in 2000. As we inhaled its deep, recognizable aroma—which we could still do together—we also recalled the night before our wedding when we had savored our second bottle.

Opus One had become our special wine, and I posted on Facebook the next day a long, detailed message about the luxury of sharing this last bottle, one of only four we had ever had, with Bob the day after his birthday when we could focus our attention entirely on each other and a peaceful kid-free and relaxing house after all the visitors and parties of the last month. I managed to take an awkward selfie of myself, Bob, and a wine glass just before making our toast to life, our life, and love: "Slainte!" In the photo Bob is trying to smile, and his beard is now white. He had grayed in his twenties but had always used a Just for Men product to keep it dark. He had no energy for that anymore, and while I offered to do it for him as I trimmed and groomed his mustache and goatee, he said he just didn't care much about it anymore. People thought ALS had turned his hair gray, which was rather comical. We got a kick out of that. Maybe it had figuratively, but literally, no, it was not a byproduct of ALS, except insofar as ALS had caused such exhaustion that the idea of spending time on beautifying had become absurd.

Bob and I spent the evening relaxing and sipping wine and writing in side-by-side chairs in the alcove by the living room bay window that would soon become his permanent residence during the day. Bob was working on a file for the kids titled, "Leftovers," with any advice he still had left that he hadn't expressed in the videos he had already made for the three of us. I started, once again, to work on the memoir I'd been "threatening" to write since my late twenties; only now it didn't resemble the memoir I'd once envisioned. That evening wasn't the date we had envisioned either. It was just us, being together. I read him the new chapter of the memoir I had started—this memoir—and he made me promise that I would continue to write whatever I wanted to write about him once he was gone.

"Tell the truth, Dee. Tell it like it is. Don't hold back. Write your memoir. Hell, write two."

"Okay, I will. I promise."

Bob had always called me "The Wordsmith." He believed in me.

The next day, the kids were returned to us exhausted, which gave us a little more respite from parenting duties as they slept on the futon in the living room for most of the day.

Two days later, on June 26, Bob realized he couldn't get

up from a chair, and I rushed to the medical supply store and charged a lift chair/recliner to arrive that same day, the leather one he had requested so he could "slide off easily"—and also so it wouldn't "stink" from what he called his "sweaty ass." It was also the one with the highest back and deepest seat in the showroom; I wanted his large six-foot, five-inch body to be comfortable.

By the Fourth of July, Bob would be getting around the house in a loaner power chair from the MDA and giving Maeve rides to John Philip Sousa marches. My father always used to blast Sousa marches on the Fourth of July as he marched around the living room, knees comically high. It was my dad's tongue-in-cheek way of simultaneously saluting and criticizing the country, as he believed any good citizen ought, and he continued to do this when Bob and I visited him at his house in upstate New York. "To be a good citizen," he would say, "one must not only love one's country, but always believe it can do better, and force it to." He always said, "Vote for the person you think is best, and then beginning the day after the election, get on them and stay on them."

27

LOSING INDEPENDENCE

For Independence Day, Bob lost his independence.

In the Fourth of July video I made, four-year-old Maeve sits on forty-four-year-old Bob's lap. He is driving her around our living room to the sounds of Sousa and trying to teach her how to salute. He holds his curled hand to the right of his forehead and pushes it out toward the camera, elbow bent at his side. The video is dark and imperfect—it closes with my zeroing in on one of the dog's bones on the floor as I try to figure out how to turn the camera off. A number of the other early videos taken with the iPad have no sound, as I hadn't yet mastered the art of not holding my finger over the mic. Oh, how I wish we could hear some of them—especially the one of the kids having a pillow fight on the futon, while Bob, in his wheelchair, jeers, cheers, and issues playful commands of who should get slugged next.

By the Fourth of July, we all lost our independence, because it was from that day onward that it became very difficult for anyone to leave the house at all. Not only did we not have a deck lift for Bob yet, but we also had begun, as a family, to face the challenges of Bob's immobility. We had had, it seemed, our last meal at a restaurant on Father's Day. It was there, at our favorite Mexican restaurant, after the chips and the salsa and the chimichangas and the mole, with our friends Jim and Eryn visiting, that Bob couldn't get up, and Jim had to help me get him to his feet, one of us on each side.

With ALS, it can be difficult for onlookers to have any idea what is wrong with the person who appears to be in fair health, until someone has to lift the person from a chair or until they watch the slow and awkward gait as the person begins to walk.

We had had our last vacation where Bob had been lifted doll-like from his fall on the bathroom floor. We had slept in our marriage bed for the last time. Bob had taught face-to-face for the last time. If sudden death takes our loved ones from us in one grand sweep—like clearing chess pieces from a board—then terminal illness takes away all the things we take for granted one at a time, at first so slowly as to almost not recognize a piece has been removed, and then so quickly we can hardly keep pace as the board begins to be upended.

While Maeve did not fully understand what was happening to her daddy, his being in a wheelchair had made it much more clear to her that he was sick, and while she did not understand much, she felt a great deal. "My daddy is sick, and the doctors can't help him, and I don't know why," she would say. When our neighbor hurt himself and had to get thirteen stitches in his leg, Maeve said of her neighbor friends, "Their daddy is sick and my daddy is sick, but their daddy is going to get better and my daddy isn't, and I don't know why." Maeve had all the same questions and frustrations as all of us. She was small, but emotionally she was probably as astute as anyone coping with ALS.

For the Fourth of July, two more friends came to visit with their daughter, who was nearly the same age as Liam. Having read my updates, they decided it would be best if they stayed at a hotel to give us some privacy. Over the weekend they visited, they delivered Bob daily coffee drinks that he had begun to enjoy as he began to struggle with the bubbles in soda. I made dinner for everyone and then my usual strawberry, peach, and blueberry pie—the closest I could get to red, white, and blue—and then it came time to go see the fireworks, and Bob opted out. Just like New Year's Eve when he had chosen to go to bed instead of watching the ball drop, he chose to stay home while we headed to the Mississippi to watch the fireworks. At the time I thought maybe Bob was just too tired, or maybe he just didn't want us to have to go to the trouble of trying to get him into the van, but I realize now he already knew he couldn't

take those back deck stairs without a lift. Sitting all day with
his thoughts, he could not conceal a wince each time he had
to say goodbye to a friend, a holiday, or anything at all. His life
had become a series of endings, and it was getting harder and
harder for either of us to ignore it, and yet my letters and the
constant barrage of visitors and enthusiastic champagne toasts
had helped us keep it at bay as much as we could, and even lead
others to believe it wasn't happening.

When we all piled into the van to go to the fireworks that
night, one friend jumped into the passenger side. As I backed
out of the garage and righted the wheel to pull from our driveway, I felt a tug toward Bob. We had always done everything
together, doubling our time to run errands instead of splitting
up because we hated being apart. The few times I traveled for
work without him, he wouldn't sleep in our bed without me;
he instead chose to sleep on the couch downstairs. We typically
went to academic conferences together and had even presented
together, having co-written and published a paper on Robert
Frost's poem "Design," which considers the philosophical debate of intelligent design. We had driven to Pennsylvania and
Georgia for conferences and flown to Colorado, California, and
Hawaii over the years. I had conducted research at the Dart-
mouth library when Liam was a baby, and presented at a conference there, while Bob entertained Liam on the grounds so
we could spend every moment I had free together. We, who had
become one, were slowly peeling ourselves apart, one missed
moment at a time.

I was beginning to literally have to go on and leave him behind, if not for myself, then for the kids and those I was trying
to entertain—as if I could continue to play the host. I was still
writing update letters in the third person with an electronic
signature by us all, despite the fact that by July, everything had
changed. I guess we were all doing such a good job pretending
that when our friend took the front seat of the van with me
on the Fourth, and noticed the accessible parking hangtag, he
said, "Hey! How'd you get that?" before we even pulled out of
the drive. I looked at him the way Bob often did—sideways,

surprised, with a smirk, and said, "Uh...Bob?" quizzically. Feeling silly, he just shook his head at himself. "Oh yeah, right."

Bob and I were doing a very good job pretending, indeed. Or, at least I was.

28

Happy Anniversary

ALS affects voluntary muscle movements. Put simply, this means that anything you can hold, like your breath or your urine, is affected. Anything you can do, like grip a glass, swing an arm, get up from a chair, is affected. You can't "hold" your heart and keep it from beating, so it isn't affected. Male erections are not affected because they are—well, at least somewhat—involuntary. Bob had had some urethra trouble as a young man, and so perhaps that made him prone to difficulty later.

When Bob was about fourteen, his sister, two years older, threw a party without parental approval. At this party there was the usual craziness and teenage drinking, and Bob got drunk for the first time. As the night went on, he found that he couldn't pee. The urine backed up, and Bob, in considerable pain, ended up at the hospital with a blockage. The explanation provided to him at the time was that he was allergic to beer. So by the time I met Bob, his drink of choice was rum and cola. He had not yet been introduced to wine, and he hadn't had a beer since that incident at fourteen. Naturally enough, I inquired further.

"What are you allergic to in beer?"

"I don't know."

"Well, are you allergic to wheat? Barley? Hops?"

"I don't know."

"Can you be allergic to beer if you aren't allergic to anything that's in beer?"

"I don't know."

"Well, this just doesn't make sense. I'm no scientist or doctor but it seems like you have to be allergic to something in beer in order to be allergic to beer. Doesn't saying 'you're allergic to beer' sound precisely like something a parent would say to keep a fourteen-year-old from getting drunk ever again?'"

"You have a point."

Bob was a brilliant logician and could reason better than anyone I had ever met, but he hadn't ever really stopped to think about his "allergy" in this way. He'd accepted the reasoning long ago and learned to drink other things.

"Okay, but maybe you want to ask a doctor? I mean, it's weird."

So, the next time Bob had an appointment, he asked. And you know what the doctor said? "Are you allergic to anything in beer?" And so it went. His "prescription" was to try beer in small doses and see whether he had any reaction. Bob didn't much like beer, having avoided it for over fifteen drinking years, but slowly he grew to like it a little bit.

Bob had scar tissue as a result of several urethra blockages, so he quickly recognized the symptoms and knew when it was time to get to the hospital.

When someone can't pee, you have to get them to the hospital as quickly as possible, before the urine backs into the kidneys, which can lead to sepsis and death. So when Bob couldn't urinate, we knew just what to do. It was a feat getting Bob anywhere now, but because of a colleague at my university who had a manual wheelchair she no longer needed, I knew that if I could get Bob down the back deck stairs, one step at a time, I could get him there, and so that's what we did.

I wheeled Bob to the deck in the manual chair, then I helped him to stand, standing in front of him, hooking my right leg in between his, my arms under his arms, and pulling him toward me. We were on the verge of toppling down the stairs and onto the driveway just when I was able to right him. Then, holding both handrails of the deck, I stood in front of him helping as we got him down those stairs, very slowly. But then I still had to get past him with the chair. I sat him on the second to last step, thinking I could pull him from that height but not from the bottom step. With the urgency of his urethra blockage driving us forward, I managed to lift him and get him back into the wheelchair, then to the van, and up out of the wheelchair again, and turn him so his butt was up against the front passenger van seat and at the near perfect height, and then I swiveled his legs inside. There were so many moves and maneuverings to get Bob into the wheelchair in the living room, out of it on the deck, into it at the bottom of the deck, out of it at the van, into it in the Emergency Room parking lot, and then into the ER that we were both exhausted. By the time Bob got to the ER, the pain had become excruciating. We needed a deck lift, stat.

Having worked out religiously for several years—and then more obsessively as Bob's illness manifested itself—was coming in handy. I was now working out six days a week and had moved from the elliptical, free weights, and the punching bag to the Bowflex machine, Bob's tenth anniversary present to himself. I had wanted something in a Tiffany blue box for our tenth anniversary, and Bob had wanted a Bowflex. We found a slender platinum bracelet with a single small diamond that we could afford to charge and pay off.

I picked out my bracelet, and Bob ordered it online and personalized the card. My little blue box arrived in time for our tenth wedding anniversary, August 10, 2011.

> You have given my life more than you can ever imagine. You're my love, my life, my wife—and I can't believe what I was thinking when I thought I was going to go it alone. I would have missed all the fun and love that is you. All my love, XOXOXOXOXO
> —Bob

Ten Xs and Os. I bet he didn't count them.

Bob thought, after his first marriage, that was it. He was going to be a bachelor. And after getting the job in Florida, he imagined himself a buff bachelor, hanging out on the beach and "going it alone." Instead, he subsequently found himself with a wife, a couple of vasectomy reversals, and a couple of kids, eleven years after we'd gone on our first date.

Bob found the used Bowflex in Missouri, and we took a long ride in the minivan to pick it up. Since our anniversary had occurred just months before he was diagnosed, he'd been able to use the Bowflex for only a few months. I was proud I was able to now use the Bowflex, and I was proud I was able to help Bob. I was learning and adapting as we went. We both were. Maybe there was a reason we got that Bowflex after all, even though it wasn't the reason we had initially thought.

At the ER I accompanied Bob all the way to the examining room and then Bob suggested I leave him. We had always been each other's eyes and ears at doctors' offices and it was often necessary. The first neurologist appointment he had decided to go alone, too, and then during the Barnes-Jewish appointment I had had to look after the kids.

We had both needed advocates with doctors at various times, but this time Bob said he wanted me to leave. He didn't want me to see them insert a catheter.

"It's not going to be pretty," he said. "I don't want you to have to see this."

"Are you sure? I don't mind. I want to be here."

"No, really. You don't need to see this. I've been through this before, remember?"

"Okay," I said with hesitation. "But I'll be right here, okay? I love you."

"I love you too. It will be okay. I'll see you soon."

Bob knew well that images of our loved ones in pain aren't ones we can easily shake. He had heard me howl during my C-section with Liam, and he had never forgotten his feelings of helplessness.

Bob's urethra troubles would continue to crop up, unexpectedly and immediately, and we would race—as quickly as one becoming paralyzed could race—to the hospital several more times.

We had the MDA loaner chair and the manual chair from my colleague, and eventually the medical supply sales representative fought with insurance and managed to push the personalized power chair through. It would arrive soon, with all the bells and whistles required of a chair in which one is expected to live and die of ALS. It had to be the right height and width for Bob's "giant sweaty ass"; it would need to recline completely for sleep and be adaptable as he lost the use of his arms, allowing him to drive and steer with his chin (or maybe even someday his eyes), and to top out at speeds of around 30 mph. As Bob's disease progressed, he began to feel a growing sense of kinship with Kristin who has MS. When Kristin next dropped over, they bonded a bit more.

"Hey, Kris, you and me."

"Yeah?"

"Let's drag race in the driveway."

"Ha!"

"No, seriously," Bob said, taking deep breaths in between each phrase. "Ready. Set. Go."

He was entertaining me and Kris, again.

"I'd beat you," Kristin said.

"You know it's bad," Bob said, "when you go to the medical supply store and are, like, 'Hey, cool! They have that in red now!'"

Bob was smiling less often and eating far less, but his humor persisted. The man who had once carried two liters of Mountain Dew around with him was now regularly requesting iced coffees from Starbucks. Now that the carbonation in soda made him choke, iced coffee was the highlight of his day.

Thanks to the amazing and generous Gio, and the incredible fundraiser that ended up raising over $20,000, the deck lift was soon installed. It became a highlight of that summer for the neighbor kids, who still didn't entirely understand what was going on, though they knew Bob was sick. Like Liam, they continued to run and frolic and mostly stayed outside. When they came inside, they didn't stay as long as they once had because Bob was often resting and needed quiet. I attempted to thank everyone for their generosity in one of my update letters:

I write these letters to you, Bob proofs them and adds to them, and I find all these words to talk to you about this most painful time in our lives, but the generosity and love of the fundraiser leaves us without words. All we can really say is thank you (which seems so ridiculously lame given the gifts of love and support you have given and continue to provide us). This is simply one of those instances when words, which we've invested our lives and livelihoods in, startlingly escape us.

The people who installed the deck lift were pros. They removed the deck boards, storing them in my garage, and installed the lift in a few hours. I didn't give the saving of the boards much thought, but the installers clearly had imagined a later time, post-Bob.

Liam and the "brat pack," as Bob fondly dubbed the neighborhood kid crew, were the first to give it a go, riding up and down, up and down, until I told them enough. We certainly didn't need to break it. The installed deck lift brought peace of mind. If there was a fire, I could get Bob out. Soon we would have a chair that fit him better than the loaner, and soon, maybe, we could start taking Bob out now and then.

Bob was still able to transfer himself from the lift chair to his wheelchair, drive to the bathroom off the kitchen, and use the walls, and then counter sink and tub, for support as he ambled to the toilet—when he didn't have an emergency catheter, that is. The hall and the bathroom were narrow enough that Bob had stable handholds on all sides at all times to lean upon. The toilet had a riser on it, so he didn't need too much muscle to lower himself down onto it. He still had sufficient leg and arm muscles to raise himself to standing, to get his boxers up, and to make his way back. As this became more exhausting, however, he started to stand by the lift chair in the living room and pee into a portable urinal.

29

POETRY

I was still talking to Michael online, and I was now talking to Bob about Michael too. Bob already knew what I had been thinking about Michael and future possibilities, just as he'd always known what I was thinking.

"I'm not sure he could step up," Bob said. "If he could, that would be great. The kids know him and love him, and he's a good guy, but I don't know, Dee."

"Maybe he's changed. Maybe he's ready now."

"Maybe. Hard to say. He loves you. He'll be there for you and the kids, no doubt. But I'm not sure he can be what you need him to be."

"Me either."

"Hey, it's worth a shot. I get that you are comfortable with him."

"Yeah. He's like family."

"That you've got no matter what."

When Bob was first diagnosed, we discussed his intellectual goals. I had assumed he would want to publish one more philosophy paper. He had recently been working on a paper concerned with the Problem of Evil, which is about being unable to reconcile a belief in God with the amount and degree of suffering found in the world. Bob had been seeking an academic journal in which to publish the paper when he was diagnosed. Did he want to return to the Frost paper we had been working on? Write one more co-authored paper together?

"I want to write a book of poetry," he said.

"Poetry? Wait, I'm the writer," I teased.

"Well, I think that's what I want to do. I've been writing

some poems for WC (Writing Circle) and I'd like to write some more. I'd like to get a book published before I die."

"A book? Wow. I never thought you'd pick poetry…you don't want to travel or complete a paper in philosophy? Who are you? I don't know you anymore," I joked. "What made you want to write poetry?"

"Your dad, I think. Well, you too, but your dad mostly. When I met him, I didn't really know anything about poetry. But that's it. That's what I want to do. That's part of what I've been doing sitting here all day. Liz knows someone in publishing." Liz was the visitor who had gifted the "Happy Plasma!" cake. "Liz says she could get me in contact with her. I'm going to do it, and Kate says she will edit for me."

"Are you sure you don't want me to edit? I can help. I mean, I'm right here."

He bent his chin down and looked up at me with those piercing green eyes and with both eyebrows raised.

"Dee, don't you think you are doing enough? I mean, shit, I can't do anything around here anymore. You've got the house and the kids and the dog and my lame ass. I don't think you need to be editing a book."

I shrugged my shoulders and raised my own brows. "You have a point."

And so it was done. Poetry it was going to be.

The poetry book became a project, partly to leave something in writing behind, I believe, and partly to keep him going.

Our relationship with Dave continued to grow, especially once the visitors, as per Bob's request, began to slow in late summer, and the house became more and more of an echo chamber. Dave had been away on a couple of bike trips that summer, his first in early June and again later in the month. He had missed Bob's birthday and didn't return until after the Fourth. We had missed him. He had become a regular at the house, and now that visitors were slowing and our writing circle was on summer break, his visits were one of the few things we could look forward to as the heat of the Illinois summer and our isolation droned on. His visits had become like the phone calls my stepmother, Terry, had made: a rhythmic repetition we had desperately needed without ever realizing it.

As the visitors began to recede and the weeks became more of a blur, it often wouldn't occur to me until after dinner what day it was and what time it was and that that meant Dave would be arriving any moment, gliding up the driveway on his bike, slipping in the back door, sweaty in his bike clothes. I would glance at the clock, realize what day and time it was, and then remind Bob that Dave would be here soon, so Bob wouldn't be caught in a compromising position, like peeing in the urinal. Bob had, by the end of summer, given up on wearing clothes and sat around in black boxer briefs. He didn't much care who saw him in those.

Instead of Dave sliding in the back door or taking two steps at a time up the front steps and surprising me, I began watching for him, and greeting him with updates, so he could be prepared for the changes that were happening daily now, especially since the update letters I had been sending out had dissipated. I had no time anymore. When Dave had left for his first bike trip, Bob was still walking. Now he was in a wheelchair and had a catheter off and on. Dave was also going to be surprised when he saw the deck lift.

When I spotted Dave on his bike, I would meet him in the driveway.

"So this is what has been going on this week. It's been quite the week," I would say, feeling exasperated and grateful to release—grateful to be talking to someone else about Bob. As we rolled into late August, other than my therapist, I was having fewer and fewer opportunities to talk about Bob to anyone, and it turned out Bob was right, as he so often had been. I needed to talk to people about him; I couldn't just talk to him anymore. I was taking it to someone else. I had to.

After Dave had the highlights, we'd go join Bob in the living room.

Over time, Bob and I learned that Dave had been living alone for about fifteen years. He had been married in his twenties, days after receiving his bachelor's in computer science. He and his wife then drove to his first job in Austin, Texas. They bought a house, and he expected children would be soon to follow. Only, his wife started having an affair and was gone within a few years. He then lived alone in the house they had bought for several more years listening to sad 80s love songs and growing to hate trimming the rose bushes that bordered the property before being persuaded by a college friend he had biked with in Europe that he should go to graduate school. Back to Michigan he moved, where he began his PhD. The university where we now both taught was his first and only academic job after graduate school. He now lived in a yellow colonial house a few blocks away from our own. Bob and I had never been to his house, nor had we ever known any of this before.

Bob and I shared with Dave our opinion that first marriages, if one divorces, often seem to be reflections of our upbringing and pasts, instead of our futures, or at least it had been that way for us and others we had come to know. Dave agreed. For folks with graduate degrees, it seems even more common. A lot of change happens when one pursues higher education. It's also a particular type of life. As Bob used to say, "It's a combination of being in the military and being an actor. Being in the military because you have to go where the jobs are, and being an actor because there usually aren't any jobs."

Bob, Dave, and I grew more and more comfortable with each other through these shared intimacies. So comfortable, in fact, that one day when Dave got up to leave, Bob said, "Hey, Dave." And when Dave glanced over his right shoulder with a "Yeah?" expression, Bob quipped, "Nice ass."

Bob would know. He didn't have one, as he frequently pointed out.

30

POWER UP

When Bob started using the power chair, we noticed that the lip into the kitchen and the one onto the deck practically catapulted Bob, so Dave took measurements, and then he brought wedges of wood over to allow Bob a smoother crossing. Every time Dave dropped by on his bike, he took note of what needed fixing, and he tried to offer a little help. We began to see Dave as "the fixer."

Over the summer, Liam's bicycle went inexplicably missing. It turned up a few days later at the church parking lot down the street, but with a flat tire and other issues. Dave took it home, cleaned it up and repaired it, and returned it along with some very cool bicycle stickers for Liam.

On the first floor there was a tub but no shower. With no way for Bob to bathe, sponge bathing was where it was going to be now, and so I learned how. Each day, able-bodied people do so many things for themselves. We not only use the bathroom and bathe, brush our teeth, floss, brush our hair, clean our ears, rid ourselves of unnecessary hairs, apply lip balm or creams, trim our nails, and so on. We eat, which means lifting utensils and plates and cups. We pour. We cut. We hold two utensils at once. We walk. We drive. We blow our noses and wipe away our own tears. We swallow medicines or vitamins. We wash and dry our hands. We dial and lift phones to our ears.

All these things, when someone is paralyzed or becoming paralyzed, are no longer things they just do. They are things that take time and effort to do, and sometimes they can't do them at all for themselves, or they can't do some of them. Anyone who has had a child is familiar with the daily care needed by a helpless infant, but their needs tend to also be a bit more basic, and their size makes things a lot simpler. When babies are born, we can carry them in one hand. Some don't even have eyelashes yet. They often don't need their nails trimmed just yet, but do before long, and it is terrifying, but manageable. They have very teeny toes. So far, though, babies don't have unwanted hair, and they can bathe in the kitchen sink. Bathing and grooming Bob was considerably more difficult.

I tried to wash Bob with facecloths and soap and water as he lay in bed. It was messy, and wet, and drippy, and water pretty much got all over the place. Also, the sink was situated on the other side of a big house, so lugging two tubs of water, one soapy and one clean, and a bunch of towels and facecloths took time. Setup and takedown took time. But mostly it was messy, and I wasn't very good at it. So, I bought wipes and some foam cleansers, which were absurdly expensive and didn't clean very well. I did a bit better buzzing Bob's hair. I got pretty good at using the electric razor, and at trimming his mustache and beard. I bought the best one we could find, a self-cleaning super shaver. Toenails were a bit more difficult. I had to be a contortion artist to do it well. Brushing teeth was pretty good, but I also wasn't great at flossing.

We could groom Bob on the front porch in the summer. He just rolled on out in his manual chair. In winter, I didn't know what we would do. Everything was complicated. There's a reason daycares and hospitals have spaces that can be hosed down. Maeve was playing with shaving cream at daycare, and I was playing with it at home. I was glad I had been working out because the bending and squatting took work and a less able-bodied caregiver would have had trouble. I was also glad I had figured out a way to help Bob transfer. Bob had gained thirteen pounds in the spring and had lost only five so far, so he was still a lot to heft. From behind, I put my arms under his and lifted him straight up. From the front, I slid my right foot between his legs, leaned in, put my arms under his, and lifted him forward to my chest, and then pivoted and placed him where he was going. I was using dance steps I'd learned in college to pivot properly. Dance classes seemed to help. So did using my legs. There were tools for this, but I had a method, which I had refined over several months from when he was taking naps on a futon in the living room and needed help standing up.

I slept with Bob on the first floor for about two weeks, and I was stumbling around blurry-eyed every day because of it. The dog's nails clickety-clacked on the hardwood floors, and while I'd never had a blockage in my urethra, my bladder had always been frequently full. Once, on a trip to St. Louis with Lee and Ping, a one-and-a-half-hour trip, I'd asked to stop three times. Getting from the dining room through the living room and then the kitchen to the bathroom multiple times a night didn't make for restful sleep. Neither did Bob's twitching. I didn't know how he could stand it; it never stopped.

After a few weeks of trying to sleep next to him, I surrendered. I was exhausted. I couldn't take care of anyone when I was tired. Bob had always said one of the greatest gifts he had given me was sleep. Observing my exhaustion one day, he gave me another: "Sleep upstairs. It's okay. You need your sleep. You always did. You are no good to anyone if you are exhausted." And so we said goodbye, again. There were so many goodbyes.

Bob and I could still kiss, but his jaw just opened. His lips couldn't pucker anymore. It was like kissing a baby when she first learns to kiss. It was tender and sweet, but not the same. He could lean his biceps around me, but he could not hug. The rest of his arms hung limp. He could not hold my hand, but I could hold his. We lay next to each other. That was something we did. We started napping together in May in the living room, and by July we were napping together, or at least lying together, in the dining room in the afternoon, snuggling. I could still rest my head on his hairy chest and hear his heartbeat. That repetition was a rhythm I wanted to hear, always.

Another song was popular that summer. "Chasing Cars" by Snow Patrol. The entire song sounded as if it were in my own voice. Our voices. In unison. We would lie together, listen, and cry, wishing the world away, as we held each other, or at least as I held him.

Bob and I had always had a healthy sex life, and we kept

having one, when we could. It was far more difficult now. We were both exhausted all the time and he was sleeping in a room with no door; but we knew every creak in that house and had gotten good at being sneaky over the years, and the kids were often at the neighbor's and would soon be going to school again. I had to be on top, but working out left me rather acrobatic, or at least sufficiently able to manage. It was easier on the makeshift queen-size with a bed rail than it would be later in a single hospital bed, though; although with the hospital bed there was a trapeze, and that would come in handy. We were beginning to fully get the line about "sturdy ceiling lifts" from the MDA handbook.

I had published a few poems by this point and was on some email lists for journals. One of the journals that had published a poem of mine sent me an email seeking submissions for what it described as a "sizzling hot" and "sexy" summer issue. They wanted the sexiest poems. I forwarded Bob the link and playfully wrote: "Write me a sexy poem." Little did I know Bob had already done so, and submitted it too. Bob's first and only poem published in a journal came out late that summer.

Emission
for D

Our sweat shows power, the capacity
of heat that our bodies need to release,
a lubrication for, and evidence of, our
rapturous frenzy. I watch you and your
body afterward, watch the tiny droplets
slowly roll down your beautiful crevices
and places where my tongue once was—
and delight in our temporary ambiguity,
knowing no distinction between where
my residual liquid ends and yours begins.

31

No Crying

As the summer progressed, I began to realize the toll Bob's grooming would take once school began again for me. As academics, Bob and I always said summer vacation was really over August 1, because that's when the prepping needed to begin. There were syllabi to create and meetings to attend, and the children, too, would need school supplies. The school system required every item to be marked with the child's name. I organized a pencil-labeling drinking party with Lee before the kids started school to make the entire process less draining by sharing the work. I did not know how I was going to manage to get myself up, get the kids up, get them ready and out the door to school, come home and get Bob up, then get myself out the door to school, race home and make lunch for us both; then, get every other thing done, like prepping and grading and errands and groceries and cleaning and laundry and cooking, and get the kids at five, and make dinner for everyone—what had become three different meals because the kids, Bob, and I now all had different needs. Kids are kids and so they had things they didn't like, and Bob now needed his food to be easier to chew and swallow because his jaw muscles had weakened considerably. And I hardly had any appetite at all and was trying to eat healthier than either the kids wanted to, or Bob could, given his need for calories and soft foods. I had no idea how I was going to keep all of this up and still have time to bathe and groom Bob. However, I had learned to ask for help, and so I did. I called the nurse at our doctor's office.

"So…I'm going back to school, and Bob needs help. I have been doing everything, and I don't know how I will be able to do it all anymore…and I'm going to have to leave him here alone for a bit, several hours, and I don't know how I'm going to do that either…and insurance says hospice is our only option, but it doesn't kick in unless a doctor tells you the patient has fewer than six months…."

She called me back in less than an hour.

"The doctor enrolled you in hospice."

"Does that mean she thinks he has less than six months?"

"I don't know, but you are all set."

"Okay. Well, thank you so, so much."

I didn't believe Bob had less than six months. I didn't want to. I hoped the doctor was just looking out for us, taking care of us, bending a few rules. Maybe she was. I hoped she was.

Meeting all the hospice caregivers in August was exhausting, but necessary, and they were great, especially our main nurse. As usual, Bob and I cracked jokes about his illness and about his impending death, and he dealt the cards straight with regard to who we were and what we wanted. Bob explained that he didn't want any religious assistance. We had that covered. We had our own way of coping, and it didn't include clergy. The night I learned my brother Sean had died, a clergyman showed up at our house. Bob told me about it later: "I opened the door and there he was. In full attire. He was in his robes. Head lowered like in some movie. It was dark. I imagined ominous music as he slowly raised his head. He said he had heard Sean died and he was here to see you." Apparently, he was the clergyman associated with the fire department. Our neighbor had called her husband, a fireman, in shock, to tell him I'd lost yet another family member, only two weeks after my father.

"Since he knew you from the university, he knew you'd lost your dad a few weeks ago. He grabbed his robes and raced out the door—to rescue us, or something. It was the last thing we needed. I thought you were dying and here's this guy on the doorstep like some sort of savior. Bullshit. You needed real help."

Bob slammed the door in the clergyman's face. They say there are no atheists in foxholes. Bob called bullshit on that too. "I haven't believed since I was in my teens and visited the children's ward of a hospital."

The hospice folks took notes. Got to know us. And then they gave us a team. Once school began, this would become my daily schedule.

6:00: Wake up.

6:05: Work out

6:35: Take shower

7:00: Get kids up and make them breakfast

7:30: Get kids out the door and to school

8:00: Get Bob up and make him breakfast

8:30: Go to work

9:00: Teach

10:00: Teach

11:00: Teach

12:00: Go Home

12:15: Make Bob lunch

1-2:00: Hospice workers arrive

3-4:45: Hospice workers leave

4:45: Leave to get kids

5:15: Come back with kids and start dinner

6:00: Eat dinner

6:30-7:00: Clean up dinner

7-7:30: Help kids with schoolwork

7:30: Give kids baths and get them ready for bed

8:00: Relax with Bob

9:00: Get Bob ready for bed

9:30: Have a glass of wine and a cigarette

10:00: Go to bed

Repeat.

My university allowed me to hold office hours by appointment only and to remove myself from academic committees. Terrence would hold it all together at work. Since we were now the only two tenured faculty in the department, Terrence truly was doing it all without me.

The hospice workers planned to send someone to bathe and

groom Bob between 9:00 and noon, and to sit with him and keep him company, but Bob didn't want just any company; he never had. Someone would show up, usually by 9:30, and they would typically be finished by about 10:30. If they could stay another half an hour or so, he would be able to ask them to do dishes or sweep the floor or let the dog in and out or take out the garbage and recycling. He determined he would ask them to make my life easier, not his. He asked me to leave notes on the table if I thought of what they could do, or to just tell him, and he'd pass it on. Hospice helpers wouldn't do big things, we were told, but they would do the little things. They might leave by 11:30, but that would mean Bob would just have to make it a half hour on either side of my departure and arrival.

In the beginning, Bob was able to make it to a commode that had been placed in the living room near his lift chair. When Bob had to go, I made sure all the blinds were drawn in the living room and no kids were going to bust in the back door—I locked it for a few minutes—and then I helped him transfer, pulled down his boxer briefs, waited, wiped him, pulled up his boxer briefs, and then raced the commode bucket across the house and through the kitchen to the bathroom and got it cleaned as quickly as I could. He had bouts of diarrhea sometimes, and so I wanted to be able to make sure I could get back in time should he have another episode.

Bob's ALS was moving fast. We were less than eight months into this thing and Bob was enrolled in hospice. The weeks between Dave's visits now felt long, very long, since a lot would change in the intervening time. The peeing by the chair was awkward, but the commode in the living room was even more awkward. Now Dave was dropping by not just on cycling nights, but on other nights too. Once summer was over and school began, and life was going on for everyone we knew, no one would really be coming around much anymore. We had sworn off nearly all visitors, except for Nana, who hadn't come yet. She offered to come when we needed her most, which she knew was going to be during the transition from summer to fall. Having been in our lives for so long, she knew what the academic year meant—she'd visited when it was in full swing a few times—and so she came during the week the kids were beginning dance classes and starting school and daycare, and I was starting school, and hospice had just begun—as had the commode and the hospital bed.

Bob wanted to accompany me to the kids' first dance classes. Maeve was so excited. She had her little shoes and leotard and Liam was psyched to learn hip-hop. After all, I had taken several videos on the iPad of them dancing themselves silly in the living room while our portable disco ball—a fun gift for our writing circle after-parties—illuminated the room.

We started early. Everything we would do from now on would take time, whether it was dressing Bob or getting him out the door. I managed to load Bob into the van and load the power chair now that I had a ramp, but it wasn't easy. The ramp weighed a lot. It was heavy and awkward to unfold and fold and put on the bumper of the van. The power chair weighed a lot and was very difficult to steer while standing beside the ramp, but given the van we had, no one could be in the chair to drive it up into the van. In fact, the power chair barely cleared the ceiling of the van once it was inside.

Shortly after we'd received the power chair, I purchased the ramp, and our friends Steve and Suzanne helped me learn how to load the chair into the van. It was quite comical, the first time. It was no longer comical.

We started the process about forty-five minutes before dance class, despite the fact that the class was held in a location ten minutes away. It was August. It was hot. We were sweaty. It was exhausting loading two kids and Bob and myself and a power chair. But we did it, and we went to the dance class, where I hoped to unload Bob and take him inside to watch the kids. Only, that never happened.

When we arrived, I realized the only parking available was parallel on the street, where even if I got the chair out, there would be no guarantee someone wouldn't park behind me and make it impossible for us to leave; or I could park in the accessible spot by the door, the back end of which butted right up to a street. If I put the ramp there, it would be halfway into the right lane of the road, and Bob would be unloaded on a corner with cars potentially turning right into him. We sat in the van trying to figure out what to do.

Bob shook his head. "You can't do anything. Don't worry about it. Just take them in. I can wait here."

"For the entire class? It's so hot."

"I'll be okay."

"We can just go home. I mean, this is fucking ridiculous. Get some accessible parking."

"It's okay. They need to go to class. Go watch them. You can tell me about it. I'll wait here."

I was so angry. "Why have fucking accessible parking if it isn't fucking accessible?"

Bob looked defeated, and he usually didn't. He could usually find the humor in just about anything.

I felt as though I were abandoning him as I walked the kids inside. It was yet another important moment we could not share together.

By the second class, Nana had arrived for her visit, just when we needed her most, as promised, so I left to take the kids to dance and was gone barely an hour; but during that hour Bob had had to use the commode. When I came back, Nana met me at the door.

"Bob had to use the bathroom."

"Shit. Were you able to help him?"

"You know it," she said, self-assured. "Yeah, I helped him. I got him on the commode and off and got him cleaned up."

"I'm so sorry."

"No, it's fine." Her eyes filled with tears. "You gotta do what you gotta do. I just felt so bad. It must be so hard for him."

"I know. I'm sorry. I'm sorry for both of you."

"Oh, don't worry about me. I just can't believe it. He's such a big guy. I just can't believe I had to help him do this."

"I know."

"It just breaks my heart." She wiped her nose and I hugged her.

Nana had been one of a handful of people I had called throughout my life, and increasingly so since my mother and father died, to talk about nearly anything, from my deepest emotions to what was going on at work. She was the first person I had called from the parking lot at Target, and yet from January until her visit, I had barely called her at all. I didn't call her because I couldn't handle her emotions. She would cry on the phone just about every time I called, and it was all I could do to hold it together. I couldn't be there for her too. She was one tough lady. She'd grown up on a farm, and as a kid she could kill a hundred chickens in an afternoon to ready them for processing. And yet, she was deeply emotional and could not conceal her suffering over Bob's illness. She loved him. She loved us together. Having to wipe his ass had pushed her over the edge.

Just before Nana left, when we all knew it was the last time she'd ever see Bob, she leaned forward over the lift chair to give him a kiss and her tears welled up again.

"No crying," Bob said. "No crying. There's no crying in baseball." Then Bob had to explain the movie reference to *A League of Their Own*.

"Okay." Nana wiped her tears away. She understood. She just loved us so much it hurt.

Bob didn't want anyone feeling sorry for him. He wanted understanding, but not pity, not even from Nana.

32

Holding it Together

When my father died, we visited the funeral home. We went with Liam. Bob carried him in and out of the private viewing room where we had to say our final goodbyes to my dad. Liam reached his hand out as Bob carried him out of the room: "Papa!" he said with longing, his hand reaching toward my father's lifeless body, covered by a blanket, still on a gurney. When we saw Scan in a similar room, on a gurney under a blanket in San Francisco, it was just Bob and me. Death, for us, had become an intimate affair.

I sat in the chair next to Bob's lift chair. "I don't know if I'm going to be able to handle being responsible for everyone else's grief. You know how it goes. At memorial services, family members stand around consoling everyone else as they come up to pay their respects. The funeral goers begin by expressing their condolences, and before you know it, the family members are consoling the funeral goers. I don't think I can do it. I certainly don't want Maeve and Liam to have to go through that, and I just don't think I can do it. I'll have all I can do to hold my own shit together."

"You don't have to. Don't do it. Remember: This shit is about us—you and the kids—I will have said my goodbyes long before. You've gotta take care of you and the kids. I don't give a shit about anyone else at that point. Don't do anything for someone else. You and the kids; don't forget that."

"Okay, I won't. Everyone who wants to see you is coming now, and has been for months. Anyone who would come would have just been here, except people from work who would only come out of obligation, people we aren't close to, or other people from this town who we barely know. I don't want to make our friends pay a bunch of money to come back here; they just came."

"Look, it's about you and the kids. You don't need a bunch of people descending on the town and having to worry about them. You are going to have enough shit to do. Like I told you before, it's not about me, it's about you and the kids. It's about everyone still living, but you are the only ones I'm worried about. Everyone else is going to be fine. You've gotta take care of you because you are the only one who can take care of the kids. We both know that."

"Okay, then I don't think I'm going to do anything. Some people may be disappointed, mainly our writing circle peeps, but they'll deal, and we can throw a party or something later."

"Yes, throw a party. St. Pat's or something. Raise a glass. Have a fucking party," he said, and he meant it.

We did manage to get Bob out a few times, despite the difficulty. Liam pushed him around Walmart with Maeve on his lap while we picked out the kids' school supplies. We managed to get a couple of friends to meet us at a local park for a picnic one afternoon; we picked up pizza and had a short visit at a picnic ramada. The kids and I also pushed Bob around the local shopping mall once. We found that the manual chair was a lot easier to get in and out of the car, but a lot harder to push around, and I realized how stupid it had been to load the power chair to go to dance class in the first place. I had fucked up. I was going to fuck up again. At the mall, we realized I couldn't roll Bob into the restroom since it was a men's room, and his arms were no longer strong enough to roll himself; that's why he needed a power chair.

Liam, at nine, became a caregiver. Not only did he help cut up his dad's food, and sometimes feed him or lift his cup to his mouth so he could suck from the straw, but he also helped him in the men's room. Bob would write one of his poems for his poetry book about his experience using the handicapped toilet.

My First Time for ALS

They say you always

remember your first time—
and they're right:
the first time feels different
and you feel different afterward,
and then, you want to do it
every chance you get.

For me, my first time was like
I was born to do it, like
I'd been doing it for a while
and it was all too easy.
Everything fit in the right place
and I knew exactly what to do,
and further, it felt at the time
as if I should be doing it,
and that it almost seemed wrong not to.

And when it was over,
I didn't feel ashamed, or judged,
or exposed; I just thought,
Oh, so this is how it goes,
this is how it's done—
and this is what
(some) people (have to) do
(legitimately). *
*use a handicapped bathroom stall.

Bob was writing and editing his book, along with Kate; that,
and the letters he was creating and editing for the kids occupied
his days and nights, when he wasn't being bathed, struggling to
eat, or having visits from hospice nurses and social workers, or
the few people still left to visit from out of town or the occasional drop-ins from locals. Bob was beginning to write about
the illness as well as his love for me and the kids, and all of it
was run through with his attitudes about life and his discipline
of philosophy. He was constantly in touch with Kate and then,
when he was ready, Liz put him in touch with the publisher she
thought might be interested in his book. Bob had said he would
contact the publisher, but if she wasn't interested, he was going

to publish the book on his own because he wanted to hold the book before he died.

The publisher Liz put Bob in touch with said her company didn't publish that sort of book, but knowing Bob's story, she offered to help him edit the book for professional publication pro bono. She also said she had a cover artist who would do a cover pro bono. It was a labor of kindness and love. The generosity of people during Bob's illness continued to amaze me.

While Bob was busy with his book and I was busy with my classes, random postcards started showing up in our mailbox.

The wife of one of Bob's high school teachers had contacted me over the summer, asking me to send her a list of things Bob loved. I sent her back the following list:

> Bob doesn't do sports and we don't watch much TV.
> Anything and everything philosophy is right up there. Nietzsche especially.
> Food: Hearty stuff. He loves homemade sauce and meatballs. Steaks. Basically anything I cook. Indian food, sushi, Ethiopian food. He loves ethnic food.
> Drink: Red wine, champagne, Jameson, Guinness.
> Music: Rush, Bagpipes & Irish music, The Pogues, The Beatles.
> Paintings: The Death of Socrates.
> Movies: *The Matrix, Close Encounters of the Third Kind, Wit, The Peacemaker, Karate Kid,* Romantic comedies (generally).
> Politics.
> Women's rights: Bob is a feminist through and through.
> We loved Paris when we were there.
> Charitable organizations: Amnesty International, Heifer. org, American Civil Liberties Union
> Anything having to do with our kids.
> And then:
> Duh. Poetry and opera. I can't believe I left those off.

The postcards that began arriving in the mail in September all featured something Bob loved, or humor. They were quotes from philosophers or silly quotes. They were signed by friends

of ours, friends who were on our email distribution list. First
we received just one. Then another one. Then several more. We
started to catch on.

"Wait. This is a thing. Somebody must have organized this."

"Did you know about this?"

"No, I didn't. But it's super cool."

It kept up for well over a week before I made the connection
to the list. No one can over-calculate the joy of receiving mail
every day from family and friends from all over the country.
These tiny messages kept coming in and lifting our spirits and
making us laugh. When our hearts are low, surprises are momentary lifts. They may not sustain for long, but those blips of
excitement, like receiving a box of fruit or a knock at the door,
were positively wonderful.

Every day when I checked the mail, we were delighted. In the
meantime, Terrence had arranged for Bob to teach an online
class at my university as a sabbatical replacement, and we had
ordered Bob finger extenders that helped to uncurl his pointer
fingers enough that he would be able to henpeck the keyboard.
Bob teased that if I annoyed him too much, he would move
those same extenders from his pointer fingers to his middle
fingers.

In a depressing visit, just before the start of the fall term,
Bob's university delivered his belongings and the mini fridge
from his office. I turned the mini fridge into the juice-box-
and-nutritional-shakes fridge, in an attempt to give the visit a
positive spin. We focused instead on what Bob would have in
lieu of returning to full-time teaching: his class, his book project, the letters he was writing for the kids, and now these daily
postcards.

Not only did the organizer of the postcards keep us guess-
ing as the excitement mounted with each new postcard, but
another entirely unexpected gift arrived in the mail in August,
just before our eleventh wedding anniversary—a box of two
half bottles of Opus One, two Opus One ball caps, two Opus
One golf tees, and a box of See's lollipops for each of the kids,
all in a gorgeous Opus One bag with Opus One tissue paper

and an Opus One wine opener by Laguiole. The opener came in a leather case and was simply gorgeous.

My stepmother, Terry, owned a wine store and worked with a distributor for Opus One. When I wrote my Facebook post about Opus One being our special bottle and shared our memories of enjoying the wine together, the distributor was so moved that she wanted to gift us something from the Opus One winery. The distributor had known Terry for years and was very fond of her. I wrote a message of gratitude in response, thanking the distributor for giving us an "unexpected extra opportunity to enjoy life." She responded, sharing that we were in her thoughts and prayers and that our story was very dear to her, as her own father had died of cancer when she was twelve. She had been writing her own daughter a letter every year, just in case she herself did not live to see her daughter's twenty-first birthday. She said our children were "blessed to have such beautiful, brave parents" and hoped Bob was dictating letters to the kids. "His thoughts and letters will be a warm and wonderful memory for them forever," she wrote. I agreed.

We would make two more good memories while Bob was still able to enjoy food and wine, I told her, and the Opus One could still bring him that "pure eyes-closed pleasure it always has." We opened one of the half bottles for our wedding anniversary on August 10th, but Bob was not able to drink more than a sip of it. He had difficulty swallowing anything anymore, and swallowing alcohol had begun to make him choke now too.

In an email describing how we had spent our wedding anniversary, I wrote to Michael:

Bob and I opened the 1/2 bottle of Opus One that was gifted to us and turned on some Pandora tunes. Bob sipped a small amount from a plastic tumbler (he can't hold glass anymore), and we sat in our side-by-side chairs with our feet up and chatted awhile. We talked about his poetry and my new memoir, and I read a little aloud to him. We then managed to go in and lie on the bed for a bit. We can hardly even get close enough for a hug these days since he's always isolated in the recliner or his wheelchair, so lying side by side is a novelty.

33

Taking Words

While Bob was still driving his wheelchair to the hallway near the bathroom, before the inevitable decline into using the commode and subsequently wearing diapers, two terrifying and memorable events occurred.

The first happened while I was upstairs on the phone in the bedroom with the door shut. It was hard to have privacy with my own thoughts without shutting the door. Bob had seemed okay, and I had always made sure he had what he needed before leaving him, but he was struggling with diarrhea, partly from his changed diet—he was smothering most things in sour cream in order to lubricate them for swallowing and partly having to do with ALS and the lack of muscle control increasing incontinence.

Bob had gone to use the bathroom and had managed to get himself to the toilet, but when he stood, he lost his balance and ended up straddling the rim of the tub like a horse saddle. Since he had lost much of his voice, and he was facing the bathroom wall—his voice needed to travel through the narrow hall and the kitchen, around the corner into the living room, and up sixteen steps of stairs, through another hall, and through our two-inch-thick bedroom door—I did not hear him for a long time. Finally, I thought I heard something, a faint something, and I told the friend I was talking to to hold on while I checked on Bob, and there he was. I could not lift him. There was no way I could lift him. I raced out the back door and was lucky to find our fireman neighbor in his backyard. In a panic I blurted out the minimum: "Bob fell. He's in the bathroom. I can't lift him. Can you help me?" He came racing in, but we needed another. Casey's apartment was a short walk away. I messaged him. We had a rescue team now, and they did just that. They both rescued Bob, and me. But I would forever feel like I had failed Bob in that moment. I should not have left him alone. I should not have gone to talk on the phone.

Shortly after this incident, at the prompting of the hospice nurse, we purchased a wireless doorbell so that if I were on the second floor or in the basement, Bob could get my attention with the push of a button. With a wireless doorbell to get my attention and a Lifeline button Bob could wear around his neck that could call an outside line, Bob would never be left stranded again. Bob could still depress a button, though he could no longer cut his own food; I was now slicing up food for all four of us.

Because we had a habit of finding humor in everything now, as soon as I was able to wrangle the doorbell from the relentless plastic packaging, we entertained ourselves with the variety of sounds we could select from: cuckoo and traditional chime, among others. Our favorite was the foghorn that sounded like a buzzer on a game show when you'd gotten the answer wrong. We, of course, chose the foghorn for emergencies and the cuckoo for getting my attention. The kids were wildly entertained by this.

While we were beginning to rely on manufactured sounds to signal danger and alarm, we were also beginning to rely on a sound machine that created white noise to drown out the sounds of the children playing and laughing, so Bob could sleep in the dining room bedroom. The combination of a cuckoo clock, a foghorn, and white noise were symbolic of various states of being in our house.

When hospice first began helping, Bob was still taking his power chair through the kitchen and making his way to the bathroom. It wouldn't be for long, but he was trying to make it last as long as he could. On one of the summer days that I went to run errands and get him an iced coffee, he made it all the way to the door of the restroom but could hold his bowels no longer. He exploded everywhere, he told me later. All down himself, and on the floor, and just everywhere. He held on to the open bathroom door and sobbed. He was so ashamed. I had told him to just call me if he needed anything and I would be right home; I was always only about ten minutes away because our small town was only about ten minutes from one end to the other, but fortunately he had the Lifeline button and he used it. He called a hospice nurse. I was only gone about an hour and a half—which had become the maximum amount of time I was comfortable leaving him and the longest I would go unless I was teaching—but this is what happened, and he didn't call me. He chose not to call me. He said I was doing enough. That's what the nurses were there for, to help us, he said, and I was doing enough. This was a gift for me; this was something Bob could do for me, or at least the nurses could.

From late August through the end of September, all the good and bad shit started hitting the fan, literally and figuratively.

Words had meant everything to me and to Bob for so much of our marriage. Talking and writing side by side kept us strong and united, which is why we often opted to go to a hotel on a date rather than into the public sphere. Slowly, however, as Bob had predicted, I increasingly took my words elsewhere. As painful as it was for me to tear myself from Bob, like two strips of Velcro adhered to each other, he was too tired, and I needed to say things I didn't want to say to him. The survivor in me also now knew what Bob had known all along—that I needed to be talking to someone else, not only when he was gone but now, while he was still here. While many people traveled from a variety of places to see us, we had only a handful of local friends who would be able to be there for me then, and who would choose to be there for me later.

My moods and needs swung like a pendulum, fluctuating over the course of Bob's illness, according to who was willing to lend an ear and how. Michael's mother, too, was dying. While Michael had been propping me up in various ways through "power chats" since January, he got his dose of what he called "Vitamin D" from me as well; I got to talk to someone who had known me and loved me for nearly twenty years in one capacity or another. Despite the challenges of my daily life, I started writing emails to Michael to help him as he shouldered the burden of his mother's terminal illness. His mother was now hospitalized and he, too, had few to whom he could turn.

Michael suggested I keep a journal, but who had the time or energy for that? Mostly, though, I had little interest. I never much liked talking to myself. I needed an audience, and he became that audience. Through emails to him, I was able to process my days and imagine my life after Bob, and I was continuing to imagine it…with Michael.

School started in late August and Bob was grateful now that he had wrapped up his poetry collection, was occupied with editing his book, and had an eight-week bioethics course to teach online for my university. ALS doesn't affect your mind, only your body, so as long as Bob could still communicate somehow, he could teach this class. Dictation tools were not going to be useful since his pronunciation had become difficult for others to understand. He increasingly produced excessive saliva, and with so much difficulty swallowing, he could choke on it if it was not cleared from his throat. He had those cool finger extenders to help him type, though, and I offered to take dictation for him if it became too difficult to type. He had always hen-pecked a keyboard, anyway, never having learned to type properly, so the technique, while familiar, was much harder to do with curled fingers. The extenders helped only so much, and it was slow going, but he was managing. "I have all the time in the world!" he would joke.

Once, while preparing to vacuum the living room where Bob hung out in his lift chair, I plugged in the vacuum and then turned and looked at Bob.

"You know, Bob, ever since you got ALS you've become a real lazy ass. You don't even vacuum anymore," I said with a flat voice.

Bob always used to laugh so hard he became silent, but now he started bouncing up and down and tilted his head back and made a squealing sound in between silences, like a seal.

"I can't even fucking laugh right anymore."

"You say that as though you ever could," I retorted.

Dave visited regularly, and I also started stopping by his office on my way to work. Dave's office was on the second floor and mine was on the fourth. Instead of taking the elevator, I started walking up the stairs and popping in his office for fifteen minutes before starting class at nine. Sometimes I even left home a little early, so I could have a little more quiet before teaching or to chat with Dave.

Dave was easy to talk to. He also had a hot pot in his office and would make me tea to take to class. During these morning chats we learned a bit more about each other's history, and I shared some of my writing with him. I mentioned that I used stories and poems to help me process my grief about my dad and my brother.

"I can't write now," I told him. "My friend Michael says I should be keeping a journal, but I just can't. I already know everything I think."

"No? But it sounds like a good idea."

"I write email updates. I guess those are going to have to be my journals. I have to be talking to someone, an audience, to write. I guess it's the academic in me."

"I can see that."

"I really started writing creatively after Dad and Sean died. I guess before that, I was the academic, Dad was the poet, and Sean was the screenwriter. Maybe I felt freed."

"What did you write?"

"I have a bunch of short stories about weird characters. People who deal with their grief in strange ways. I have one about a woman who attends funerals of people she doesn't know."

"I'd like to read it."

"Really? I'll send it to you."

Dave had read it by the next time I saw him.

Dave and I also did our share of griping about our university, and when I quoted Herman Melville's character Bartleby the Scrivener's line, "I'd prefer not to," Dave shared that he had read that story and loved it too. We were finding some things to talk about other than Bob.

Soon I settled into my school routine. I dropped Liam at

the middle school he was now attending, dropped Maeve at the daycare, and went about getting myself to work and back for Bob. Having time to cook was becoming a lot more difficult than it had been over the summer, and I was needing to order takeout or come up with very simple meals for everyone. Bob was eating a lot of hamburger with sour cream, something he would not have enjoyed when he was well but he was managing to get down, and I was doing whatever I could for the kids and me, but I was eating less and less and less and smoking more and more and more.

The kids and I carried our food into the living room to sit with Bob. I had positioned one of the couches to face him, with an end table in front of it. The kids and I often sat there, using the coffee table for our plates and drinks. Liam always ate with his daddy. Sometimes, depending on what we were eating, I would sit at the kitchen table with four-year-old Maeve, because of the inevitable mess at mealtime. Liam and Bob had some alone time this way, without me or the distraction of Liam's little sister. When I first saw Liam lift a spoonful of food to his dad's open mouth or bring a strawed cup to his lips, my heart both warmed and broke.

When I sat in the kitchen at our high-top table, around which so many years of writing circles and parties had taken place, I could turn to my right and see Bob across the room, about thirty feet from me, which was useful when our now-infrequent guests arrived. Bob sat nestled in the bay window, in the space that had become his. It was from this angle—as he started to stand to urinate in a plastic hospital urinal or to use the commode—that I could keep an eye out and keep guests on the other side of the table out of eyeshot. But the distance was between us. While hugging when I was pregnant and had a belly the size of two watermelons, Bob and I used to joke, "Do you ever get the feeling that there's something between us?" Now there was. There was the distance from the kitchen to his chair, now that we weren't taking meals together all the time. Not only had the lift and wheelchair interfered with our being together, but now he had a hospital bed for one. The hospital bed they delivered had to be swapped out that first day for a big and tall bed, but even that didn't really have room for me. He was growing more and more isolated, inside a sort of bubble, where not only was our physical communication becoming more limited, but also our verbal.

When I started to realize that my schedule and Dave's Wednesday night rides meant we didn't see him, and most often, anyone else from Wednesday to Monday, Dave offered to start dropping by on other days. Bob and I decided Friday nights would be good because it would feel like a kick-off to the weekend. Hospice didn't do regular visits on the weekend, so Saturday and Sunday I had a bit more time to prepare meals and catch up on things than I did during the week, but we were also lonelier then. If Dave dropped by Friday nights, we could have some company but still have our weekend to ourselves. Dave, a longtime bachelor and not much of a cook, offered to bring us pizza on Friday nights. Dave's pizza delivery started with one Friday night, but then it became a regular thing, and something to look forward to at the end of the work week. Bob couldn't eat the pizza, but it was great for me and the kids, and then I'd only have to make something for Bob. Bob and I had always liked to have a drink, but without Bob to drink with, I was no longer drinking more than my one glass of wine at night on the deck with a cigarette or two before my ten p.m. bedtime. One of our friends had called me a "party pooper" when I shoved him out the door at ten one night since there had been a time not long before when I was willing to stay up as late as four a.m. on a writing circle night, knowing full well I had to teach at eight the next morning.

I had always wanted to savor the best moments. I had known for a long time how short life could be and was.

34

MOURNING SEASON

After August 30th, we were officially in the mourning season for my family members. From then onward, I would be not only contending with Bob's illness, but recalling the losses of my other four family members. This was going to be worse than my fortieth year. We were going to be knee-high in shit.

It wasn't long before Bob often couldn't transfer to the commode quickly enough and began wearing diapers as backup. I forgot what euphemism we had in the beginning—perhaps we used the brand name—but before long Bob was insisting we "call them diapers because that's what they are." Bob was always unflinching about reality, perhaps because of his training as a philosopher. We were on a train heading toward a brick wall, and when it hit, I would lose him but somehow survive the crash, or so he promised me, and he was not going to turn away. He was going to stare that fucking wall down.

Bob's favorite band of all time was Rush, and he and our friend Glenn went way back in their shared affinity for music. Bob had played drums in college and belonged to various bands that played covers at local bars. He had had a lot to say about the dynamics of bands and how personalities typically vied for a "who's on top?" position, which frequently caused friction in groups. As the drummer, he could recede, quite literally, to the back of most sets, and he liked it that way, just as he had liked cultivating a certain "look" to accompany his height, which caused apprehension in others.

Rush was coming to St. Louis, and he and Glenn, and Glenn's sixteen-year-old son Connor, had scored tickets some months before. The concert was scheduled for September 22, the anniversary of my father's death. We were going to meet Glenn and Connor in St. Louis, attend the concert, stay in a suite at a hotel, then return home the next day. Glenn and Connor would be flying in from the Albany area. As Bob struggled more and more with daily activities and eating, he made it very clear that he needed to make it to see that concert and to see his poetry book, which was now in its final stages, come out.

My thoughts had become preoccupied with Michael. We were talking nearly daily now, with his mother in the hospital taking her last breaths and Michael facing decisions about life support. He was leaning on me and I was leaning on him. Bob and I talked more about the possibility of my getting back together with Michael in some capacity after Bob was gone. More and more, it seemed to Bob a strong possibility. Of course, Bob and I were having these conversations entirely without Michael's awareness.

One day Bob said to me, "Why don't you write him? Then you would know. You should just tell him what you are thinking and see what he has to say."

"Really?"

"Yeah, just put it on the table. Then you'll know what he's thinking. No sense wasting any time on him if he's not interested. You deserve the best, Dee. After all, you got all this," he gestured toward himself, and then tilted his head back and squealed again in laughter, his voice having entirely weakened and changed.

"But if I do, and he's not interested, it will make our relationship weird again, and we are good friends."

"Yeah, but if you don't, you'll never know, and you'll be wasting your time thinking about it."

"That's true."

"And besides, if he's not interested in you and the kids, fuck him, well not literally," he squeaked, "but fuck him, you know? You deserve everything. You are hot, smart as hell, and kind. You have put up with me and look at all this shit you are doing. He'd be fucking crazy to say no, so if he says no, then move on. At least you'll know."

With Bob's encouragement, I began to write it out. Writing

was a way to focus my energies, so one night, I did what Bob said, and I tapped out a lengthy letter to Michael. It started with what we had once been, what we'd been through since then, albeit from a distance—my brother's death, then, just days before my writing, Michael's mother's, and we were still on this track toward Bob's death—and then it came to a close with, "So, I was thinking: What do you think about maybe giving it a go again?" After I had written it all out, a few long pages, I sat next to Bob and read it aloud to him.

"Perfect."

"Really?"

"Yeah, send it to him."

"But it's weird. I don't know. I mean, it felt good to just get it out and on the page, but I don't know if I'm ready to send it. Maybe I don't ever have to send it now that it's out and on the page."

"Look, D, you aren't going to know until you just put it on the table. If he's not interested, you can move on. You have so much to offer, you deserve so much, and the kids. They don't need some deadbeat dad. If he's not going to be there for you, you don't want him, and you need to cut him loose and move on."

"True." I said I'd sleep on it.

The next day I told Bob that while I'd written the letter and it felt good to get it down, I didn't think I'd send it. It felt like too much. I wasn't sure I wanted to lay out so much not knowing how Michael was feeling. Instead, I thought I'd catch him online the next time and just lay it out in brief. "Sounds good," Bob said.

After dinner one night, Michael popped up online. I poured myself a glass of wine. "This is it," I shouted to Bob from the kitchen. "He's online." "Go for it," he said from the living room.

After greetings and a bit of small talk, I broached the subject with Michael.

"You've really been here for me these past months as we've gone through so much together. So…I was thinking. Do you think maybe…after Bob's gone…at some point…down the line…we could maybe give it a go again?' I don't remember the exact phrasing, but it came out something like that, haltingly.

There was what seemed to be an interminable pause as the cursor blinked on the page.

Then, "I think we are good like this, Dee. I think what we are is good." I felt socked in the stomach. All the hope that there was some "afterlife" after Bob that had been building inside since early January just evaporated.

I wrote back, "Yeah. I guess you are right."

Part of me had expected his answer. Some part of me had always known the truth, but I had hoped. I had hoped that someone would be there for me, and Michael was familiar and seemed easier, easier than being out there again. Michael had been raised by a single mother, and he assured me that I didn't need anyone, that I could do it all on my own. I knew he was right, but I didn't want to. I had never wanted to. That's why, when faced with the possibility of divorce, I had left previous marriages before having children. If divorce happened, I wasn't going to be able to stop it, but it wasn't going to be anticipated. If it was anticipated, then I needed to leave before children.

Now I'd done all this work to have this life I had dreamed of when I was young, the kind of life I saw in movies, albeit a less conventional one despite the appearance of our two kids, a golden retriever, and the 1895 yellow Queen Anne on a small-town street in middle America. I wanted stability for me and for the kids, while we hashed out Nietzsche quotes in the living room and I tapped out literary criticism and stories and poems. I wanted it all, and I had had it with Bob, and I was terrified of never having it again. Mostly, I wanted my kids to have a family. It was just us as it was, and we lived in a town where everyone had family. I wanted a partner to help me raise the kids, and I knew finding that was going to prove incredibly difficult. Finding Bob had been difficult enough, and that had been before moving to a small town largely populated by married academics. Bob and I always said how grateful we were to have moved there as a couple because being single would have been a bitch.

Our single friends assured us we were right.

That night, Bob and I talked as I readied him for bed.

"I'm sorry, Dee."

I shrugged my shoulders and stared at the floor. "It is what it is."

"I know, but I know you are disappointed."

I shrugged my shoulders again and looked Bob in the eyes. "I don't know why I thought he could do it. He didn't deserve me then and doesn't now. It just seemed like it would be simple, you know? Easy. Like we could just try to pick it back up. It seemed...comfortable, safe."

"He's just not up for it. Look, he'll be there for you and the kids, you know that. That part's good. But it's just not who he is. He was never going to give you what you need. And you deserve that. Really, I'm sorry."

"Thanks." I laughed. "So, uh, do you think we are weird? I mean, don't you think this is weird? Here's my dying husband consoling me over my disappointment over another guy's rejection. We are so weird." I smiled, big.

"We are awesome. This is how it should be. Look, if I weren't sick, none of this would be happening; this fucking disease. I'm going to leave you. It's true. And there isn't a damn thing I can do about it. I love Michael. He's a good guy. If it would have worked for you two, I would have supported it. If people don't get that, then they are the ones who are fucked up, not us. If you love someone, really love them, you put their needs first. Look at you, wiping my ass. You didn't sign on for any of this, Dee. Neither of us did. But this is what it is. I'm sorry about Michael, but if he doesn't want you, fuck him. You deserve so much more. And who knows? Maybe you don't even want a dude."

I started laughing.

"There was that chick at Applebee's we both thought was cute," Bob added.

I shook my head and giggled. "You always make me feel better."

As the Rush concert drew nearer, we got more and more

nervous about how the logistics were going to work. We had a rhythm to our days now and most of it was starting to work itself out, but we had a few dates on the calendar that caused some trepidation. One was the Rush concert, and another was visitors day at Liam's school, and Liam really wanted us to be there.

35

LONG CONVERSATIONS

Days before we were due to visit Liam's middle school, Bob had to get another catheter put in. I had gotten very good at flushing and maintaining his catheters. Caregivers have to learn to be nurse's aides, and fast. Urethra blockages had become a routine thing, albeit an unexpected emergency every time. Catheters are horribly uncomfortable and invasive and yet Bob had no choice.

Bob had necessarily become accustomed to losing his privacy. He was being bathed by various women. As he said, dignity was not something you got to keep when you have a terminal illness. He joked about how we humans can get used to anything, even peeing in the living room or having someone change our adult diaper. We may not like it, but we aren't given any choice. He was just relieved that I didn't have to do it all anymore, even though I'm sure he'd have preferred for me to do it.

When the catheter went in just before the planned visit to Liam's school, Bob sat Liam down to talk about it.

"Are you okay going to my school with your catheter?" Liam asked.

"Yep, sure," Bob replied.

"Because Mom was asking me if I still wanted you to come, even though you had your catheter, and I said yeah I still want you to come. I mean the only time I wouldn't want you to come is if you were dead."

"Yeah, I don't think I'd be able to come then, buddy." Bob squealed, his body shaking up and down as he laughed.

"But I'd still want you to come even if you couldn't see or if you couldn't talk or if you couldn't hear."

"Okay then. I'll be there."

Then Liam was off to play, seemingly unimpeded by adult issues around death and dying. He, like his father, just seemed to "call it like it is."

Getting Bob to Liam's school in mid-September was very hard. We had to get shorts on Bob and get him groomed, and then I had to load him and the manual chair into the van. We used the power chair and deck lift to get him to the van, but on the other side, at the school, I would use the manual wheelchair to unload him. Once again, the accessible parking was still not that accessible, as it was a great distance from the building. We couldn't stay long because of Bob's limitations, but we managed. We checked in at the front office, and then we went to find Liam.

Liam was out on the playground, which meant maneuvering our way through the building to the outside area, which was not very accessible either. While Bob had lost eight pounds since enrolling in hospice, he was still a lot for me to push around, especially if there was any sort of incline or decline. I could wheel Bob to a certain point once we got through the several doors in the building and outside, but I was halted by wood chips and grass. We scanned the large play area for Liam while I stood next to Bob outside in the sun and heat. I finally walked out toward the fields and play area to try to find him, leaving Bob alongside the brick building and sheltering my eyes from the sun. I was roughly fifty to seventy-five feet away from Bob when I found Liam and shouted to him and gestured toward Bob. Liam took off in a dead run toward his dad. I realized what a moment this was and managed to snap a photo of the joy on Liam's face as he hugged his dad.

It's one of my favorite pictures of their love and strength in this battle. Bob's chair is parked perpendicular to the building and Liam's arms are around his dad's neck with his back toward the camera. They are in an embrace of love, and there is calm appreciation on each face. It was one of those moments when the entire world went away, like the moment we all clung to each other in Barnes-Jewish Hospital that day. For Bob and

Liam, there was no playground, no other kids or teachers, or even me. It was just the two of them in this moment where Bob had come through for his boy. Liam was entirely present with Bob; the entire shattering world had receded.

Bob was growing increasingly frustrated by his inability, and who could blame him? Hospice was coming five times a week and various medicines were being increased, one of which was a relaxant to help with Bob's anxiety and frustration, but also to help calm him as he tried to swallow pills and breathe. His throat muscles were so limited that even swallowing the smallest of pills required a concentration so intense that sweat would bead on his brow. Soon I would give him his medicine in liquid form and suppositories. Morphine, the primary drug for terminally ill patients, had arrived in a liquid form. All of life had become effort for Bob, and the more effort it became, the less interested he was in most things. He still wanted to talk to me, and he still wanted to hug the kids and talk to them, but other than the Rush concert and awaiting the published copy of his poetry book, there wasn't a whole lot motivating him.

Around this time, Bob's sister checked in with me. She said she hoped I was okay, and that she wasn't sure "if that was a stupid question."

"Of course I want to be asked how I'm doing…everybody does," I replied. "Some days are better than others. Essentially, I'm a single mom, a full-time teacher, and a full-time nurse. I am tired and stressed all the time. But it is what it is and we are still doing pretty well, all things considered. We still manage to sit down to dinner every night as a family, for example, mostly to home-cooked meals. So, somehow we are keeping things going."

I was exhausted, but we were managing. It was true. My eyes, with Bob's, were on the prize of the Rush concert.

Dave still dropped by with pizza, and, having learned he liked hard cider, I picked some up for him to enjoy with his pizza. Bob and I had become so housebound and the visitors had dropped off so considerably, and each day we faced yet another physical or mental challenge, that the idea of having a drink over pizza on Friday night just seemed like such a relief and such an opportunity to be "normal" even though life was anything but.

I would get Bob fed and cleaned up before Dave arrived with dinner for the rest of us. I would meet Dave at the door to let him know how things were going. Then we would go and sit with Bob a bit and talk about the week and general goings-on at work, and sometimes our pasts, and then Dave and I would head to the kitchen. I sat so that I could view Bob in the living room with just a turn of my head. Dave would sit across from me on the other side of the table so that if Bob needed any-thing, he would have privacy.

Dave and I would talk about work, about past relationships, and about university matters. We would talk into the evening, with me occasionally going in to check on Bob or assist him, and even asking Dave to stay where he was while I cleaned Bob up by changing him, or helping him transfer to the commode, wiping him, and emptying the bucket. "Sorry," I would say as I ran through the kitchen to the bathroom with the commode bucket. It was a pretty unappetizing task and rather personal for a guest to have to witness, especially if we were eating. Dave took it all in stride. "It's okay. Really, don't worry about it," Dave would say. As the clock got closer to nine, I would let Dave know we should wrap up the evening as I was going to have to get Bob to bed. The kids were often already passed out in the living room.

After one of these nights with Dave, but before the Rush concert, Bob rolled into his dining room bedroom in his power chair so I could help him get ready for bed. As I lifted Bob from the power chair, his back turned to me, he said, "You two can really talk."

I thought for a moment. "Yeah, I guess we can."

Bob turned his head towards me. "You should pay attention to that," he said, and then winked, and turned away from me again.

I rolled my eyes and chuckled, looking at his long back, his neck, his sweet bald head.

"Are you saying I should hit on Dave?" I joked, to Bob's backside.

"Well, we both know marriage is a long conversation," Bob said in his increasingly nasal voice, gasping between every few words.

"You know this is weird, right? I mean, we're really weird."

"Yeah, I guess so…just pay attention to that. It's not always easy to find someone you can talk to, as we both know."

"Okay." I smiled. "Okay."

36

SOWING THE SEEDS

One of our last visitors was Tama, a former philosophy colleague of mine, and friend of ours and Dave's. Tama was the
colleague who had gifted us the Ping-Pong table that Dave
had delivered to us years before in his pickup truck. We'd first
met Dave over dinner at Tama's house, despite the fact that we
taught at the same university. While Liz had helped me to plant
flowers earlier in the spring so that Bob would be surrounded
by life and beauty, now Tama and Dave helped me to ready the
deck for fall and winter by emptying and storing the pots.

Bob had planted a seed, and it began to grow. I thought back
on the summer. Just after Bob had been diagnosed, when I had
been joking about how he was ditching me and I didn't know
how I could ever find someone else in this town in the middle
of nowhere, I told him, "You know, Dave is the only guy at
work who is single and I find even remotely good looking."
We laughed about the dearth of eligible bachelors in our town.
Bob said, "Well, at least you're bi. I mean, that opens up some
possibilities." We laughed. "You have double the odds I would
have," he added.

Though I'd only had one brief relationship with a woman in
my early twenties, I'd dated and kissed a few others, so he had
a point.

"I'm not even sure I could be with a non-academic now," I
said. "I've gotten so spoiled with us having the same schedules
and taking our summers to write and read and be with the kids.
I may have to meet someone at a conference."

"You are an HPA, you will have no problem."

Bob liked to call me an HPA—his own acronym for what he
had dubbed me: a "hot piece of ass." It sounds crude when I

type it, but coming from Bob's mouth, it wasn't. It was playful. Bob was the greatest feminist I had ever known. Given that I was his wife and we had absolute trust in each other, it was a compliment, not meant to be demeaning at all. It was rather fun, actually. I had my own acronym. We could speak in code.

A few days after Bob had planted the seed about Dave, I recalled Dave's return after his first bike ride in Michigan in July. I asked whether he had met anyone. Since he'd been hanging out with Bob and me for a few months and rehashing his past relationships for the first time, he admitted that he was opening up to the possibility of finding someone again. Dave told us he had never talked so openly and in such detail about his past before. It's as though we all came into each other's lives because we all found something we needed in this friendship the three of us had formed during the sweltering months of summer.

After his July bike ride, Dave told me that he'd met two women, both of whom he found attractive.

"There were these cute women who rode a tandem," he said. "They were both really cute, but I especially liked one of them."

"Yeah?" I felt a surprising sink in my belly.

"Yeah, and then my friend teased me."

"About what?"

"Dave, you know they are gay, right?"

Dave had had no idea they were a couple. While I wasn't consciously thinking of Dave in a romantic way yet, I remember a surprising twinge of relief at this news. But I shrugged off the feeling and returned to Bob and my life and duties in the house as Dave rode away.

Somewhere in the back of my mind I was certainly conscious Dave was single and might still be so when I lost Bob, but I hadn't fully explored the notion. I wasn't ready. I was still trying to hold on tightly to what I had. I am aware that sounds contradictory, since I had been speculating about Michael ever since Bob told me he wanted me to find love again. But Michael was familiar, and he lived in California. He was over there—*way* over there, at a safe distance. Dave was right in front of me, of us, more and more with each passing week. That was scary.

It was mid-September when I followed up on the conversation with Bob again.

"Are you saying I should trade a chest and biceps for legs and an ass?" I asked, referring to the crack he had made about Dave.

Bob tilted his head and moved his bent fingers up to his goatee in a familiar reflective pose. "I'm just saying you should think about it."

We sat a few moments in silence while I thought about it. "I just don't think Dave would go dancing in the gay bar with me," I said, finally.

"You never know," Bob said.

"Yeah, I suppose not, but I don't see it."

Bob tilted his head again. "I could see it."

"Really?" I giggled, imagining it myself.

Dave was so unlike Bob. He was quiet and reserved, gentle and soft around the edges. And at six feet tall and narrow of frame, he seemed small compared to Bob. He dressed differently—in button-down collared shirts, preppy instead of grunge. But he liked to read and he was interested in my writing. He liked classical music and opera. He was an academic. And he had a vocabulary. He surprised me with his vocabulary. Most of all, though, Dave was kind. Kindness was the quality I noticed the most. In a message to Michael, shortly after this conversation, I wrote: *Cyclist friend has been amazing. He reminds me of Bob in his sensibilities and generosity.*

37

RUSHING

September 22 was fast approaching, and Bob was getting excited about the concert and listening to Rush all the time. I had lined up my colleagues and friends to help—Lee as a driver back-up, and Terrence, who loved Rush too, to help get Bob inside the concert and bounce anyone who would give a guy in a wheelchair any shit. Bob had ordered a black T-shirt that read *Got Peart?*, a take on the old *Got Milk?* advertising. Neil Peart was the drummer for Rush and Bob was a great fan of his music. He used to pretend-drum to Rush on every available surface. He once beat a tune on a car seat when we were first dating. My dad, who was driving, said, "Do you hear that?" "That's just Bob, Dad. He does that." Bob had respect for Peart not only as a drummer, but also because of what he had survived—Peart had outlived both his wife and his daughter. Bob couldn't imagine doing the same.

On the morning of the concert, friends Steve and Suzanne sent us an email wishing us good luck getting Bob to the event. Everyone knew what a goal this event was for Bob. I wrote them back at 10:19 a.m.: "Bob says no go. He's been suffering from incontinence since yesterday and says it's too much of a headache." This was an understatement. Hospice typically visited Monday-Friday and so the previous day's aides had gotten Bob spiffy, knowing this was the big weekend. The venue was two hours away and everything had to be carefully orchestrated just to get the timing right.

I needed help loading and unloading the power chair into the van, which we needed so Bob could maneuver the crowds himself. We needed the manual chair too, just in case. I wanted people on the inside who could help clear a path should Bob need to make an emergency exit, so Terrence, Glenn, and Connor would manage that—they all had tickets to the concert. We needed to check out the venue when we got to St. Louis so we could figure out the best place to pull up to the curb and unload Bob and the power chair. My friend Lee and I were going to wait outside, ready at a moment's notice to zip up to the curb and rescue Bob if anything went wrong.

The team was in place, but Bob woke up having wet himself right through the diaper, and his clothes and bedding were soaked. Everything smelled of urine. An aide wasn't coming and we were on the clock. Bob was also having some issues with his bowel movements, and we needed to be on the road by shortly after noon to pull this off. I was on the phone with Glenn a number of times that morning, letting him know we may not make it to St. Louis, since he and Connor were flying in from Albany and expecting to stay at a hotel I had reserved in my name. Glenn could rent a car and come up for the night, or he could use the hotel suite I'd booked, if I could get them to let him in, since it was too late to cancel. I was taking Bob's cues. It was up to Bob, but I hated to see him miss this. Our friends wrote back at 10:39 a.m.: "Please tell his bladder for us to not be in such a rush. XXX"

Shortly after 11:00 a.m., I decided I should try calling hospice. Bob's spirits were down, but I thought we could still do this, with help. Could they possibly send an aide, even though we weren't scheduled for today? Did they have extra supplies they could send? Pads for the cloth seats of the minivan? Extra diapers? Maybe some sort of rubber overlay to help Bob get through the concert, or could we double up the diapers? Could he get an emergency bath? Could this all happen in the next two hours since we were due to leave? Bob had recently taken to calling the hospice workers "the medical mafia" because they seemed "to know a guy" when they picked up the phone and managed to get equipment, meds, etc. to us in minutes or hours.

At 11:39 a.m., I wrote back to our friends: "I am trying to make this happen. RUSHing around like a lunatic. Cross your fingers again!"

I was scheduled to pick Terrence up around noon. We were to meet Lee at his house shortly after that. Ping was coming to stay overnight with the kids. Things were further complicated by a note from Liam's school that informed us that he needed an instrument for school by Monday and had chosen the viola. Our friend and cellist, Megan—who had gifted Bob with a private concert in our living room—offered to take Liam to get his instrument. I was so frustrated by instructions from Liam's school that year for anything and everything. Whatever he needed by the next day or the next week always seemed impossible. I was labeling crayons and pencils and putting together Styrofoam solar systems when I had a dying husband at home.

We were still determined to try to get Bob to the concert. I got him back into bed so he'd be ready for a bath if hospice came through. I kept him company for a few quiet moments before going to check on hospice.

Bob looked at me intently: "On the inside you're a tank. On the outside you are the *Mona Lisa*. Therefore, you are a Mona Lisa Tank."

Hospice called and said they were sending someone immediately. About ten minutes later, a car came flying into the driveway and parked sideways, as the police do in the movies.

The hospice aide zipped into our house and cleaned Bob with speed. She told me to ready the van. We were going to make this thing happen. I got back on the phone. "We're on," I reported with glee. I loaded the van with our overnight things, pulled it from the garage, placed the pads on the seat, and told Terrence that Bob and I would come get him first. I was issuing instructions to Ping and to the kids, making notes, and letting the neighbors know in case Ping needed help. The aide finished with Bob and he was back in his lift chair ready to go. Moments before we were about to leave, I opened the front door and checked the mail. There was a package for Bob.

Bob's book had arrived: *After Thunder: Poetry from the Edge of Fatherhood and ALS*. It was September 22, the sixth anniversary of my poet-father's death, and here was Bob, posing in his lift chair with his book on his lap, the sun shining in from the bay window, and a giant grin on his face. He did it. He had completed a book of poetry.

It was now time to go; the aide said she would stay to help me. She got Bob in his power chair while I finished readying the van, thanking Ping, and saying goodbye to the kids. There was a random red cowboy hat among the kids' things, and the aide placed it on Bob's head and then wheeled him to the back door. She got him on the deck lift. While I stood in the driveway with the passenger-side door open awaiting Bob, as the kids ran around playing, I snapped a picture of the two of them riding down the lift, Bob with that silly hat far atop his bald head, since it didn't fit him at all, and the hospice aide crouched down on his right side, smiling.

Lee drove while Terrence and I sat in the back seat, the power chair and manual wheelchair behind us. Terrence and I snapped a selfie; my face is gaunt. I am so thin.

Rush tunes blared from the stereo—Bob had brought his iPod—and I used my iPad to snap a short video of the back of Bob's head, Lee driving, the music blaring, and Bob's face in the side-view mirror. I sat behind Bob. I often leaned forward and put my arms around his neck, and kissed or stroked his head, neck, and shoulders from behind.

We checked into the hotel, met up with Glenn and Connor, ate some pretty good take-out Chinese food at the hotel, and then got the four concertgoers to the concert with ample time. There is another great picture of Terrence, Glenn, and Connor standing around Bob's wheelchair outside the venue, with Terrence giving Bob rabbit ears from behind. It took all of us to do this, to get here. I still struggled to steer that power chair down the ramp, as it weighed several hundred pounds. If it fell off the side, it would hurt me or I would damage it. We didn't have an accessible van, so we managed, which meant reclining the chair as far as it would go, putting it on high speed to get it over the lip of the ramp, heading into the back of the van, and then quickly slowing the chair down before it rammed into the back seats.

It was a challenge that caused my heart to race every time.

Getting it out in reverse was even harder. Doing this at night in the center of a city on a busy street in a space we weren't even supposed to be parked in was even more challenging, but I was determined to snap this iconic picture before Lee and I leapt back into the van and sped out of there as if we were driving a getaway car.

Lee and I had a long time to kill before the concert would end, and we had to stay relatively sober so we could still drive and do all the work, but we could also stock up for later. We would all surely want some booze when this was over.

We stopped at a liquor store that was more like an emporium. We wandered around like kids in a candy store, stocking the cart with fun beers for later. Seeing the range of hard ciders, I called Dave to see if he wanted to replenish his supplies. It was the first time I had called him, and it felt a little strange.

"Hello."

"Hi, Dave?"

"Yeah?"

"It's Deirdre."

"Hi. How's it going?"

"I'm here in St. Louis for the Rush concert, and Lee and I are at this place getting beer and stuff while everyone is at the concert, and they have a huge cider selection. Way more than the couple of brands available in town. I was wondering…do you want me to get you some?"

"Sure. That would be nice."

"What kinds do you like? Apple? Pear? They have all kinds."

"You pick."

"How much?"

"A six-pack is good."

"Okay," I said. "I already have a couple six-packs in the cart for when you come over."

"That's really nice. Thanks for thinking of me."

I felt a flip in my stomach.

After I got off the phone, I went back to the cider section. I kept finding Lee and the cart and adding another six-pack.

After checking out, we headed back to the hotel to await the call from the guys that it was time to get them. I had bought almost entirely cider.

When we got to the hotel, Lee and I realized we didn't know what beers people would want. In order to have variety and enough for all of us who would be drinking, we decided we would haul the drinks and snacks we had purchased in the manual wheelchair. It could be the party chair! We snapped a picture of the wheelchair qua grocery cart, too, by the elevator.

Everyone was high after the concert. It had been amazing. Bob was happier than I'd seen him in months. Here he was with one of his longtime best friends and some of our best local friends, and he'd seen Peart in person. We would also sleep together in the same bed for the first time in months. To add to how awesome all of this was, we were staying in an accessible room with a shower Bob could be wheeled into. The next morning, I put as many towels as I could on the floor outside the shower stall, got Bob naked, and rolled him into that shower. I made the shower just the right temperature for him, and I let him sit in there as long as he wanted. Bob closed his eyes and savored that shower as he'd once been able to savor a glass of Opus One. It was absolute bliss for him—almost as good as sex; it was his first proper shower in over two months. I went to the other room with the guys for at least fifteen or twenty minutes to give Bob privacy while he hung out in the shower. When I returned, there was water all over the floor; he was so damn happy to feel that water. I used every spare towel to mop up the mess. It was so worth it.

After we said our difficult goodbyes to Glenn and Connor, we started the two-hour drive home. It was one of the longest drives of my life. While Bob was still very much alive and in the front passenger seat, where I could continue to rub his shoulders and his bald head from behind while Lee drove, or lean forward and kiss Bob's cheeks, or whisper, "I love you" in his ear, I knew that two of the things he'd been staying alive for were now behind us. He had published his book and he'd seen Rush. He had his online class to finish up for my university, but that was duty, not love, and beyond that, I didn't know what could keep him going through the long winter that lay ahead of us.

The day after the concert, Bob began celebrating his book.

On September 26 we received another email message from Steve and Suzanne. Some of our friends understood our gallows humor from the start and had ridden it out through the various and numerous storms. Steve and Suzanne were two of them. They wrote:

We hope you enjoyed the concert that you rushed to see. We hope that, what with the visitors in town, you didn't feel too rushed. I would have come, but I've been rushing around, trying to prepare for classes next term. I feel a little rushed. But the rain has been severe here, keeping me inside, where I hear, during the heaviest of storms, an odd, rushing sound outside. If I were high, I guess the sound would be kind of a rush, but sober, not so much.

I would write more, but I have to rush off now.

XOXO, S&S

On October 1, Bob pushed his book in an email to our friends on our update list:

Bob + Media Whore = BUY (several copies of) MY BOOK

The reviews are in…

"Bob who?" – *Harper's Monthly*

"How did you get in here? Call security." – *Newsweek*

"What the hell is ALS?" – *Time*

"Look, I don't have time to read every piece of crap that comes across my desk." – *USA Today*

"Why would I even review this?" – *Popular Mechanics*

So, be sure to get your copy today!

On October 7, Bob emailed all our friends again:

When I first made the announcement about the book (9/30), my book-rank was somewhere around 30,000. As of today (10/7), my book-rank is 1009. Granted, I have no idea what any of that means—but it still sounds pretty cool.

It was pretty damn cool. People had rallied around Bob's book and it was kicking ass.

38

Waiting for Me

I hadn't written an email update in nearly a month because there was no time left for anything but maintenance of our lives—Bob, the kids, my teaching, the house, the laundry, the cooking, the errands, the picking up, the dropping off, the groceries, the gas in the car, the calls to my therapist, the meetings with hospice nurses and aides, the trips to the hospital, and the drives of thirty minutes when I cranked up the radio, rolled down the window, and smoked a cigarette, hoping that the inhale and the exhale would somehow center me. It was a calming breathing exercise, even if I would have been better off just taking deep breaths rather than filling my lungs with nicotine.

Those moments alone in the car, however brief, where I randomly wandered the streets of our town hoping no one would see me smoking—I can't believe I was actually concerned about that—and wanting to avoid contact with anyone else so I wouldn't have to make any kind of small talk about ALS, were my precious moments alone, free of responsibilities, free to rage or cry or be as desperate as I wished without little eyes on me or feeling Bob's concerns about me.

Bob's decline these past months had been rapid. By October, I was shocked at the speed with which ALS was progressing. Every day the nurse discussed additional options with us, regarding medications that would help him breathe, help him relax his muscles and not panic when he didn't feel he was getting enough air, and help him rest. There were more liquid medicines and more suppositories, in ever-upped amounts. I was losing him.

I followed the head nurse, our favorite nurse, to the back door one day to talk to her privately.

"How long do you think he has?"

"That depends. I've seen some people hang on if they have a goal."

"Something they are trying to reach?"

"Yes."

"I'm worried the Rush concert and his book were his only goals. I think he's done. That's all he was looking forward to."

"I can see that."

"Do you think he could make it to Christmas?"

"If he really wanted to, he might be able to make it to Christmas," she said.

"I don't think he really wants to," I said.

She held my hand and looked at me with deep concern as my eyes filled with tears and I tried to hold back my emotion so Bob wouldn't hear me crying around the corner.

"He's ready," she said. "He's waiting for you."

"You think so?"

"Yes. I know so."

"I told him I would be what he needed me to be. I told him I would step up."

"Maybe you should talk to him."

"Okay," I said, reluctantly.

We said our goodbyes and then I wiped my tears away, trying to hide my emotions, returned to the living room and kissed Bob goodbye, and then left to pick up the kids at daycare. My fear was pumping through me.

In the minivan on the way to the kids, I felt as if Bob had died, as if I were on another numb drive. I was numb, but processing the nurse's words over and over in my mind. I was sobbing. This was it. He was leaving us. This was it. I needed to be who he needed me to be. I needed to step up. I didn't want him to have to wait for me. He was calling the shots. This was his shot to call. If he was ready, I needed to be too.

After the kids went to bed that night, I sat down next to Bob.

"The nurse says you are waiting for me, that she thinks you are ready," I said. "You don't need to wait for me. I can do this.

I wasn't ready for any of this. But I did it. I'm doing it. I stepped up, and I'll do it again. Whatever you want, whatever you need, I will step up. Don't you wait for me. I'll be ready when you need me to be," I said, through tears.

About a month before, I had mentioned to Bob that I had passed a very nice-looking cemetery in town. "Would you like to go see it? I mean, if the kids decide they need a place to go, do you want to pick the place yourself?" Bob was glad we had this house, this small town, and I had a tenured position. He believed we were where we needed to be for his illness and death. Everything we had needed throughout his illness was expeditious, nearby, and more affordable than it would have ever been in New York or some other big city. We believed that part of why we lost Sean was due to the lack of accessibility and the exorbitant expense of medical care in San Francisco. So many people needed treatment, and there was only so much access.

Bob also felt reassured by our neighbors, who had become a communal family, with the kids running from place to place and in and out. He believed, or at least wanted to believe, the kids and I would stay there forever and be safe. It gave him peace of mind. So a cemetery wasn't entirely out of the question as it had once been for my dad and brother, whose ashes were still in our closet. After all the moving, perhaps we were where we were finally going to stay. "No, I don't need to see the cemetery," he said. "It's really up to you and the kids. You can stick me in the closet if you want. I don't care. Really."

I looked at Bob and said, "Oh, come on, I can't have a closet full of ashes!" I laughed and shook my head. "People think I'm weird already, with Dad's and Sean's still in there."

The ashes in the closet were always on my mind then; I hadn't felt right about sticking them in a closet at first. I was just very confused about what to do with them. It was funny, in a macabre sort of way, and I had frequently made jokes about them to others in the six years since my father's and brother's ashes had taken up residence, but there was also a deep absence that placed them there. I had moved over thirty times in my life, even though I was now living in the house I had lived in the longest—six years at that point. While my father had lived all but the final months of his life in New York, the rest of us had been nomadic. My brothers, my mother, and I had had no particular place to call home for long; we were without a shared place to come from—to call home with a capital *H*—a place to return to, a place where people have to accept you, even if reluctantly, as Robert Frost referred to in his poem "Death of the Hired Man." All of us had come to call home wherever it was we were standing and trying, however temporarily, to take root.

Bob, grinning, said, "Of course you can! You can show people." He directed his hand to distinguish between various positions of ashes: "Here are my dad's. Here are Sean's. Here are Bob's." And then with as much of a sweeping gesture as he could then manage, he swung his right arm, now bent at the elbow, hand irreversibly curled, in front of him, from the left to the right, and said, "and here are all the ashes of every man I've ever slept with!"

Bob leaned forward in soundless laughter with strained breaths, his laughter expressed through his entire body.

"All right then," I said, joining in his laughter.

When Dave came over that weekend for pizza, I told him what the nurse had said. We talked in the kitchen, within earshot of Bob, as I watched around the corner for what Bob's needs might be. I sometimes whispered. Eventually, we also laughed and joked and had a nice time as we tried a few of the ciders I had hauled back from St. Louis. At some point we even got on the subject of horoscopes and Dave's astrological sign of Taurus. After we looked up Dave's sign, we looked up mine—Scorpio. As I was reading the descriptions aloud, we happened upon the "compatibility section" and I started reading it aloud. I don't know what website I was on at the time, but the general consensus of Taurus and Scorpio is that they are both strong signs and will inevitably have their battles, but that they also can share a deep passion. As I was reading some aspect of our signs to Dave, I heard some squeaking sounds coming from the living room, and I turned to my right and saw Bob with his head back, mouth open, shaking up and down in sobs.

"Excuse me. Bob needs something."

I went to Bob. "What's the matter?" I stroked his face and hugged him.

He waved his arm at me to go.

"Are you sure?"

He waved his arm at me.

I asked again. Again, he waved his arm at me to go.

"Okay. Let me know if you need me."

I reluctantly returned to the kitchen, but soon asked Dave to go.

"Are you okay? What happened?" I asked Bob as I was helping him to bed.

"I was just sitting there and I was thinking, she's moving on. She's moving on."

"I'm so sorry," I said. "Dave doesn't have to come over. I didn't mean to be socializing in the other room without you. You told me to do that. To keep trying to be 'normal,' but you just say the word and I won't do it anymore."

He shook his head. "No, it's not that. It's what I want you to do. I am glad you can have this time where all of this goes away and it's just normal life. You need that. We haven't been able to leave the house at all. But I just had this moment as I was watching you laugh from across the room where I realized I was looking at my life from the outside. That used to be my life. That used to be me in the kitchen with you."

I sat next to him on the hospital bed and held him close and we ached and cried together.

As I kissed him goodnight, Bob said, "Dee, I want you to keep doing what you are doing. It's okay. It's what I want for you. I just needed to feel that. It's okay."

39

NOT READY

On Monday, when I arrived at work, I saw Dave's pickup truck parked in the lot, and I felt excitement that he was there. I dropped into his office chair and told him about how Bob was declining by the day now. A few weeks before, we had had a sort of falling out (albeit a temporary one) with a good friend who was the "next of kin" on our hospice call list. This friend had walked into the dining room as I was changing Bob's diaper, and when I told them firmly, "You need to leave now," our friend had tried to make light of the situation. When I repeated my instruction, even more firmly, while maintaining eye contact—as Bob had encouraged me to do in such situations—the friend left, feeling scolded and hurt. I was fiercely protecting Bob's privacy, but I had also never spoken that way to our friend before—our friend, who had felt on the "inside" and didn't seem to understand why, in this particular instance, the inside did not include this level of intimacy.

As a result of this bump in the friendship, Bob asked me to bump Dave up as our backup on the hospice emergency list. Dave would be second after me from now on. Dave, who seldom used his cell phone and had never sent a text in his life, was now leaving his phone on at all times, and I was texting him periodically.

When I went home that Monday after work, Bob was struggling to breathe. When the nurse came, she asked if he wanted some oxygen, and he said he did. She said it might help him a little bit. The oxygen arrived that afternoon.

I looked at Bob when we were alone again. We were still fighting to keep our humor alive.

"You know, we are in the mourning season. We've passed my mom's anniversary, August 30th; Dad's, September 22d; and now Sean's, October 6th. We've only got Paul's left on Halloween. If you wanted to keep it neat, you could get out before November 1st, the Day of the Dead," I teased.

He laughed, as much as his lack of air would allow him.

"You wouldn't, you know, ruin the holidays for everyone forever then," I joked.

I'd found a way to lie next to Bob in the hospital bed, even though it was a tight squeeze, but I had lost a lot of weight—nearing thirty pounds in the nine months—just as Bob had gained during my pregnancies. So whenever we had the opportunity in the afternoon, after the nurses and aides and the medical mafia had left, and before I had to go get the kids, we would lie down together and snuggle. It was an effort because it meant transferring Bob yet again, after the regular morning and afternoon transfers, but it was worth it.

We were still enjoying an active sex life. I would have to do a thorough job of bathing him before I could initiate lovemaking. As Bob said, now that he was wearing diapers, he seemed to always smell like urine. No one else could smell it, but if there was going to be foreplay, it needed to be preceded by a good scrubbing. It can be difficult to transition from cleaning one's partner's private area to then making love to him, but I just changed hats, as we all do every day, switching from one role to another, from lover to mom, teacher to friend. I got the cleaning done, washed my hands and put away the supplies, and then nestled my head on his hairy chest, closed my eyes, and breathed his natural scent deeply. Then I was back to sexy Bob, the man I loved, the man who was my other half.

On Tuesday afternoon, I felt that same nervous energy I usually felt during times of crisis. I paced the house, feeling incredibly anxious. I was in between therapy appointments, and Bob's illness was rapidly advancing. Bob suggested I call Dave.

"Dave did say I could call him anytime."

It was the first time I had called Dave since the day I had called from the liquor store.

I went upstairs to our bedroom where I always went to have privacy on the phone and called. "Hi, Dave?"

"Yeah?"

"This is Deirdre."

"Hi. How's it going?"

"Not well. Bob isn't doing well."

"I'm so sorry. What's going on?"

I explained that things had gotten even worse since I had stopped in his office on Monday. It had only been a day, but Bob did not look good. His color was changing, and I could hear him struggling, even with the oxygen hospice had supplied. We talked awhile, Dave asking me questions, and then he said that if I wanted to come over for a bit, I would be welcome. I told him I would check with Bob and come over for a short time before picking up the kids from daycare.

"Dave invited me to come over," I told Bob after getting off the phone.

"I think you should."

"Yeah?"

"Yeah. I think it's a good idea."

"Are you sure?"

"Go. Get out of here. Talk to someone. It will help."

"Okay. Do you need anything?" I felt like I had when I left my mother years ago. I was running. I had to talk to someone. I had to get away for a minute. I was also craving a cigarette.

"No. I'm fine. Go. You don't have long before you have to get the kids."

I drove the few blocks to Dave's house, recognizing it by the two potted red geraniums on either side of the front door. I knocked. He invited me in and led me to the living room.

I did most of the talking, rehashing the last week of our lives at home and explaining that I thought Bob was close to the end. Dave listened and offered his help.

"There's nothing you can do, I don't think, but thanks anyway," I told him. "I just needed to talk. And having you on call is really helpful. If you could just keep your phone turned on because I don't know what's coming next. It's all been so fast.

I told Bob he didn't need to wait for me. I guess he took me seriously."

Losing Bob one degree at a time was killing me. There was a part of me that just wanted it over with now, and I knew Bob did, too. It was all just too painful. We had been living with the reality of his death for months, and we had said all we needed to say. We were both so over this disease and all the bullshit. Bob was so tired. I was so tired.

Bob had told me early on that I needed to point out things to him—that I had always been his other set of eyes and ears, and he needed me to be that throughout this illness. It had been so difficult to become that person—to be the one pointing out his limitations—but I had been trying to do that for months, and it was painful but honest. I was the one who told him when he needed the accessible hangtag. I was the one who told him when he couldn't take stairs anymore. I was the one who said it was time for the wheelchair.

I was the one who sat down next to him and said, "You said you didn't want any life-extending measures because you wanted this bullshit to end as soon as possible, but you are using oxygen. Do you want to use the oxygen? Is that extending your life? Do you want it?" We hadn't really talked about it. The nurse had seen Bob struggling, and Bob—the man born with asthma—had just gone forward with the suggestion. We had never really talked about it; he had never really thought about it. He looked at me. "No, I don't. It's uncomfortable to wear and annoying to hear and I couldn't sleep last night. I don't want it." He took it off that day, and the nurse upped the anxiety medications and the morphine. Another day passed. Bob grew weaker and his skin more discolored.

Then, that Thursday night, after the kids went to bed, Bob told me he thought we were getting close. He asked me if I was okay. "As okay as I'll ever be. I am never going to be ready for this, Bob. I wasn't ready for any of it and I'm still not, but you are calling the shots."

When the nurse came that Friday to make sure we had everything for the weekend, I raced to the door so I could talk to her before she left. "Bob says he doesn't think he'll make it through the weekend."

"He will," she said. "I can usually tell. He looks pretty good. I think he'll be okay until Monday."

"Are you sure?" I inquired. "He told me he was going to start preparing the kids."

She looked concerned. "I think he'll be okay, but if he's not, call. We can get you whatever you need, or just be here. I'm going to a wedding this weekend, but there will be another nurse on call, not one you've met, but she's very good and she will get you what you need."

"Okay."

It was around two p.m., three hours before I had to pick up the kids. I climbed into bed with Bob, and we held each other and cried. And then I decided we needed to make love. I knew this was probably the last time, if Bob was right, and he was always right, and I was going to make it count. It was beautiful. And when it was over, I collapsed into him.

The Last Time Making Love

He is still—unable to move.
The work you used to do together
now yours alone to do for you both.
The laundry, the cooking, the shuttling
of the children to and fro, the furniture
rearranged, and now your husband
lifted by you and moved
where we now must go.

You look into each other's eyes
knowing there is little time for such
things in these last bare hours; there is barely
enough air to pass through him to achieve
the goal—what you could early on spend
a weekend enjoying, you had to later
achieve in quick fixes before the young steps
on the stairs or the sudden tap at the door

disrupted all.

But here, now, you grip the bar that
helps him move and climb his body
knowing every smooth and bristled surface,
you repeat in your mind not to
ever forget his warmth, his scent,
or the crevice in the center of his chest
where you found your home.
Do not avert your eyes—
know that this has to be forever.

The leverage of the bar becomes
part of both of you as you, willing to do
everything for the man you love
will these punctuated moments:
be beautiful, be perfect, be the lasting
few minutes to an end that makes
you both whole. In the temporary joy
that comes, you both experience a release,
a pleasure knowing that this time, at least,
time did not matter and
the parting was satisfactory.

Spent, you lie on his chest,
beads of sweat joining in the crevice,
and you both rest in the last after love
made with the assistance of a hospital bed
equipped with railings and a bar for leverage.
It is the final respite between hospice visits.

After, the children will enter this doorless
dining room and return you to the movements
that will remind you your eyes are no longer
able to gaze at the same horizon.

40

Ready Almost

It wasn't until Bob was sick that I realized that our song, "Time to Say Goodbye" by Andrew Bocelli—the one the piano player just happened to know at that restaurant in Indialantic on the night of our wedding—would come to seem like a foreboding foreshadowing of what was to come. Who knew when we'd met that our time to say goodbye would come so soon?

On Friday afternoon, Bob asked me to tell Liam after school that Daddy said it was time to say goodbye. We thought Maeve was too young for me to say such things to her. We were probably wrong, but I think maybe we were right. I will never know for certain.

Liam and Bob had alone time. Liam drew a picture for Bob in pencil. Bob was wearing a Guinness shirt and crying.

I stumbled through it all as in a dream. Every minute seemed to last an eternity. Every minute had been the entire week. From Monday through Friday of that week, it seemed a month had passed. Time had slowed to a crawl, again.

I was putting one foot in front of the other and doing the things, all the things, and Bob and I were talking everything through and things were happening, but I was numb, so numb. I was in so much pain. Bob was in so much pain. The ache had become so great I was beginning to be ready. I wanted Bob's suffering to end. I wanted all of the suffering to end. I felt like Prometheus, bound to a rock and having my liver eaten every day only to have it grow back and be eaten again. I wanted the pain to stop. Of course, mine would never stop until I was myself dying, but Bob's pain would, and mine would ease when his suffering ceased, wouldn't it? That must be at least half of the pain, right? Watching the love of my life suffer?

Losing Bob began to feel like tearing off a bandage slowly, ripping the skin with it. Despite facing the loss of the love of my life, I was now bracing for the final impact and was nearly ready for his death to come. Bob was too. We both wanted to rip the bandage off already.

From the beginning, I had wanted death—my own, not his. I had wanted him to go on, to be the one to go on, because I had no will to do so myself. And from the beginning, Bob had been shoving me out of the grave. I felt there was a hole already dug, and I could be the one to lie in it. I was ready, I had told him, in the beginning and repeatedly, to die myself. I had had enough. I could not do it. I could not outlive my family and him.

But Bob had spent every moment since his diagnosis not only shoving me out of the grave but handing me flowers and wishing me well. Every time I had figuratively placed a foot in the grave, he had territorially declared it his. Sometimes he lauded me, sometimes he praised me, sometimes he cajoled me, and sometimes he made me laugh, like the time he said, "Aw, c'mon, Dee, seriously? You think I should be the one left behind? You know how much I suck with money. You know the kids would never get new clothes and their hair would be a mess as I sent them off to school without their teeth brushed. You know I would never date anyone else and I would just be miserable and in this house depressed, and you know that wouldn't be any good for the kids. You can do this. You've done it before. You can go on. You can even love again." He acted like I was a professional griever and he was a novice. I could do this, but he couldn't, or so he thought.

I had survived before. It was true. But it takes a will. Without the kids, I wouldn't have had the will. With them, I needed to survive and endure for them. I didn't know what we were going to be or how we were going to do it, the three of us, but I knew I had to stick around for them.

And Bob did have a point: he wasn't very good about remembering things at the store.

When I was teaching and still in graduate school, one of my students lost a parent—her father—while she was out to dinner with my geologist colleague and me. When I dropped her off at the dorms, she got the call that her dad had died. My heart ached for her. It was late August, approaching the anniversary of my own mother's death, and she was younger than I had been when I had lost my mom. I had so much empathy for her that I drove over an hour and a half to attend the wake, and I brought her a teddy bear as a gift. I knew that when someone died, holding something or someone could help, so I gave her that bear. She still has it.

Sometime in September, I suggested Bob order two giant bears for the kids, as well as something for later that they could have and keep. The week that had slowed to a crawl, the first few of the gifts arrived. Bob had ordered a pocket watch for young Liam and one for him when he was older, both engraved for his "Amazing Boy." He had also ordered a statue of *The Thinker* for Liam to have whenever I thought he would most appreciate it. For Maeve, he ordered a music box purse for now and a nicer music box for later. Inside the nicer music box, he put a Mae West quote on a slip of paper: "I myself have never been able to find out precisely what feminism is: I only know that people call me a feminist whenever I express sentiments that differentiate me from a doormat." Bob also ordered a statue of *The Dancer* for Maeve. For himself, Bob ordered a black T-shirt with the painting *The Death of Socrates* on the front. He had showed it to me one evening and told me he wanted to be cremated in that shirt. In the painting, hung in the Metropolitan Museum of Art in New York, Socrates is surrounded by his students, his disciples, and holds a cup of hemlock in his hand. His wife is seen in the background, ascending the stairs. I have a photo of Bob holding Maeve in front of that painting at the Met from the summer of 2011, mere months before his diagnosis. Their backs are to me but much of the painting is visible.

Bob finished the grading for his eight-week class at my university and, remarkably, printed his grades for me to submit on his behalf.

Bob had spent most of his last few days sleeping in his chair. Some writing-circle people came over that Thursday. He was saying his goodbyes, I realized later. That night, we had our writing circle after-party while Bob slept in the background. With Bob's limited oxygen intake, he no longer had the ability to stay awake for more than very short periods at a time.

Dave came over with pizza that Friday night, as always, and we ate dinner while Bob slept. Dave left early, saying he would drop by or call the next day. He told me to let him know when a good time would be.

The kids needed Halloween costumes, but I couldn't imagine facing Halloween at all. Halloween—the anniversary of my eldest brother Paul's suicide—was only a few weeks away. Casey dropped by late Friday night to see how we were doing, and when I told him Bob said the end was near, he offered to take the kids out to get costumes the following day to give Bob and me some time alone.

I hadn't written an update in nearly a month. How could I send a note when Bob died, if he died soon, if I hadn't written an update in a month? How would people be prepared? Despite how I dreaded the task, I dragged myself to the computer and wrote an October 13th update.

It had been less than a week since Bob had at first accepted and then refused oxygen. If the days of summer had dragged, then this week had simultaneously been excruciatingly slow and lightning fast.

The weather had turned and the forecast predicted pouring rain all weekend long. The weather matched the solemnity of our house. Most of our humor was gone, though I was still trying hard, so very hard, to make jokes; so was Bob.

I was readying Bob for bed when I asked him, "Is there anything else you want to say to me?"

"Not that I can think of," he said.

"Are you sure? Nothing at all?"

"I think a sign of a really good marriage is that you have always said everything you wanted to say."

"True."

"Oh, wait, there is one thing."

"Oh?" I asked, eyebrows raised.

"Yeah…I'm a really great dancer," Bob said, and lifted his head back to let in more air as he squeaked out what was left of his glorious laugh.

Dave joined us Saturday evening. After the kids had been tucked into bed, Dave and I gathered around Bob's hospital bed. Dave sat on the futon on the floor, and I sat on the edge of Bob's bed. Bob was really struggling with his breaths and talking was tiring, even though he wanted us near. He asked that I read some poems aloud and requested some of my father's poems. He also wanted me to get his new book and read some of his own poems to him.

One of the poems Bob wanted to hear by my father was one I had read over my father's body in the front room of the house, before the funeral home took my father's body.

I'm Ready Almost

I'm ready almost to receive
someone who's overstayed his leave, the
absent guest, the out-of-sight-if-not-of mind,
the never-gone-when…
Guess:
Canny chameleon, present whereabouts
unknown; at major races, waver of
the checkered flag; stentorian ring-
master to a bumbling throng; accomplished
portraitist to skinny bums and fat-bummed
kings, to rectors yet to be accused
of peculation of church funds; itinerant
butcher (and to hell with that), clearly
a person of parts; of all trades, jack;
to each of us
most things.

How will it go? Easy-does-it? Sudden? Slow?
A steady diminution of
concentric rings?

I think I'll sit
for it,
my po-or-trait,
wide-eyed
perpendicular,
and stiff.
Don't want to miss
one metaplastic minute of
narcotic ecstasy,
confectionary bliss.

On second thought make mine
vehicular
and swift.

I read. We talked. It was quiet. There were awkward silences.

Breaking the silence, Bob quietly asked, "Does anyone know any good jokes?" Then after a moment, "Not you, Dave, we know you only know bad ones."

Bob tried to laugh. I really laughed. Dave took the jab with a smile and a knowing chuckle. Dave knew a lot of jokes, a lot of jokes one finds in a joke book. We all knew this about Dave. Dave told what is commonly referred to as "dad jokes."

"I just want to die in peace," Bob added one more dig at Dave's jokes, we all knew playfully. This made us laugh harder. Here Bob was on what was ostensibly his deathbed, and he was still making jokes that made us laugh.

Bob grew tired and Dave went to the kitchen while I readied Bob for bed and kissed him goodnight. Then I, too, retired to the kitchen to have a drink with Dave before he left for the night.

The next day was another day of rain and waiting for what Bob had signaled would come soon. He had been requesting more liquid morphine drops, and I had had to call hospice so they could send more medicine. Now Kristin, having read the update from the day before, offered to take the kids to the movies to get them out of the house.

The previous night had been Bob's last burst of energy and humor. He was spent. He was now sleeping except for brief moments when he opened his eyes. The lack of oxygen had taken an expedient toll and the morphine and anxiety suppressors had calmed him into nearly continuous sleep.

At one point, Bob gestured weakly with his arm to sit up. I propped him with pillows. His voice had been hard to hear the night before, and I had had to translate what he was saying at times to Dave. Now he was struggling even more. He gestured for me to come closer. He whispered to me: "Never...quit... fighting...for you...for the kids," he said in between labored breaths.

"I won't. I promise," I could hardly utter.

The pressure in the house was becoming impossible for me to manage. It was so hot and rainy outside, but Dave sat on the front porch with me while I cracked open a beer in the middle of the day and smoked a cigarette, the pressure of anticipating Bob's death becoming something nearly impossible to withstand.

Late in the afternoon, I checked on Bob, and he was struggling even more to breathe. I administered more morphine to relax him. I felt that I shouldn't leave his side anymore. Dave had dinner plans with his neighbors and said he could drop by later if I needed him, and he left.

With the kids still gone, I sat with Bob, and when I left the room, I returned to check on him more and more often—every five or ten minutes, or so. He hadn't been eating much at all the last week. It was simply too hard to swallow. He'd had only a few bites to eat in the last couple of days. He was having trouble taking in any water as well, choking as he tried to swallow.

Late afternoon on Sunday, Bob began gasping for air. I knew the end was near. I would not leave his side again. He was starting to have that raspy sound that people always say signals the end.

Suddenly Liam surprised me by appearing in the doorway to the dining room.

"What's the matter with him?" he asked, horrified.

"He's dying," I carefully and cautiously said.

His eyes widened in surprise.

"I'm so sorry." I hugged Liam close.

I left Bob and went to the kitchen where Kristin was waiting, having just returned with the kids from the movies. I explained to Kristin that I thought we were near the end, and I needed to get back to Bob. I thanked her for taking the kids. Silently, I wished they had stayed away longer because I didn't really want the kids home when Bob died. I had hoped they wouldn't be there to see him go.

Kristin left, and the kids and I went to sit with Bob. I stood at his bedside, stroking his arm or his head, trying to relax him.

Liam said, "Shouldn't we call Dave?"

Surprised, I asked, "Do you want to?"

"Yes."

"If you want to, then you should. Tell him it's okay, your mother said to go ahead and come over." Liam ran out of the room to make the call.

Dave was such a short ride away; he was at our house in what seemed like minutes.

I was standing by Bob's bed, stroking his head and arm and soothing him. "It's okay," I told him. "The kids and I are going to be okay."

Maybe it would be better if I sat on the futon? I thought. *Maybe he is holding on for me.*

Often when people are dying, they don't want their loved ones to witness it. When I had left after being by my mother's side all day, my stepfather turned toward the door to respond to a nurse, and it was then that my mother took her own last breaths.

When Bob took his last breath, Liam, Maeve, Dave, and I were sitting on the futon on the floor beside his bed.

Minutes after Bob took his last breath, there was an unexpected knock at the door. A colleague had been to St. Louis and was delivering some Korean barbecued pork buns to our house. Maeve beat me to the kitchen and blurted out, "My daddy died." I had hoped to keep it to ourselves for a night.

My father had been rushed away from me. I didn't like how death was dealt, and I wasn't going to have it so this time, if I could help it. I had asked the hospice nurse a few weeks before whether I had to call in a certain amount of time after Bob died. "Is there a law?" I asked. I had been told there wasn't. "You take the time you need. You call when you are ready."

I knew how swiftly death was handled. It was deftly handled by the ants in the Frost poem "Departmental," which I had taught numerous times and had experienced firsthand in Florida when a colleague died over spring break, and I witnessed from the adjacent glass office the expediency of reassigning her classes and rummaging through her files for materials and student marks so that life and classes could go on. Death is often so departmental, as Frost pointed out with his militaristic ants. I wouldn't have it so. I wouldn't have people taking Bob swiftly from us, or turning our night of mourning into a cleaning up affair.

It was around seven p.m. when Bob died. If I called now, we would have people in our house until at least nine. It could wait. This was our time, the kids and mine.

In the moments after Bob's last breaths, Liam handed copies of Bob's book to Dave and me. Just as when Liam had proclaimed our Barnes-Jewish trip as "the best vacation ever!" he seemed intent on making everything immediately better, as if holding Bob's book in our hands and reading his words would bring him back to us. In some ways, I suppose, he was right.

I gave Liam his pocket watch and Maeve her music box purse and told them Daddy had left these for them.

Dave and I sat with the kids awhile. Then Dave said goodbye. He would check on us the next day.

After putting the kids to bed, I kissed Bob's body goodnight and slept on the futon on the floor beside his hospital bed, comforted that it was the one where we had first made love, on our first date a dozen years before, in his graduate school studio apartment in upstate New York.

I held Bob close in my mind and kept his body close in proximity as I forced myself into sleep.

I was beside his body all night long and reassured he was still mine, still with me.

Bob had died on his own terms, at home, surrounded by family. He said I was calling the shots, but he had called the shots, and I had followed them. He had spent months preparing me and had made sure I wouldn't be alone.

When I awoke the next morning, the sun was shining.

41

THE LAST UPDATE

After I had called Bob's family and our closest friends, I called my colleague Terrence and said I wouldn't be in to work for two weeks. Then I wrote an email to "Bob's Muscle Team."

October 14, 2012

Dear Friends and Family:

Bob died yesterday around seven p.m. He was at peace and ready to go—he had done everything he wanted to do as well as everything he had to do (he even finished his grades for his online class and printed a copy for me). Liam and Maeve and a friend of ours and I were by his side. A memorial party celebrating life, generally, and Bob, specifically, will be held at our home at a later date (TBA).

The kids are doing even better than one would ever expect…and are grateful for the gifts Daddy left for them. In addition to his book (which Liam grabbed a stack of immediately and began handing out), a few moments after he died, I gave Liam the pocket watch Bob had purchased for him, which is engraved, "For my amazing boy and the amazing man you will become. I love you—Dad 2012," and Maeve the music box with a ballerina dancing he had purchased for her. They also have some stuffed cuddly things on the way. We will all need something BIG to hug.

Thank you for all of the love and support you have provided and for continuing to be a part of Bob's Muscle Team. We owe it to him to live our lives as fully as possible and to make the world a better place. He showed us how.

I'll be in touch about the party. Until then, I encourage playful expressions of sympathy for Liam and Maeve. Surround them with love. They are going to need it.
love,
Deirdre

Then the kids and I stood around Bob's bed and said our words to him. I called hospice around nine a.m. As I had anticipated, someone was out to the house immediately—thankfully, our favorite nurse. The funeral home that had handled both my father and brother was called, and the hospital bed, commode, and medicines were all removed from the house. Bob's power wheelchair was placed in the front office, which had once been my father's room, and where Bob had found my father's body. By noon, I had an empty dining room and no husband.

The room couldn't be a dining room again. There was no going back. So, I turned the futon that the kids had been sleeping on back into the couch it had once been and shoved it into the dining room. I moved in a coffee table. I moved out the dresser and end table. Bob's bedroom, former dining room, would be the "Wii Room" or "Wee Room" for the children, I decided. It would be filled with joy. Just as the fridge from Bob's office had become the party fridge when it was delivered to our house that summer after Bob alerted his university he would not be returning to work, this room would become a place of youthful voices and joy, not death.

A friend made sure balloons were sent to the kids. Liam ran around the neighborhood the day after his dad died with the balloons and his pocket watch, and Maeve with her music box. The neighborhood kids decided to sign the balloons as one does a cast when someone breaks a leg or arm. They expressed their sympathy to Liam and Maeve on the balloons. "Sorry about your dad."

Bob had died on Sunday night over Columbus Day weekend, which meant the kids and the "brat pack" all had Monday off. I kept Liam and Maeve home Tuesday, but on Wednesday they bravely went back to school while I planned my visit to Social Security. It was one of the primary goals of the week.

As that first day wore on, I realized no one would be coming with food. Despite my letters, very few people had taken to dropping by lately.

I called Alyse from my writing group, and learned that they had been planning to gather at a nearby pub that evening for a memorial for Bob.

"Or you could come here to the house," I offered.

"We didn't know if you'd want us to," Alyse replied.

"It would be nice," I said.

I hadn't understood why no one had called me. Would they have gotten together without me if I hadn't called first? I'll never know. What did occur to me are two things.

One was that people just don't know what to do when someone dies. They are afraid of doing the wrong thing, so they often just go silent. It is often the same when someone is sick. We just freeze. It's as Bob described: it's like staring into the eyes of a chicken. We go blank. I'm guilty, too, despite my many experiences with death.

The other thing that occurred to me is that no matter how much I say I don't have family, it's very hard for people to understand. One of my writing circle friends told me months later that for some reason she just thought family would be there and she would be interfering if she showed up too soon. She didn't know why she thought that. We'd been friends for six or seven years already. She knew me when my dad and brother died. She knew they were the last members of my immediate family. Still, for some reason she just thought my experience would be like so many other people's experiences; someone would show up, maybe Bob's family, but Bob had wanted only me and the kids there, and we had decided not to have an immediate memorial.

The day at home was solemn and overwhelmingly quiet. It was isolating and lonely and the clock ticked slowly. I moved furniture. I tried to right things. Other than Dave dropping by after work, there wasn't a single knock on the door until I invited the writing circle folks to the house, and we spilled onto the deck after the kids went to bed to reminisce about Bob, drink, and smoke cigarettes.

As the week wore on, a few more people started to appear. Enough time had passed that they knew they could come, and they brought food, or raked leaves, or just talked to me. Dave dropped by each day to see how we were doing, or called to see if I needed anything.

Going to the funeral home was like old hat now. I walked up to the door as if I owned the place. The door opened just before I reached for the handle, but I couldn't see the person opening it. It was as if it had opened itself. I couldn't help but think of the Addams Family. I was so comfortable at the funeral home, in fact, that I cracked a joke. "That could be kind of creepy, you know," I playfully said as I entered. I knew the drill. This was my third time in six years. I had this down.

I arranged for the kids and me to visit Bob's body one more time in a private viewing area just as Bob and Liam and I had visited my father. Bob was then cremated in his Socrates T-shirt, but I kept his wedding ring. The day of his cremation, I sat at my kitchen table, drinking midday again. I knew this was it. I'd never set eyes on his gorgeous eyes or body again. I'd never smell that scent at the center of his hairy chest that was the place I put my nose and inhaled and felt safe and home. His body was gone forever.

I made it to Social Security where, despite all my preparations, I learned there was still more documentation I needed that had been left at home.

I rearranged furniture and made it through the first nights without him. I had been able to leave the house. I went out for beers and fried food with a friend while Dave watched the kids. I had begun to eat again. While out that first time, I just happened to bump into the person who had installed the deck lift. He saw me and approached the table to ask about Bob. I told him he was gone. He said he could remove the lift when I was ready, and offered me some money back. I wasn't ready. I wanted to keep his chair and the lift. I wanted to keep something, as irrational and unnecessary as both were; I wanted to keep those things. For now, they needed to stay. Too much change. Too fast. Too much.

I was alone in our huge house without him. Just me and the kids and the dog and 3,200 square feet of space, missing a husband, a daddy. Just me and the kids.

Somehow one night—I think a night or two after Bob died—the kids, Dave, and I all ended up in the master bedroom, in a pillow fight. Dave started the pillow fight in the living room, but we ended up in the master bedroom because that's where all the pillows were. It reminded me of the night the kids stood on the open futon in the living room with Bob in his lift chair inciting a riotous pillow fight while I filmed. It was a much-needed release of pressure and pain and brought momentary joy. We all needed some momentary joy. Long-term joy was harder to come by.

I signed up for a couple of things shortly after Bob died: A wine club that delivered a case monthly, and I continued a fruit club order a philosophy professor of Bob's had gifted us after the diagnosis, which was also delivered monthly. I considered ordering cheese, but it was too expensive, more expensive than the wine. Still, I wanted something random showing up on my doorstep now and then when I least expected it, the way Dave once had. I wanted to open the door to the front porch and have a good surprise on a day I didn't think I could go on.

About a month before Bob died, he said to me, "Dee, when I'm gone, I want you to get that bracelet you saw at the jewelry store when you last went to get your diamond cleaned. I bought you the Tiffany one for our tenth anniversary because we couldn't afford the tennis bracelet, but I wanted to get you that one. I want you to have it, if it's still there." It had been over a year since our anniversary.

"That's ridiculous. It's too much money," I said dismissively.

"But I want you to have it," he said. "If it's still there, please get it."

42

A Good Marriage

Dave came over to keep me company on Friday night as he had for weeks now. I started to feel flips in my stomach when I saw him. I recalled the day I saw his truck at work and my stomach had fluttered with excitement. The more Bob and I had joked about Dave, the more I had started to think about him. Now when I hugged Dave hello or goodbye, he put his arms around me tightly. I really missed being hugged like that.

When Dave came over for pizza that Friday, we were alone for the first time. The kids were running around the neighborhood, and we sat on the front porch to talk while we had a cider and beer.

I was excited about Dave coming over. It was so soon, but I had started to recognize feelings for him and they felt right. I knew it was soon in days, but in my heart, it didn't feel so soon. I'd been losing Bob since December. Bob had been talking to me about finding someone else to love since the day after his diagnosis in December. I was missing Bob every minute of every day, and yet I was feeling flutters when Dave walked into a room. I had never been good at keeping words or feelings to myself, and I wondered how long I was going to make it without saying something.

We were sitting on the porch and I was so close to telling Dave what Bob had said about him, about how for the last month or so, we'd been making jokes about him—Bob and I—about my trading a chest and biceps for legs and a butt, but mostly about how marriage is a long conversation, as Nietzsche said, and we could talk, as Bob had said. Just when I was about to summon the courage to say something, Dave looked at me and began:

"I want to tell you how much I've grown to respect you and Bob in these many months. I have so admired the way the two of you have handled his illness and how much love you've shown for each other. It's really been remarkable, and I've been grateful to be a part of it. I've been happy to get to know each of you, and to get to know Bob better before he died. I've just been so impressed by both of you and the love you had. In this time I really feel I have come to know you, especially, and I'm wondering…now that Bob's gone…if maybe…if maybe you thought the two of us could create something like that."

"It's funny you should say that," I began. I told Dave what Bob had said about us being able to talk, *really* talk.

We moved to the kitchen table, our knees sometimes touching beneath its surface, as we continued to talk. Dave ran his finger in soothing circles across my palm and stroked my wrist.

Knowing it was getting late and nearing the time for him to leave, and aware of the growing electricity between us, Dave asked if he could kiss me. I said yes. He leaned forward and we shared our first awkward almost-teeth-bumping kiss.

The next time Dave and I kissed, it wasn't awkward. It felt as if we had been doing it all our lives.

43

Finding a Place

Bob's mom took the first picture of Dave and me together, while we stood on Dave's porch during her first visit a few weeks after Bob died. Without words, she gave us her blessing.

When I went to the local jeweler to get my ring cleaned, about a month after Bob died, the tennis bracelet Bob had wanted to buy me was fortuitously still in the case. It was an awful lot of money, but I closed my eyes and heard Bob, and then I bought it. I hardly wear it, but I have it for Maeve, and one day it will be hers. Bob had wanted me to have it; I want Maeve to have it.

Dave and I took the kids trick-or-treating in his neighborhood on Halloween, and we self-consciously held hands as we walked behind them, and they ran door to door.

Soon it would be the Day of the Dead and then my birthday and then Thanksgiving and then Christmas. The season of mourning would not end for me that year.

While I began to control my smoking over time, and before long quit again entirely, I couldn't set a clear end point to my mourning. It was messy and it was forward and backward and zigzag and often ugly. I do know, however, that for me mourning is the period between death and grieving, when I am emotionally hurtling through space, and physically through life, often in a vehicle, puffing on cigarettes, untethered. Once achieving some stability, I would move from mourning to grieving, and the latter, unlike my period of mourning, is forever.

In the video Bob made for me to watch after he died, he is sitting on a chair in our master bedroom in his usual clothing, but there is some sort of a dark spot on his shirt that I couldn't quite make out. My video is clearly the last one of the three he made—one for me and one for each of the kids. He must have made it sometime in May, probably around the anniversary of our first date twelve years before. I know this because of the way he speaks, and that he was still able to climb the stairs. I know this because of the stage of his ALS.

When I later zoomed in on his shirt to figure out what the dark spot was, I realized what he was wearing. I had given Bob a card for one of our recent anniversaries that had come with a pin. The pin reads: *I'd be lost without my wife*. Bob was still making me laugh.

Near the end of the video Bob made for me, he asserts meaningfully between choked gasps and tears he wipes away with his curled fingers: "You are going to have to find a place for me."

I finally know exactly what he meant.

44

June 22, 1968-October 14, 2012

In Memory of Bob and Gestures Toward Life and Love

Bob had a tattoo on his left arm which was inspired by Ni-etzsche, and which he designed. The tattoo formed the symbol phi, for philosophy. The symbol was formed with an ouroboros (a serpent eating its own tail), which to him represented the tree of knowledge, with a sword vertically through it, which symbolized Nietzsche's Übermensch or warrior, Zarathustra. Underneath the symbol were the words, *Never Quit*.

Hours before Bob died, he gestured to me to come closer. He wanted to say something and wanted to be sure I would understand him. I sat on the left side of his hospital bed and leaned close to his mouth with my ear. With his right hand, which had become curled by the disease, he gestured weakly toward me, working hard to utter and emphasize the following words: "Never…quit…fighting…for you…for the kids," he said in a barely audible whisper. Then he gestured toward the T-shirt sleeve on his left arm and waved his hand upward to indicate I should raise the sleeve to reveal his tattoo. He ran his curled fingers along the bottom of it. "N-ev-er quit," he said slowly as he traced the words. These were his last words to me, followed by a kiss.

Bob spent the ten months of his diagnosis preparing those

he loved to say goodbye to him. He did not spend his remaining time mourning his own death. Instead, he chose to spend his life celebrating life. When you find yourself on a train headed toward a wall, you can either collapse on the cushions or pour champagne. We chose to pour champagne and keep on pouring it, a response similar, I imagine, to the musicians who kept on playing as the *Titanic* sank.

Bob said to me the Friday before his death, "You made my life my life." Later that same day he would ask me to prepare Liam to say goodbye to him. Throughout his illness he continued to be as other-focused and selfless as he had always been when healthy, urging us all to keep on living and loving, and to begin imagining how we would continue to do so when he was gone.

The week after Bob died, I found myself flipping the pages of *The Portable Nietzsche*. In a passage from Thus Spoke Zarathustra, "On Free Death," it reads: "Many die too late, and a few die too early." It goes on to read: "I show you the death that consummates—a spur and a promise to the survivors. He that consummates his life dies his death victoriously, surrounded by those who hope and promise. Thus should one learn to die; and there should be no festival where one dying thus does not hallow the oaths of the living. To die thus is best."

Liam, Maeve, and I are doing well because Bob lived and died victoriously—with truth, honesty, and a forever concern with and for the well-being of others. He spurred me and the children on with his promise that we should go on living, go on loving until it is our time to, as he put it, "get off the bus." He did not drag us into the grave with him, even when I, at least, was eager to join him. Instead, he kept kicking me out of it and handing me a bouquet.

In one of the notes Bob left for the kids, he wrote: "Meaningful lives come from who you know and what you do with the limited amount of time you have. So, make it count. Be fulfilled and help others along the way."

Thank you for all the love, joy, and support you provided throughout these many months and now: physical, emotional, material, and monetary. Thank you for continuing to raise high a glass with us and laugh—full-belly-doubled-over-laughs. May we all continue to live our lives "with blood," as Nietzsche said, and as Bob did and often reminded me to do—with passion, honesty, strength, and an appreciation for each other and life itself.

ACKNOWLEDGMENTS

This book was born of memory and love and would not be possible without the support of my partner in all things, my husband Dave, and our remarkable, resilient children, Maeve and Liam, who sacrificed hours with their mother in order for her to spend time on its creation. I am grateful first and foremost to this home team who made this book possible and never doubted the importance of my writing it and remembering Bob as the gregarious, generous, wise, and beautiful human and father he was and would have continued to be if it weren't for the devastating disease that is ALS.

Liam and Maeve, I am honored to be your mother, and this story is firstly for you.

Bob is alive in our children, those he taught, those who knew and loved him, those who admired his intentional living, even from afar, and those who remember him. Bob, this book is also always for you, so that you continue to be known by those who do not have the blessed fortune to remember you.

To Bob's family, my family, who trusted me with Bob's love and life and has held me even closer in his absence, I appreciate you, I love you, and I am honored to be a part of your lives. Thank you for always believing in Bob and in me. Thank you, also, for putting up with our quirks and differences and loving us wholly, sometimes even despite them.

To Bob's mom, Mary, special thanks for holding me up through phone lines and in person when I was falling, and for welcoming Dave to the family as your "son-in-law." You have always helped to remind me who I was, and with each passing year, I have learned more and more where Bob came from, and how he learned to love so deeply, through all that you are and continue to be for us. Thank you for all you have given to me, Dave, Liam, and Maeve.

This story is for all those affected by ALS; this story is for all those whose ALS stories remain untold.

Thank you to the Muscular Dystrophy Association and the ALS Association for their critical support during Bob's illness, both in words and deeds, and for the fight they are still fighting for all those affected by ALS.

Thank you to hospice for doing the greatest life and death work for strangers with utmost integrity, generosity, and empathy.

Thank you to Dr. Dana Altman and nurse Julie, the medical team who not only took care of Bob, but took care of us.

Thank you to my therapist during Bob's illness, Diane S., who always heard me.

Many, many thanks to friends and family who traveled to see Bob or reached out to us while he was sick, filling our lives with humor and joy and making all the minutes a little easier.

Friends and family who have graciously allowed me to share your beauty in this book, I thank you for being there for us during the beautiful ugly and for understanding the inevitable loneliness inherent in all grief. No matter how much company surrounds, grief is always, always solitary.

Dear Kate, thank you for always listening to me, putting up with me, and most of all loving me.

Chelona, thank you for your light, and for guiding me during one of the most difficult times of my life.

Terrence, thank you for being an incredible colleague and dearest friend through all the good and the bad.

Giovanna, thank you for always reminding me I was never alone and for teaching me how to ask for help.

Linda, thank you for being the first reader of this story, and for always teaching me, not only directly, but indirectly, simply by being you. You are a forever inspiration.

I have close and faraway friends who encouraged, consoled, and uplifted me when I most needed it during this project and were always a click or a dial away. They make me a better human and always seem to know just what to say. I don't know what I would do without you, John, Roxanne, Nader, Brian, Beth,

Maggie, Carrie, Debbie, Marissa, Rick, Susan, Liz H., Liz S., and Leslie.

To the core members of my very first writing circle, thank you for bringing joy and laughter into our house, and for always asking for more: Casey, Terry, Alyse, Rebecca, Heather, Katie, and Lee.

Thank you to our Florida team, Kate (again), Lynn, Suzanne, Steven, Chris, and Barbara for letting no distance keep us too far apart.

To my neighbors and friends, Sarah and Jon, Jillian and Cole, thank you for being there for three of the major losses of my life, and helping me to shelter Liam and Maeve from the storms. I will always be grateful for the village that cradled all our children. Special thanks, also, to Sarah and Jillian for repeatedly encouraging me to tell this story.

I am remembering Myron's Dianne who always wanted me to tell my stories. I wish you were here to read this one.

In appreciation for Donna Kaz and her Creative Nonfiction Workshop, and the sister writers I met there, workshop leader Terri Muuss, and workshop participants Rebecca, Joy, Dallas, Laura, Cyn, and Clara, who encouraged me to further refine this manuscript and submit it. Their thoughtful and inspiring feedback ignited my final revisions.

I am grateful to the English, Literature, and World Languages department and Ferris State University for its support of my writing residencies at The Writers' Colony at Dairy Hollow and at The Golden Apple Artist Residency where the first completed draft of this memoir was born. The generosity of The Writers' Colony's current director, Michelle Hannon (and former residency director, Linda Caldwell), as well as of Golden Apple director Shelley Stevens (and her partner Greg) are notable. I thank all of you for welcoming me to those beautiful and peaceful places and continuing to support my writing. I am also grateful to the journals where two excerpts from this book were previously published: The Writers' Colony at Dairy Hollow's journal, *eMerge*, and its editor-in-chief, Charles Templeton; and *The Coil* and its editor-in-chief, Leah Angstman. Thank you also to Kate Garrett, editor-in-chief of *Bonnie's Crew*, for first publishing "The Last Time Making Love," and to Glenn Lyvers, editor-in-chief of Prolific Press, for first publishing "Emission for D."

I am grateful for the bravery and generosity of Tim and Kaylin for sharing their ALS journey in the Often Awesome series. Their unflinching honesty and documentation of Tim's illness not only educated us on the realities of ALS, but helped Bob make his own end-of-life decisions.

My appreciation to Jennifer Johnson, photographer extraordinaire, for my author photo.

Thank you to my editor, Jaynie Royal, and the team at Regal House Publishing and Pact Press, managing editor, Pam Van Dyk, cover designer, C. B. Royal, and proofreader, Elizabeth Lowenstein, for their belief in this story, their invaluable guidance, and for ferrying it to you, dear readers, whom I thank for sharing some of your precious time with me.

I am grateful for the guidance, support, and love my team at Smith Publicity, Kellie Rendina, Katie Schnack, and Courtney Link, have given this book.

Please join me in spreading awareness of ALS, supporting those who are fighting an ALS battle, and raising funds to research a cure. Liam, Maeve, Dave, and I have been walking for ALS as "Bob's Muscle Team" for the past six years. A portion of the author royalties from the sales of this book will be donated to our walk or an ALS Foundation each year. Thank you for joining us in the fight against ALS.

If you need support for your diagnosis with ALS, please contact the MDA Resource Center at
https://www.mda.org/care/mda-resource-center
By Phone: 1-833-ASK-MDA1 (1-833-275-6321)
By Email: ResourceCenter@mdausa.org